THE ORGASMS OF HISTORY

3000 Years of Spontaneous Insurrection

Text and story board by FREMION
Drawings and Illustrations by VOLNY

With GUILLAUME KEYNIA helping out on
"The Souvenir Album of Buenaventura Durruti"

Translated from the French by Paul Sharkey

Edinburgh • London • Oakland

The world is already in possession of the dream of a time of which it now must possess a consciousness so that it may actually live it.

Guy Debord,
Society of the Spectacle (1967)

There is only one way to be radical. The wall needing to be demolished is enormous, but it has been so sapped by so many breaches that soon it will take only a single shout to bring it tumbling down. May the redoubtable reality of the third force, the individual enthusiasm content in uprisings, at last step out of the mists of history!

Raoul Vaneigem,
Treatise on Living for the Use of the
Younger Generation (1967)

I tell you this, that one must carry chaos within oneself, if one is to be able to give birth to a shooting star.

Nietzsche,
Thus Spake Zarathustra (1883–1885)

THE ORGASMS OF HISTORY

Every time that the proletariat gambles upon changing the world, it stumbles upon the global memory of history. The installation of a council-based society—hitherto mixed up with the story of its crushing at different times—tears the veil away from the reality of its past potential through the feasibility of its immediate realization.

Raoul Vaneigem
Situationist International (1969)

It is criminal to embark upon even the slightest attempt to change society, no matter how limited, without bearing in mind certain old experiences of the "movement."

Francis Pisani
Libération (1979)

The chief protagonist is the people (...) I have seen how the party leaders, the heroes of conventional history, neither foresaw nor made provision, that they were the instigation of none of the great achievements, and especially not of any of the ones which were the people's unanimous handiwork at the start of the Revolution. Left to their own devices by its supposed leaders, in such telling moments, the people discovered what needed doing and did it.

Michelet
History of the French Revolution (1847-1869)

The production of this book is dedicated to the memory of Jeff Urban, a comrade and friend of the Anarchist community. Jeff fought injustice all his life. A veteran of the "White Night Riots", Jeff was a working class hero to the end when he took his final stand against the state.

Jeff will be missed by the Bound Together Bookstore Collective and the San Francisco Anarchist community.

CONTENTS:

Let us understand one another. First, this book. This is not the work of a historian. History is much too serious a matter to be left in the hands of academics. We are not here just for the fun of it. This book is the handiwork of the committed. A subjective book, extremely so. An enthusiastic book, enthusiastic even in its criticisms. Every insurrection, every experience related here was one that we should have liked to see live its natural span and reach its conclusion. Though we may be weaklings, and though we may be determinedly autonomous, individualistic individuals affiliated to no organization, we are nevertheless "up" for any uprising or experience which might coincide with our own time on earth. To our enormous delight, it has fallen to us to "be on the inside looking out" (in May '68, or in Le Larzac) or to have thrilled to what we were able to follow, albeit only at some distance (China, Portugal, the Diggers in San Francisco).

Let no one kid themselves: a book is no substitute for a rifle. But it can help to train one's sights that bit better. A book can never be a substitute for an orgasm. But it can help to while away the time between attacks, be they political, social or, amorous.

This book is the saga of *Freedom Through the Ages*, the saga of these millenarians of counter-power, of alternative societies, or of their high hopes. "Beloved liberty, you fought alongside your defenders…" "The aim of society is happiness for all…" And all that sort of thing. Which of us has not had this inkling (never articulated and forever relegated to a later date by the analysts, philosophers and, historians) that it is the same battle that has been fought out over so long, coming to a resolution only in a few fleeting glimpses of happiness to be bolted down quickly?

This is a rough draft of a history handbook for free human beings: one intended for disobedient children (along with their parents) and it is illustrated with pictures for pasting not just in the margins of their liar's copybook (history at school) but for adorning the walls of their memories.

It is a history of widespread self-management, or of attempts in that direction. For upwards of a century now, Marxism (in its current form, at any rate) has been striving, and Christianity for the past 2,000 years, but we who have been striving after self-management of our lives, our times and our space ever since the very earliest beginnings of mankind, under a multitude of names and with various degrees of success. We have nothing to learn from anyone except ourselves. That is why this book is here.

WHAT'S IT ALL ABOUT?

The powers that be have been much the same in every civilization down through the centuries. Those who wield power bear a pretty close resemblance to one another. Those who strive to bring them down are much alike.

Between feudalism and bureaucracy, between capitalism and private western imperialism and the State capitalism and imperialism of the "socialist" countries, there are few, if any, essential differences. What sets an emperor apart from a Russian Communist Party secretary, or the absolute power of a five-year-old prince from that of a republican president hog-tied by lobbyists? Or the clout of the medieval Church from the clout of a contemporary multinational? The power is the same, the procedures are the same, and the same sorts of men are at the top.

Now, what differences are there between the people's aspirations at these various times and in these different civilizations? None. The Roman peasant driven off his land has the same aims as the peasant in Le Larzac, and in the U.S.A. The dropout of the 1960s found himself in much the same position as the English dropout of the 1640s, and a similar fate awaited the women, the proletarians, and the slaves.

Their aspirations yearned for the same basic freedoms: the same sort of free education, of repression-free sexuality, of equal rights and inter-personal relations, of shared organization of social life, of access to the land and to resources, a common taste for festivity, fraternity, and wholesale liberation. The only thing that has changed is the coat of varnish painted over these. For millennia past, under every regime, such notions have been popping into people's heads and those heads have been taking up arms to fight to ensure that they prevail, or merely to prevent them from being snuffed out altogether.

When all is said and done, this history of counter-power is a success story, for those notions have not been extinguished. And yet, from Inquisition to Gulag, from slavery to wage-slavery, from slaughter to brainwashing, we have been subjected to a number of attempts to wipe us out. None of them have worked. Our ideas and our experiences are planted in a growing number of minds, and fire and lead can never eradicate them all.

In this book, we have had to choose. Very much so. We have discarded hundreds of topics and whittled them down to just twenty-nine. But we ought to make it clear that for every one of the twenty-nine, there are others equally as good. If we have passed over some jacquerie or another, some insurrection, some commune or another, such and such a phalanstery—this should not be taken as implying that we have forgotten about them. They live on in our memory and the ones described here are merely well known or little-known samples.

Merely to list our possible subjects would take up several pages of this book. The reader will note that, with the notable exception of Etienne de la Boétie, no theoretician has merited a place for his theories. Words count for little, and it is actions that sometimes expose the important dichotomy between thought and action in a single individual, no matter how outstanding.

Nor is this some anarchist or libertarian catalog. True, the latter were often participants in the events described, but not to the exclusion of all others. They represent merely theoretical rough draft for a much more expansive and significant phenomenon, or even the swan song of the proletariat's classical mode of organization.

From the Brethren of the Free Spirit to the "Muchachos" in Nicaragua, from Fra Dolcino to Guevara, from the Tuchins to the Provos, from the Rustauds to the Metropolitan Indians, from Modern Times to Kronstadt, from New Harmony to the I.W.W., from Prague to Asturias, from Rabelais to Watts…freedom's history is a rich one. "The history of every society thus far has been only the history of class struggle," Marx and Engels stated. That dictum is only true on the basis of the understanding that these two classes are, roughly, the class of the oppressed (oppressed in some fashion or another) and that of those who (through some totalitarianism or another) oppress them. We have not gone into a detailed examination of each and every chapter in this saga. The aim of this book is not to offer the definitive account of each subject. You can find that in the books listed in our bibliography (we have decided not to burden the text with footnotes, as these would have become too frequent). Its purpose is merely to whet your appetite to know more.

In the case of some of these topics, most people are ignorant of them. In others, they may think they know it all. In fact, and like ourselves before we dove into them, they know nothing. Or their information is mistaken. The university tells them lies, through omission, through outright falsehoods or merely by offering only isolated morsels of the reality. It has often fallen to this book to patch information together in order to afford it clarity.

To take but one example-the doggedly Jacobin view that historians impose upon the French Revolution borders upon therapeutic zealotry: let us leave Robespierre's corpse to molder, and let us study the real revolutionaries as such, not those who were constantly applying the brakes to them. (And I will not even mention those historians who give pride of place to Danton or La Fayette!) There is simply no way to express the unfathomable cretinism of the average academic, his crass ignorance and weird shallowness. How many such dangerous hacks are there for every one of the honest spirits imagining what a useful university might be like?

Every one of us must reclaim his memory, his past, which is our national heritage. The history of kings and their wretched conflicts leaves us cold. It is our history that matters to us. May this book provide a skeleton to be fleshed out continually.

There are various ways in which this book may be read. The laziest will make do with leafing through the pictures, the credit for which is due to the talented Volny, whose clarity of line and painstaking dimensions are a marvel. The more courageous will read it from cover to cover in order, which is to say in chronological order, so as to sense the dizzy delights of the ascent to the marvellous days that lie ahead of us.

Finally, others, who I find more to my own taste, will read this book in the most anarchically disorderly way (in fact the least anarchic way), a chapter here, a chapter there, according to their whim and fancy. They will be right to do so, for each story stands on its own, even if, deep down, it may be absolutely dependent upon the rest. Pick a topic, return to it, and one may well acquire a taste for discovering its forerunners and its successors, which may at first glance have seemed so unprepossessing. To each his own.

You will overlook my mistakes, if there be any. They can be laid at the door of the historians who first broached these topics, historians who I, inadvisably perhaps, have taken on trust. There is a rigor in the likes of Leroy-Ladurie which commands respect, even if one does not subscribe to his particular appreciation of history. In the likes of Francis Pisani or André Prudhommeaux, there is a tone that simply will not countenance falsehood. There is no denying that there is something priestly about the likes of Nettlau and above all else luminosity to certain texts he wrote under pressure. Potential mistakes will not in any way alter the underlying basis of this book.

ORGASMS?

The title of this book contains echoes of Wilhelm Reich, that "excellent educator of young people," whose book *The Function of Orgasm*, for all its imperfections and its age, remains essential reading. In it, he spells out the several stages of orgasm: the slow, almost exponential growth of pleasure, right up to the point of abrupt, uncontrolled explosion, followed by the final, rather rapid release, the ebbing of excitement, and the onset of relaxation.

Looking at this breakdown, one is struck by the resemblance to a schematic breakdown that one might devise of the uprisings described below. They, too, boast a stage when the struggles (slowly but inexorably) are hatching and building up. The explosion when it comes, comes abruptly, and is hard to control, even for those who unleash it. Once the explosion is over, there is an undeniable easing of tension, an ebb tide heralding the very palpable torpor of the aftermath of pleasure: it is, generally, at this point that repression swoops or that the salvage teams arrive on the scene. Like the lover, the revolutionary, if his orgasm was a full-blooded one, likes to rest upon his laurels. These are the orgasms this book describes.

Away then, with the hoary image of revolution as a once-and-for-all success: and with the notion of love as an ongoing orgasm. Sure, the orgasm may be short-lived, but it is damned fine while it lasts.

The only hitch, as we shall see, is the salvage teams. To follow up our analogy, let us quote Reich himself, who watched the birth of such salvage operations in psycho-analysis right from the start: "Just as Jesus's primitive Christianity was transformed into a Church and Marxian science was turned into fascist dictatorship, many psycho-analysts were transfigured into the most ferocious enemies of their own cause."

A FEW CONCEPTS

Certain key ideas will be found to recur throughout this book. Often they are of my own devising, but even history can stammer. Commune and Jacquerie are notions that have always and everywhere been in currency. We will find the Diggers unearthing the same ideas time and again in a variety of locations.

Under the French Revolution, there was an obsession with reviving the names of antiquity and this was often an opportunity to pay tribute to revolutionaries of long ago: Babeuf was to become Gracchus, in memory of the Gracchi who devised the notion of "proletarian," of which Marat then Marx were to avail before it was redefined by the Situationists. Yokel means a peasant who must not merely be exploited but also has to be held up to ridicule (which offers a partial legitimization of exploitation). This was to be a term long in use.

Not for nothing did Rosa Luxemburg and her colleagues identify with the slave, Spartacus: there was the same exploitation, the same insurrection. As for the word Provo, which dates back to 1965–1967, it has since been used by heaps of people, particularly in Ireland at the present time.

In this book the reader will find repeated references to self-management. It goes without saying that misuse of this term is quite deliberate. In that sense, it is a quite recent neologism that people, such as Edmond Maire, have a lot of gall to claim (as he did on TV a year ago) that he invented it, when his trade union only started to show any interest in it a decade after May '68, and then only in a bastardized form.

Self-management is when individuals take their own fate and future prospects into their own hands, without any specialist intermediary, and it is as old as the world itself; except that in the 20th century we have, in every respect, an acute awareness of it. Its time has come. This notion which is winning people over with the speed of light is still the favorite bogeyman of all bureaucrats. This—to quote the C.G.T. (in 1980)—"empty formula," is a formula that has nonetheless been around for 2,000 years under a variety of names and all over the planet. We have no scruples about describing as self-managerial struggles dating from several centuries ago, before the emergence of the term itself.

Likewise the term *council* or indeed *soviet* (soviet means council in Russian) is not to be taken in its perverted, Leninist sense. Councils, or soviets, are not, as Debord indicates, a theoretical construct but have been thrown up by workers' and peasants' practice, being direct democratic assemblies, self-managing assemblies. We will not go into a description of them here, for they are adequately described in the body of the text.

Suffice to say that these assemblies are the sovereign decision-makers in matters affecting their own fate, and they are answerable to no one. "Direct democracy" is radically opposed to so-called "liberal" or parliamentary democracy, in the sense that it operates without intermediaries. Everyone decides for himself, and where there are mandated delegates, they are subject to instant recall should they step beyond the general consensus. Augustin Cochin, even though he was a man of the right, even spoke of "pure democracy."

It will readily be appreciated that the term insurrection is employed in its broadest sense. The construction of a phalanstery is a social insurrection that is on a par with factory occupations and the same goes for the launching of a parallel school. We do not understand the term insurrection to mean just hand-to-hand fighting.

In the book there will be much talk of peasant uprisings. It ought to be said that rarely does the peasant put himself to trouble needlessly. When he stirs himself, it is in order to call everything into question. It is no accident that the peasant should be a self-manager in even the least of his unrest. Moreover, class historians, fans of the State to a man, are forever taking him to task for his anti-Statism (and with good cause!), labelling him "reactionary" because he rejects bureaucracy, no matter its provenance (this, moreover, is one point upon which left and right are in agreement: championing the State bureaucracy).

"To be governed"—Proudhon tells us—"is to be watched over, inspected, spied upon, directed, legislated over, regulated, penned in, indoctrinated, preached at, supervised, estimated, evaluated, censured, and commanded by creatures who possess neither the credentials nor the expertise nor the virtue. To be governed is to be, in every operation, in every transaction, in every movement, noted, registered, recorded, catalogued, stamped, weighed up, subscribed, patented, licensed, authorized, annotated, admonished, thwarted, reformed, rectified, and corrected. It is, under the pretext of public usefulness and in the name of the general interest, to be taxed, tried, held to ransom, exploited, monopolized, embezzled, pressurized, bamboozled, and robbed: then, at the merest suggestion of resistance, at the first murmur of complaint, repressed, fined, vilified, vexed, tracked, harassed, battered, disarmed, garroted, imprisoned, shot, riddled, judged, convicted, deported, sacrificed, sold out, betrayed, and to top it all, toyed with, played for a fool, outraged and dishonoured."

What could we add to this flight of oratory? Every one of us knows it. To go pretending that there is no way out of this is to bury one's head in the sand lest one see. La Boétie or Brecht came up with snappy encapsulations of it, in the wake of which we need not labor the point.

HISTORY

"For peoples, History is and remains a collection of stories," says Enzensberger in his remarkable book on Durruti. And he goes on to add: "History is an invention of which the stuff is reality. But it is not just any invention. The interest it arouses rests upon the interests of the tellers and it allows the listeners to draw a distinction between their own interest and their enemies' and to identify them with greater precision...Only the authentic subject of History casts a shadow. And casts it in the form of collective fiction."

In fact, history, as a scientific discipline, is primarily the history of history's rewriting. Which is to say, of the rewriting of the real, of the facts. This book is no exception. It is not a book of history (the discipline) but it is a book of history (the history of human beings). It has been rewritten in a particular sense. Like all the rest, except that it is up front about it.

I mentioned earlier that we should, each of us, be our own historian. Everybody ought to reclaim his memory, the memory that casts him as an actor in the realm of his own history, his own reality. We can and should "pursue history (and many another things) outside of specialized offices...history users, in particular struggling workers can recapture possession of their past, without being placed in a position of passive dependency upon specialists." (*Cahiers du Forum-Histoire*, 1977)

This is one of the reasons why one-fourth of this history book is made up of drawings, illustrations based upon documentary evidence and comic strips. The abominable visions imposed by the graphic Lavisses or in the style of Job (even if Job was a remarkable artist) of our nation's history—visions that are still prevalent— must be replaced by modern images more attuned to reality. I hope that Makhno as portrayed by Volny will eclipse the attractive Charlemagne of the 19th century illustrators, that the inflated Joan of Arcs and Napoleons will give way to the authentic heroes of freedom, to the admirable Durruti, the courageous Sébastien Faure, the astounding Jacques Roux, to a Maillard even more incorruptible than Robespierre, etc.

EVOLUTION

In human history, some periods can be particularly eventful. Orgasms can sometimes come fast and thick. For instance, we will see the libertarian idea go into a decline after 1795; for a long time, almost a century. We will find this decline letting up after the eradication of the Paris Commune. Similarly, after 1939, the movement was dead in the water up until Stalin's death. The very notion of freedom, much like the idea of happiness was none too common until just before 1789. Previously, the word had been around but indicated merely the opposite of a condition of slavery.

Most of the important jacqueries occurred between 1320 and 1420. After that, revolutionaries were decimated by the plague and by the Hundred Years' War and their voice was not heard for almost 120 years. The enormous death rate also ensured that there was more land to go around and thus eased the poverty problem. Insurrection was to mount a big comeback between 1520 and 1707. Followed by a silence that lasted until the Revolution.

In the interim, Louis XIV and others had nursed the modern, centralist, totalitarian State intro existence and this is the regime under which we are still living. Anti-statism superceded anti-feudalism. We ought to appreciate that the character of the struggle stayed the same even through the changes in the nature of the enemy.

As Y.M. Bercé was to say, the alternative communes and all who represented the "Republic of the little men against the great."

In point of fact, in peasant revolts the rebels were often to be found being led by a nobleman or professional soldier. Most of the rebels would have been incapable of leading an offensive. They were aware of their lack of expertise in military matters. The big novelty in 1789 was finding the bourgeois for the first time at the head of the peasants and workers. The peasants needed a victory over the towns, and that took military leadership. If the urban proletariat would join them, they could win. If not, they wouldn't. The wondrous simplicity of history. The bourgeois alone had the arms and it was therefore essential that the workers and peasants ally themselves with them. But in the end this worked to the sole advantage of the bourgeoisie, as Marx was quick to point out.

On two occasions at least, in the 20th century alone, a new phenomenon was to surface. Internationalization of the revolution was to spark worldwide attacks upon the world's powers that be. We are living in stirring times.

In the period around 1917–1921 and again in 1968, the entire world came within an ace of being turned upside down, and was, for the duration of a brief orgasm. In the wake of the Russian Revolution and its hijacking by the Bolshevik bureaucracy, we find soviets being set up everywhere, within Russia itself (Makhno and Kronstadt), in Germany (in Bavaria and in Berlin), in Hungary, Italy, and Argentina, not to mention the formidable achievements of libertarian educators and a cultural effervescence, before, during and immediately afterward that is without parallel in history. These actions generated Dadaism, Futurism, Surrealism, Expressionism, etc.

In 1968, this was to be even more the case. Such essays on worldwide upheaval, spontaneous uprisings everywhere at once, are a good indication of what the struggles of the future are going to be like. We must live from now on with a planetary consciousness.

THE STALINISTS

Some may be struck by our daring in this book to employ the term "Stalinist" with regard to events that took place several centuries in advance of Stalin's birth. "Stalinism" needs to be seen as an archetype of totalitarianism and authoritarianism, of which Stalin was the most consistent of enthusiasts (he took the idea to its logical conclusion). In every age, there have been libertarians, bureaucrats, and advocates of revolution through compulsion. ("Even the best of things, if secured by compulsion, becomes the worst," says Vaneigem. And he goes on to say: "Emancipation has no foes worse than these, who mean to change society and yet, while exorcising it, cannot quite disguise the old world they carry in their hearts.")

We must now speak of the left. (There is a "good left," just as there are "decent folk," from whose ranks the kapos, the gaolers and all the informers are recruited).

There are left-wing folk who have a filthy habit of cracking down on revolutionary uprisings. It was the left that cracked down on the Spartakists, and the Communists who mopped up the Spanish Revolution before letting power fall into Franco's lap. Thiers, in his day, was a man of the left, a republican. The Jacobins were to exterminate all the other revolutionary tendencies before waking up, once they had their own heads on the block, to the fact that they had wiped out all who might have defended them, and we all know the part played by the contemporary Socialist and Communist parties in cracking down on the far left in 1968, as well as in Italy and in Germany, or the part Soares or Antunes played in Portugal.

It has to be said that there is a complete irreconcilability between forms of governing systems. The one leads on to soviets, in which no one can make a career for himself, and the other to bureaucratization of society in its entirety. Capitalism, socialism, communism, nationalism, and autocracy…they all lead to ongoing social straitjacketing. These "rigid systems" share a common enemy in flexible arrangements wherein the individual can go his own way in a society that has many choices to offer. Karl Mannheim distinguishes between two sorts of utopia the old, socialist-communist one, and a newer one, which we might call chiliastic, which seeks to satisfy desires here and now, granting everything right away. In fact, the Utopians are very frequently breathtakingly Stalinist. Anyone who has troubled to read their visions of the future cannot but be scared by them. The counter-Utopians who are the subject of this book, are, by contrast, incapable of describing other than by building it, unless it is by evoking their nightmares (Orwell, Huxley, Junger).

However, every revolution needs the traditional left, if only to throw it overboard. When not immersed in the most brazen of class collaboration, Marxists, socialists and communists serve, as Debord has it, as a "replacement ruling class," the B-team, for the commodity economy. The parties of the proletariat then become the party of the proletariat's owners.

Once the unrest has been crushed, they then salvage the ideas in its baggage, which they have just been fighting against, for the purposes of redirecting proletarian energy. It is no accident that they are forever prating about past struggles and claiming them as their own. Winstanley, Fourier, Thomas More and others all have their very official busts in Moscow's Gorky Park. And will we be seeing Durruti or Cohn-Bendit joining them soon? It is only a matter of waiting until their powers of mobilization have faded. Their historians, regularly taken up by the universities, like to depict attempts at self-management as experiments in "primitive communism" or "proto-communism," which is rich. Bureaucrats can often be seen cheering on the revolutionaries, while massacring them as they go. Or eliminating them politically. Central authority then passes, very temporarily, to these "left-wing" forces, but the restoration of the old order is not long delayed. A change of vehicle might have been the intention, but what one gets is a change of ignition key (which soon adapts to the lock after a bit of filing) and the carriage of State gets underway, which is the essential point as far as the bureaucrats are concerned.

In the silencing of the revolutionaries, there are no methods that are off-limits. There are examples galore of this. Sébastien Faure once said: "Anarchists are neither utopians, nor dreamers, nor madmen, and the proof is that, everywhere, governments hound them and throw them in jail to prevent the true message which they spread from reaching the ears of the disinherited, whereas, if libertarian teachings were based on chimeras or dementia, they would find it so easy to expose its irrationality and obscurity."

To be on the safe side, the soviets, the peasants, and the urban population will be disarmed. Arms must stay in the hands of armies and police forces, be these red or white. From Soares to Allende, this has always been the tactic of the moderate social democrat, as well as of the Stalinist bureaucrat. Come the inevitable ensuing fascist onslaught, the people are left defenseless and massacre is rendered easily (as in Chile).

Once upon a time it was good form to praise Marx to the skies. These days it is good form to spit in his face. The venerable economist does not deserve such undue regard, any more than to suffer the indignity. And in any case, he is worth more than any of his disciples. What is known today as "Marxism" is in fact Leninism, a bastardized form of Jacobinism, and its chief theoretician was Stalin. To be honest, Marxism—well, no one knows what it is any more. Wasn't it Marx who anticipated this when he declared that he would never be a "Marxist"?

If, for just five minutes we can forget about the "sound and fury, signifying nothing" represented by the one-time Stalinists who have turned into the all-purpose anti-Marx (just the way there is an anti-Christ), it has to be said that outside of the chronic paranoia by which the philosopher was seized during the days of the International (seeing anarchists all over the place, trying to cheat him out of his own International), his system boasted a few startlingly bright and astonishing insights.

For good reason: he had borrowed them from others and oddly enough, the man fated to become the greatest destroyer of the libertarians of his day was to hijack virtually all of their (at that time) scattered ideas. He borrowed heavily from the Saint-Simonians (the notion of class struggle, the role of history as the basis for all political science, the driving force of the proletariat, the organization of labor, the notion of the "producer" and the expression "man's exploitation of his fellow man," and indeed "To each according to their needs, from each according to their means"). And he admitted as much, too.

On the other hand, he carefully hid what he had borrowed from Winstanley (the withering-away of the State, the oppressive structure of society with regard to appropriation of the soil), from Proudhon (scientific socialism), from Owen (the influence of man upon his environment and education, the hour's labor as the basic unit of measurement—Owen was also to have a considerable influence upon Engels' thinking), from Babeuf, Fourier, Victor Considérant (*The Communist*

Manifesto is almost wholly plagiarized from him), Flora Tristan (it was only forty years after her that Engels was to discover the importance of women's role in society), and from Becker (scientific communism). Not to mention the borrowings that he did acknowledge from Ricardo and Hegel, which were anything but libertarian.

The striking thing is to notice just how much he was limping along in their wake. It could be argued that he could scarcely have done otherwise than make use of these works, but that he drained them of their underlying implications in order to graft his own moderate ideas upon them. In respect of mores especially, he is startlingly conservative (as were Proudhon and Considérant).

But enough of this digression.

LEADERS?

The role of leaders in uprisings and other alternative ventures has always been a matter for controversy. The authoritarian case is absurd—one does not impose a revolution at the point of a rifle: but the classic libertarian one, which refutes the role of leaders, is out of touch with reality. Each and every assault upon the old world throws up individuals, be they inspired or naturally talented, who drag the others along in their wake. The role of a soviet is to make the best use of these while preventing their temporary authority from being perpetuated and turning bureaucratic. Independent individuals have no need of lasting leadership. The essential thing is that the persons issued with a mandate should genuinely reflect the wishes of the members of the council. Fourier came up with a splendid definition of this absolute independence: "No obedience is owed to any leader whose election might leave one cold."

There will be leaders in any insurrection and often they will be charismatic figures (like Durruti, Makhno, Marat and, Saint-Just). It will fall to many of them to perish in battle. Others will survive, but in defeat. Finally, a few will accede to power. Which will corrupt them. To a man. The issue of leadership is going to be on the movement's agenda for a long time to come.

FAILURE?

"Ever since the world began, there has scarcely been a single year when every people has not felt the need to shrug off the yoke of aristocracy in order to recover its natural rights, and yet how few are the revolutions attempted compared with the many that have been yearned for! And of the revolutions embarked upon, how few have succeeded! And among the latter, how few have achieved their objective without having been dodged or annihilated later on by the aristocracy!" (Cabet, *Journey to Icaria*).

"No revolution thus far has been a success: none has abolished class. Thus far, proletarian revolution has not succeeded anywhere, but the practical process whereby its project is made manifest has already led to at least a dozen revolutionary upheavals of extreme historical importance, to which the title of revolutions has conventionally been awarded." (*Situationist International*, 1969).

These two quotations leave an all too widespread bitter taste in the mouth. All of these orgasms are all very well and good but they do not add up to much. Our first answer to such a remark is that orgasms need not always be designed to sire children, but rather for sheer pleasure. Victory also comes in the form of the oppressor's never feeling safe and secure and of tyrants living in a state of fear. It took millions of years for the megalosaurs to become extinct and the great megalomaniacs may well take as long. The expectation that an experience should last and be forever fixed is a rather bourgeois outlook upon the world. A successful revolution requires ongoing combat. Freedom does not exist. It is liberation that exists, a process of ongoing amelioration. The movement has no final stage. The ideal socialist, communist or, anarchist society is a vision of which any drunkard could be proud.

That being so, should we speak about the Paris Commune (with its three weeks of victory) as having failed, or of the defeat of the Sans-culottes (with their several years of successes)? Furthermore, it has happened that some revolutions have enjoyed long-term success. The Pitauds won, after a fashion. The Remensas achieved their aims. And often ideas that are crushed pop up again within the very societies that cut them down. Virtually the entire philosophy of the Native Americans has resurfaced in the white communitarian movements in the U.S.A. Often too, these revolutionaries, ill-equipped for their historical role, stop on the edge of the abyss, the abyss of freedom yawning at their feet. There is a morbid fear of going too far, of a leap in the dark. Revolutionaries would in fact like to pause for breath on the edge of the precipice before making that leap. And it is at that point, when they are transfixed by the yawning abyss, that the dyed-in-the-wool butcher-crats catch up with them. It is a pity. One of these days the leap will have to be made without the hesitation. Freedom is a hard taskmaster and reaching it is a lengthy and complicated business. But that is good, really good.

It is a good thing to educate oneself about one's own history. It is even better to make one's own history. May this modest volume also serve as an exhortation, at best, to put into practice what our forebears have done. To that end, a study of where they went wrong might be salutary. The next time, we can leap into radicalism with a single bound. Let him listen who will to this message..."To reach the good guys, that is my aim" (Emile Pouget, *le Père Peinard*, 1899).

Greece, 4th and 3rd centuries B.C.
THE CYNICS

> Our goal is to arrive at that ideal state of perfection
> wherein nations will no longer have to submit to the
> oversight of government or to some other nation;
> which means the absence of government, anarchy,
> the highest expression of order. Those who are not of
> the belief that the earth may one day dispense with
> authority have no belief in progress either.
>
> Elisée Reclus

> Our comrades had not read Marx and were scarcely
> familiar with all of Proudhon's theories, but common
> sense was their guide.
>
> Gaston Leval,
> *Espagne Libertaire '36-'39* (1971)

Run a finger down the long list of Greek schools of philosophy and you will find scarcely any with anything left to say to us, anything to concern us in this day and age. Truth to tell, most of their ideas and theories lost all sway centuries ago. What survives is the personalities: if Socrates (who left scarcely any writings behind) is still a figure of legend for 20th century man, this is due more to his charisma (as evident in the accounts of his life) than to anything he had to teach.

But no matter the power of the Socratic legend, in any man of taste, it is overshadowed by the figures of Diogenes (the most famed Cynic) or the unjustly ignored Crates.

The founder of the Cynic school was Antisthenes, who was to be the first to say himself that he was a dog. There was a rationale behind this: Antisthenes delivered his speeches in a gymnasium known as the Cynosargos (or agile dog). It was from its name that the Cynics were to borrow their own. They always said of themselves that they were heavenly dogs, and to argue that the shortest route to godliness was to imitate the beasts. That notion, very novel in its day, has worn very well, in that one finds it throughout the passage of time, from the Libertines of 1620 up to the Hippies of 1966. It should be noted, also, that Antisthenes was a bastard, and that his disciples were virtually all outcasts, tramps or slaves, crackpots or deformed persons. In any event, they bore no resemblance to the other philosophers who were model types.

Antisthenes set the pattern for the well-dressed Cynic: a double cloak, called the tribon, a beggar's pouch around his neck (in which to carry his food) and,

1

perhaps, a staff. He was to be the direct mentor of Diogenes, Crates, and even Zeno (known as Citius), the leader of the Stoic school. Contemporaries of the Cynics, the stoics shared a number of common features with them: Zeno was to talk about an ideal world as a "huge meadow where men will graze with equal entitlement."

The ideal of the Cynics was a simple one: as frugal a life as possible, in terms both of a single garment and of their food. Some even went to the extreme of living on grass and water alone and sleeping under the stars. Virtue was the highest good. They sneered at the vanity of this world and shunned glory and wealth. It was the very essence of gods that they were beyond all need.

Their world was torn between Vice and Virtue, but between these two there was also the Indifferent, which was neither one nor the other. These were philosophers well ahead of their times, because today in the West we are still stalled in a Christian universe of Good and Evil, with no middle ground between them.

But who were these Cynics? Isn't it a bit of an exaggeration to depict them as the first anarchists? Doesn't that amount to shameless annexation of a few likable ancients?

Let's turn to Diogenes. He was a banker's son, his father a banker who counterfeited money. When Diogenes found him out, he ran away to Athens. There he came upon Antisthenes and followed him, to the great annoyance of the latter who wanted no truck with disciples (this was to be an ongoing feature of the Cynics— they had no interest in power in any form). Diogenes proved so insistent that one day Antisthenes caved in.

The date of Diogenes's birth can be fixed with certainty as 413 B.C., so he was an adolescent when Socrates drank his hemlock. He was very quickly to eclipse all the other thinkers of the day, by virtue of his personal demeanor as much as by his writings.

Our knowledge of his life as well as of the lives of his colleagues comes from the hefty volume written by Diogenes Laertius on leading philosophers. All of the anecdotes and quips attributed to Diogenes are drawn from that book and some of the contents are questionable. Which of us has not heard more than once about the barrel in which Diogenes lived? In point of fact, Diogenes slept, masturbated, and spoke wherever he happened to be at the time—often on the Pompeion or under the Zeus portico. He went barefoot, even through the snow.

He really was a dog. As he explained: "I lick those who feed me and bark at those who do not and I bite the ones that misbehave." Whenever he would eat on the open road and passersby would call him a cur, he would reply: "You are the curs because you huddle around me while I am eating." Plato, a contemporary, resigned to finding himself overtaken on the left (or, rather, in wisdom), was to say of Diogenes: "He is a Socrates gone crazy." Elsewhere we read: "He is a much wiser fellow than Socrates, but I am Socrates' successor. I wouldn't have been able to succeed Diogenes."

There is also the story of his encounter with Alexander the Great who introduced himself proudly with "I am the great king Alexander". To which Diogenes replied: "And I am the cur Diogenes." He also struck terror into Demosthenes who was Athens' ideological champion against Philip of Macedonia (Alexander's father). He pursued him into an inn and pointed to the fleeing Demosthenes with the comment: "Behold the leader of the Athenian people!" Alexander tried to win him over with kindness and asked him what was his heart's desire, only to hear the reply: "Step out of my light".

Alexander's father, Philip, felt the lash of his tongue too. Diogenes was brought before him as a prisoner of war and Philip asked him to identify himself. Diogenes replied, "I am the spy of your greed." Philip was so shocked that he had him set free.

Diogenes flouted the law and spat in the face of a rich man who had urged him above all else never to spit on the ground, because it was the only place other than the ground which he had found filthy enough. "In my life I strive to do the opposite to everyone else," he announced, leaving theatres by the entrance and entering via the exit. Eating or screwing in the public thoroughfare, he offered this rationale: "If there is no harm in eating, there cannot be any harm either in eating in the open: now, there is nothing wrong with eating, so there cannot be anything wrong with eating in the street."

He prized candor and freedom above all else. And he knew how to poke fun at philosophers: Plato was left lost for words every time their paths happened to cross. When Plato offered a generic description of man as a featherless, two-legged animal, Diogenes brought him a plucked chicken. Plato then amended his definition by adding the qualification "with flat, broad nails!"

During a meal one time, someone tossed him a bone as if he was a dog. Diogenes scuttled over to him on all fours, lifted one leg, and urinated over him. He poked fun at the rich and wealthy, sneering at the inhabitants of Myndes, a tiny village enclosed behind huge gates: "Keep those gates well shut, lest your town take to its heels."

There was an orator who was droning endlessly on and on. Diogenes therefore drew out a smoked herring which simply reeked, thereby distracting the crowd's attention. "Behold how a halfpenny herring has stolen Anaximenes's thunder." On the other hand, he announced to a man who reeked of scent: "Take care lest the fragrance from your head betray the stench from your life."

Not that the gods got away unscathed either. Or religion. One day he stumbled upon a decent woman prostrate before a statue. He stood behind her and informed her that if the (omnipresent) god could see her ass in the air he would be sorely offended.

He had a low opinion of human nature. His pessimism was absolute but sometimes gleeful. He was not always listened to when he was speaking, so he started to break into bird song, thereby grabbing the attentions of the passersby.

3

All he had to do then was to hurl abuse at the rubber-neckers, claiming that they would listen to any nonsense, while matters of importance left them cold.

"Ahoy there, men!" he would cry out in the street. A crowd would gather. Then he would turn them all away, saying: "Men, not trash!" Often, they would come back. The story about his carrying a lantern in the broad daylight is well known: "I am searching for a man," he told the crowd huddled around him. At the Olympic Games, in accordance with tradition, the herald would announce "Dioxippus has thrashed men." To which Diogenes would retort: "He has thrashed only slaves. Men are my stock in trade." And on returning from the Games, when asked whether the Games had drawn crowds, he would say that, yes, they had, but that the men had been few and far between.

In this light the acceptance of disciples was out of the question. One day a would-be disciple was particularly persistent. Whereupon our hero reached out to him his favorite weapon, our friend the smoked herring, tying it up and holding it out to the greenhorn, telling him to follow him and drag the creature along. Panicking, the petitioner would toss the herring away and slink away to Diogenes's sneering words: "A herring has ruined our beautiful friendship."

He never asked his friends to lend him money. He asked only that they hand it over to him, so poor Proudhon was not much of an inventor and certainly was not the first to suggest that "Property is theft." When asked to name his favorite wine, Diogenes would answer "Other people's," a joke that certain radio performers are still trotting out as if it were the latest wheeze.

On the other hand, one day he saw a child drinking from a cupped hand. Diogenes tossed away the bowl he carried in his pouch and confessed: "I am beaten. This child lives more simply than me."

The most inspired, most radical episode in Diogenes's life and teaching (and in a true dialectician, the two are interwoven) came the time when he was captured by pirates while sailing toward Aegina. The pirate chief, Scirpalos, sold him in the slave market in Crete. The crier who peddled the merchandise asked him in the presence of the would-be buyers what he could do. "Command!" shouted Diogenes at the startled fellow. He immediately pointed to a wealthy Corinthian by the name of Xeniadis and said: "Sell me to that fellow, for I can see that he is in need of a master." Xeniadis bought him and found himself being told by his own slave that he, Xeniadis, was the one who would have to take orders.

Impressed, Xeniadis entrusted the education of his children to Diogenes. They learned horsemanship, archery, the use of a slingshot, the javelin, the sciences, poetry, prose, and the writings of...Diogenes, not to mention Cynic philosophy. He turned them into good students and Xeniadis never wearied of saying everywhere he went that his home had been visited by a genius. Having a kind master, Diogenes stayed with him up until his death at the age of 86 in 327 B.C.

Diogenes was active right up to the end. When people asked him to rest awhile, he explained that one does not slow down as one nears one's goal, but rather breaks into a sprint. His ideas about death are, moreover, very modern, even in our day. He reckoned that cannibalism was nothing out of the ordinary, since one eats the flesh of animals and since the Cynic thinks of himself as an animal.

Here he was wholly consistent with the Cynic and Stoic tradition, which argued that the dead should be eaten, as should one's own limbs, should these be severed. A family would eat its dead so that nourishment might not go to waste, corpses being of no more account than, say, hair that had been shed or nails that had been trimmed.

On sexuality, the Cynics have rarely been matched for tolerance. Everything was allowed—homosexuality, of course, but also bestiality, masturbation, and open copulation, even in the temples. "would to heavens that one had only to run one's belly to banish hunger!" he told a person who had upbraided him for masturbating in full view. And when it was pointed out to him that he was a frequent caller to brothels he retorted: "The sun is a welcome visitor to cesspits." The holding of women in common was essential. "The first man to happen by will avail of the first woman to happen along." Man and woman were equals, so they shared everything in common, especially identical garb, the effect of which was, nevertheless, to make the girls look mannish. It could be said that Diogenes was a bit of a misogynist. But he also recommended incest (the myth of Oedipus made him laugh), first because he was also an advocate of common ownership of children and then because he was not ashamed to pleasure his mother by rubbing his genitalia against hers. Brothers, sisters, parents—everyone was to take his pleasure wherever he found it. It was the pleasure that counted, not the morality. Zeno was also very insistent upon this count. Prostitution was a matter of no account.

This mixture of utter animality, which is a striving toward the *natural*, toward the *wild*, with the reflective element, the element of *culture*, a striving toward the *civilized*, was to be a recurrent theme. In this regard the Greek Cynics are unwitting revolutionaries of enduring concern to us today.

Inimical to family, marriage, and social roles, even in the sense so dear to Vaneigem, they took the line that passions were the worst of evils. The wise man will strive all his life to detach himself from them and to eradicate them from his makeup. More and more pleasure was what was needed, and the human being was expected to turn away from that which made him human. Man is to revert to animal status, freed of passions, which are the source of all conflict.

Above all, libertarians long before anyone else, the Cynics reckoned that man ought to strive for complete autonomy, for autarky (autarkeia). Diogenes had a slave of his own by the name of Manes, who one day ran away. Diogenes did not go after him: "It would be a queer thing if Manes could live without Diogenes and Diogenes could not live without Manes."

5

We have no difficulty understanding the charm and the fascination that he exercised over his contemporaries. A peerless orator, he literally hypnotized his listeners. A certain Androsthenes came to see him and never left his side again. His father, Onesicritos of Aegina, then dispatched his other son, Philiscos, to seek out the first. Philiscos stayed as well. Whereupon Onesicritos came himself to fetch them home. Only to stay behind with his sons.

After the death of Diogenes, his disciples squabbled over who was to have the honor of burying him. He, who had requested that his corpse be left to the dogs (as they had earned it) was to get a tomb, a column surmounted by a marble dog.

Finally, it ought to be borne in mind that Diogenes also invented something that has taken twenty-five centuries to get underway. Asked by someone what his country was, Diogenes replied: "I am a citizen of the world."

Diogenes had his disciples and he also had his friends, some of whom well deserved him. Take Menedemos, a very handsome slave, or Monimos, another slave who feigned madness and looted the bank owned by his master, until the latter drove him out. Leaving Monimos free to follow Diogenes. He was fascinated by this Diogenes whom he had never seen: and it should be pointed out that the person whom he had heard speak of Diogenes was none other than Xeniadis, Diogenes's master. Metrocles was to die, smothered, by his own hand. (Remember that they praised a sort of yoga.) To begin with, Metrocles had been a follower of the Peripatetics, the fashionable philosophers, and especially of Theophrastos. One day an ailing Metrocles happened to fart in the middle of a philosophy discussion. He was so ashamed that he locked himself in at home and began to starve himself to death. Fortunately for him, Crates (of whom more anon) called to see him after gorging on a large portion of beans. He tried to console his friend by telling him that it could have happened to anybody, that it was quite all right to fart and offered him a demonstration right there and then. Impressed, Metrocles started to eat again, to venture out, to philosophize. He turned his back on the Peripatetics, making him a fine target for the Cynics. That is what philosophy is all about.

Metrocles had a sister called Hipparchia. She was to become the leading female figure among the Cynics. It is astonishing that no feminist group has thus far swooped on this extraordinary woman. She saw herself as the huntress, Atalanta, or so tradition has it. As much of a Stoic as she was a Cynic, she was to come up with a strange notion of the role of women.

It is said that at a feast in the home Lysimachus (she went everywhere with the Cynics, something of which a very dim view was taken at the time) she poked fun at a certain Theodorus, known as Theodorus the Impious, explaining: "Whatever Theodorus does and regards as no injustice, Hipparchia may do without injustice also. Now, since Theodorus can beat himself without doing any harm, Hipparchia, in striking Theodorus, is doing no harm." History does not record whether she brandished her fist in his face to demonstrate her point. But Theodorus, unable to

6

come up with a counter-argument, could not think of any way to shut her mouth other than to lift her skirt, calculating that this would confuse and annoy her. Hipparchia did not flinch, but explained that she had opted for philosophy and the Cynics and had therefore given up being a woman and was therefore indifferent to all of this. Theodorus was left floundering for a reply.

Hipparchia, who must have been very beautiful because she was much sought after, spurned all such offers and fell in love with Crates, whom we encountered earlier making recruits by munching beans. This Crates was an even more amazing character. Unlike the slaves, outcasts, tramps, and poor folk who were his comrades, he came from a wealthy family but joined the rabble after giving away his fortune. Fond of the good life, he was very ugly, so much so that his appearance at the public baths would provoke laughter.

It is said of him that one day he pinched the buttocks of a gymnastics teacher (another version of the story says that it was Menedemos) to the latter's great chagrin. "Are they not as much yours as your knees are?" Crates retorted.

On another occasion, Alexander whom the Cynics appear to have genuinely intrigued, asked Crates if he would like him to put the country back on its feet. Crates asked him, stingingly: "What for? There may well be another Alexander to destroy her."

This was the man with whom Hipparchia fell in love to the great chagrin of her family. The family brought pressure to bear on Crates to get him to make her understand that she could do better for herself. To no avail. She stuck with him. So Crates, who used to parade around in public with his face all written over and reading Homer in gales of laughter, stripped off all his clothing, stood naked before her, and muttered to her: "Behold your husband and all that he possesses. It is for you to decide, because you cannot be my wife unless you share my way of life." After that they were a couple.

Not that that was an end of the scandal. Hipparchia and Crates made love in public view. They had no reason to hide away, of course. Hipparchia donned the uniform of all the Cynics, accidentally inventing the unisex get-up twenty-five centuries ahead of time. From then on she was to be one of the most remarkable Cynics.

By Crates she was to have a son, Pasicles. When the boy reached manhood his father took him to see a prostitute so that he might achieve an understanding of what real marriage, a marriage stripped of passion, was all about. It cannot be argued that mankind has made any real progress since.

Moreover, the fragmented and, alas, often misrepresented, message of the Cynics resonates down to our own day like an echo from a forgotten world, a world in which intelligent men and women who had taken control of their own lives started to live as they deemed fit, which is to say, better. All together, in accordance with "natural law."

But now it is high time that we moved on from the days when the approach was frivolous to more serious matters.

7

Rome, 73-71 B.C.
SPARTACUS

Slaves who are ready to put up with anything are spared nothing by the tyrants.

Georges Darien,
La belle France (1900)

It's hard, I know. Freedom always is. It's slavery which is easy!

Emmett Grogan,
Ringolevio (1972)

When all is said and done, is there anything so banal as a slave revolt? One might well conclude that slaves were invented for the sole purpose of revolt, that slavery exists only to spur people into seizing their freedom. Ancient Rome, like most of the civilizations by which our contemporaries are so enthralled, was founded upon such slavery, without which everything would have collapsed.

The theorists and philosophers of which our textbooks boast so, and our high-minded exegetes have rarely rebelled against such blatant and cruel exploitation of one's fellow man. So those civilizations were not as advanced as all that—no more than our own at any rate (and we know what we ought to think about that one).

In the first century before what the Situationists term "the brat from Nazareth" (and who is scarcely anything more than one enlightened masochist among the many, albeit one blessed enough with unrivalled spin-doctors who were well ahead of their times), a Thracian slave in the friendly giant mold revolted along with 74 of his colleagues.

Spartacus very quickly won the day. His raids sowed panic, as the wealthy were dispossessed and the fighting ended with the Romans being routed. Spartacus' band very soon numbered between two and three hundred rebels.

That revolt was but one among dozens. Before Spartacus, there was Eunous, and Aristonicos, and Salvius, and Athenion, and others. Spartacus, the unchallenged ringleader, and a warrior of note, marshalled his troops on Vesuvius. There, thanks to the flames, the smoke and the darkness, their camp (or the site at any rate) could be seen from a long way away. Making it easy to rally to his banner.

His band included slaves of every nationality. This was one of the first revolts by an international proletariat, the like of which would not be seen again for another two thousand years (see our chapter on May '68). They included Gauls, Germans, Thracians, and Romans, too. All of the greater and lesser highway robbers threw in their lot with him. The local peasantry, whilst not quitting their fields, supported them, acted as their intelligence and provided their sustenance. They numbered almost three thousand.

8

A Roman praetor by the name of Claudius Puncher attacked them with an equal force. Spartacus waited for night to fall, then made a surprise raid on his enemy's camp, scattered the enemy, and made off with enormous booty.

Forced deliveries (requisitions) and looting—that was how Spartacus imposed levies on the local proprietors in order to make ends meet. In every village he captured, he started by throwing open the jails, freeing the slaves, who, most of the time, joined his band. He would hand over their captive owners to them. We can only suppose that good use was made of the gift.

On the other hand, Spartacus was personally opposed to looting and to all needless acts of barbarism. But it is hard to restrain a crowd incensed by years of slavery and the lust for vengeance. And it is hard to explain to uneducated folk denied all access to civilization that only the enemy should be attacked. So the looting persisted, as did the cruelty. Spartacus did what he was able to get his troops to ease up on this score and sometimes he succeeded.

Another praetor, Publius Varinius Glaber, came after them with four legions. He managed to corner them and while Spartacus escaped, his lieutenants, the German Oenomaus and the Gaul Crixius, were defeated. Whereupon Spartacus doubled back, took his enemy unawares in Salines, and crushed him. Several towns were looted, among them Metapontus.

The rebel forces by now numbered seventy thousand men. But they were overcome by vengeance and they made the mistake of destroying everything in their path, instead of retaining reserves. Throughout the victorious slaves' adventure, their revolt was to remain founded primarily upon warfare and the emphasis was on the military side of their revolt. That was to be their shortcoming. After all, the Roman Empire itself was founded upon that, and the rebels did not challenge what was the very basis of the system by which they were exploited.

In spite of the recruitment of huge numbers of slaves and peasants, the revolt was to prove unproductive. A lull in the fighting offered them the opportunity to carry out an experiment in communal living. The troops set up camp near the town of Thurium, which they had the wit not to destroy, and they lived in harmony with the local inhabitants. This was made feasible by the fact that by now they were very rich (from looting) and were in a position to pay cash on the barrel for everything.

Spartacus' intention was to build up a counter-State there, one that would be fairer and more peaceable and not based on slavery. He circulated a manifesto to this effect, promising equal rights for all. He was the forerunner of all who were to come after him and who follow him still, two thousand years on. It is no coincidence if today the mere name of Spartacus resonates like the gong of every revolt, or if that name was utilized during the German Revolution of 1918–1919 and if everyone, right or left, claims him as one of their own.

Spartacus and his men were by then too numerous. No one dared attack them. They also occupied the towns of Croton and Cosenza. Not until the following spring were fresh troops dispatched against the communitarians. Now, for them, the time had passed when they might tend the fields that they had shared out equally, or live together peaceably and in brotherhood.

This time, there were two consuls—Gellius and Lentulus—each commanding an entire army. Spartacus decided that they should scatter across the empire, starting with a break for the Alps. His second in command, Crixius, reckoned that the better course was to stand their ground and fight alongside one another. Without hesitating, he launched an attack with 30,000 men whilst the remainder of the army fled northward. Gellius clashed with Crixius, whilst Lentulus dogged Spartacus' steps. Crixius defeated the Romans and crushed Gellius. But at this point he made a huge mistake: revelling in his success he laid on a feast for all his men. The rash conquerors over-indulged themselves with alcohol and in orgies (which just goes to show how their former masters' "civilization" had colonized their consciousness).

Gellius had only to return and to seize his chance to massacre them. Twenty thousand slaves were slaughtered in this ambush, Crixius at their head. Celebrations are an expensive item for him who has yet to finish his revolution, as Saint-Just was to demonstrate later.

Spartacus once again provided evidence of his shrewdness. He learned of Crixius's fate while he was being chased by Lentulus, whereupon he turned to face his enemies, one by one, before their forces might link up. He beat them one at a time and captured 300 Romans into the bargain, whereupon he set off on his victory march.

News of this advance, which nothing seemed capable of halting, sowed panic throughout the north. The praetor Mantius was swept aside, the pro-consul Cassius's troops slaughtered and Cassius himself killed. Spartacus was left with no enemy force to confront. He capitalized upon this respite to lay on some funeral games for his friend Crixius.

During those games, which were inspired by the Roman games, he set his (Roman) prisoners to fight as gladiators, thereby devising an extraordinarily potent symbol of his revolution. This role-reversal was to remain one of the chief obsessions of peoples in revolt, in every civilization, throughout human history (see especially our chapter on the League of Villeins). This blend of humor and vindictive cruelty is the absolute index of all great revolutionaries (Makhno, Durruti, the Red Guards, Zapata, the Communards, etc.) From the gallery, even as their former masters were duelling with one another, the ex-slaves, ex-gladiators themselves, guffawed and called out "Kill! Kill!"

In the course of the games, Spartacus thought twice of it, changed his mind, and decided, given that fortune had been on his side, not to break and run but to march against Rome. The praetor Arrius was sent against him, only to be crushed; after which there was not a single warrior in the whole of the empire who would agree to succeed Arrius and defend Rome.

It is at this juncture that the great mystery of this revolution comes into play. Arriving before the gates of an undefended Rome, Spartacus neglected to take the city—for reasons unknown. Certain historians depict the rebels as being "stunned" by the capital and by their adventure, cowed by what they were about to do, and by the profanity implicit in their intended action. Their hesitancy marked a turning point in the revolution; one that was to prove fatal for them. A certain Crassus reorganized the Roman army and the resistance. Now it was too late to seize the city with ease.

Spartacus and his men retreated toward their point of origin in the south. They thought of moving to Sicily to settle there. But again they made a tactical error. No one saw fit to alert the Sicilians to their coming. There were no boats available to ferry them. For some obscure reason, the Sicilians were to refuse to furnish any. The rebels were cornered.

Crassus pursued them. Spartacus sensed that the conflict would be horrific. He would show his horrific side. He had a Roman captive brought before him and had him crucified in front of his troops. "As a warning to the others," we are told by Appian, "and to warn them of the fate that they should expect in the event of defeat."

And the battle, when it came, truly was horrific. Spartacus realized that his only chance was to break the morale of the Roman army by killing its commander, but the latter kept his distance. In the confusion, Spartacus ventured too far, a step too far. He was overpowered and killed by superior numbers.

Now it was his troops' turn to face a debacle. Most of them took their own lives rather than outlive their greatest adventure. After the removal of one's chains, it is a hard thing to return knowingly to them. There were few who took to their heels. The insurrection was over. For a few months, one of Spartacus' lieutenants, Publipor, waged sporadic attacks with a handful of survivors. But their heart was no longer in this guerrilla war and it petered out completely. The repression proved very severe. Six thousand of the runaway slaves were taken as prisoners. Every one of them was to be executed, by hanging or crucifixion, all along the road that led from Capua into Rome. That picture was to impress itself upon many minds and it dampened the instinct to revolt for a long time.

"The Spartakist revolt had not effectively overcome the division of the old society into two classes, those who wielded the sword and those who wielded the tools," as was pointed out by Andre Prudhommeaux who drew comparisons between the Roman Spartacists and the ones in Germany twenty centuries later. Spartacus was not necessarily so far-sighted. He was neither an intellectual nor a theoretician of revolution. Merely a slave who had had enough of his fetters. Just like all the others of whom we will be speaking. That was enough to ensure that his name has come down to us, a name as familiar as the name of a friend.

> Egoism does not say to the people, in order to eradicate poverty: wait for a court of law to award you a gift on behalf of the community, but rather tells them: seize what you need, take it. The land belongs to whoever knows how to take it, or whoever, having it already, knows how to hold on to it. If he seizes it, not only does he have land, but likewise the entitlement to it.
>
> Max Stirner,
> *The Ego and His Own* (1844)

In the wake of Alesia (52 B.C.) Pax Romana prevailed, not just in Rome, but throughout her colonies, of which Gaul was one. This "Roman peace" was one of history's most protracted wars, dragging on for four centuries. Whilst the Gallic nobility and wealthy merchants duly collaborated with the occupation, (a habit they were never to lose), the serfs and peasants fought on, rebelling regularly against the invader, region by region.

Aside from economic pillage and persistent banditry, the German invasions ultimately destroyed the freshly gathered in harvests and made famine a constant presence. In the Roman army, made up essentially of mercenaries (less than ten percent of the strength being Romans), there was widespread loss of morale and discontent:

only looting still held any charm for the troops who deserted or mutinied en masse.

The peasants took to the brush when they could no longer bear life in the fields. There they were joined by the deserter soldiers who placed their military expertise at the disposal of the peasants who knew the terrain like the back of their hands. This dangerous mix of soldiers and peasant insurgents was to become the Bagaudi, a Celtic term that means something like "coming-together of the people" or "Rebel republic." In the remoter areas, they set up a sort of self-adminis-tering republic, the Bagaudicae, where all decisions were made communally, where magistrates were elected and their verdicts monitored by all, and where power lay in the hands of the assembled peasants and soldiers. They lived in accordance with "natural law."

On every side they were hailed as the liberators which Gaul sorely needed. They got agriculture up and running again and revived the economies of the regions they liberated. Once again, the reassured inhabitants could work the land. The blight of looting and butchery was eradicated. Slaves were emancipated, serfs set free.

This republic, upon which our history textbooks are careful not to dwell, was to survive for several decades on the banks of the Loire, in the West and Southwest, and in the Alps. Within those areas there lived a community of workers whose produce maintained the Bagaudi army fighting on its fringes—a phenomenon often to recur, particularly in the Makhnovshchina, sixteen centuries later.

Whilst the first massacres of masters and grasping governors began around 283 B.C., and whilst the pro-Roman magistrates and collaborators fled, life was gradu-ally reorganized.

A number of Bagaudi leaders were former Roman soldiers, ex-comrades of Meternus who had led a significant revolt at the end of the 2nd century. But the name Bagaudi does not crop up until something like 268 when, in concert with another mutineer, Victorinus, a wealthy Gaul who proclaimed himself emperor, they besieged and sacked Autun.

By 283 the movement was up and running. Armed with their peasant tools, the Bagaudi torched the great estates, looted the rich townships and ransacked villages. Those masters who escaped their vengeance fled to the better-protected, larger cities.

Their main leaders were two Roman officer-deserters, Amandus and Aelienus. The Bagaudi army encamped on an island at the junction of the Marne and Seine rivers, near where Maisons-Alfort would be today. From this impregnable stronghold, they made raids on Paris and the surrounding region. Unused to guerrilla warfare, the Roman army was at sixes and sevens. It frequently walked into Bagaudi ambushes and the legion commander Constantian lost his life in one.

In Rome, the emperor Diocletian, having determined to put paid to this, dispatched the skillful general Maximian against them: Maximian was to deploy the tactics that have now acquired classic status: split the rebels, pen them in isolated pockets, and destroy them one at a time. This system worked and the massacre was soon underway.

On the site of what is now St.. Maur des fosses, Amandus ensconced himself in 286 in an impregnable fortified camp where he and his last remaining troops were to hold out. But hunger forced him to attempt one final sortie which

13

culminated in disaster.

Amandus was killed in the fighting. So was Aelienus. The movement was sorely wounded. A generous Maximinan spared the lives of the survivors who surrendered after their military leaders had been cut down. Generosity? No, let's not delude ourselves. Maximian was well aware that the Bagaudi had taken a heavy toll in Roman dead; and that cheap manpower had to be replaced from somewhere.

In spite of this grave setback, the Bagaudi were to fight on against the Roman occupation for another two centuries. Right into the 5th century, there were sporadic skirmishes in the countryside and an alternative (albeit precarious) lifestyle organized in accordance with "natural law."

Between 404 and 417, there was heavy fighting along the Atlantic shoreline from Normandy down to Gascony. In the surrounding forests the Bagaudi lived as free men, with the support of the local population. When the serfs in turn refused to pay an additional levy to their masters (in the wake of the invasions in 406–409 of the Vandals, Suevi, Burgundians, Alans, and Visigoths), the Bagaudi repaid the favor and rallied to their cause.

Under threat, the Romans withdrew from Britain. Whereupon the Bretons allied themselves with the Bagaudi armies to drive out the last representatives of the central authorities in Rome, before administering the entire region for themselves. The whole of Armorica became independent, not to mention the Loire district, both of them Bagaudi strongholds.

The leader of the Armorican revolt was a Gaul called Tibattus. With Bagaudi help, he managed to expropriate the wealthy estate owners and collaborating nobility and to set the slaves free. They all took over the liberated estates, managing and farming them on their own account, thereby demonstrating that destruction and reconstruction cannot be dissevered if a revolution is to be a success.

Not until 437 was Tibattus captured and executed. But a severe blow had been dealt to the decomposing Roman system, more assuredly, perhaps, than by the incessant invasions from without. Even more effectively, the internal erosion caused by the empire's moral, social and political decadence undermined its remaining crutches. The Roman Empire melted away and vanished to widespread indifference.

Normandy, 996-997
THE NORMAN PEASANT WAR

> It is a characteristic of all minorities that they cling to the memory of revolts and indeed of struggles which never attained their objectives but which were the handiwork of a few rebels pitted against more powerful foes.
>
> Max Nettlau,
> *A Short History of Anarchy* (1934)

The beginning of the reign of the fourth Duke of Normandy, Richard II, witnessed one of the most ancient of known self-managerial movements, or at any rate, the oldest one from which any plainly articulated document has come down to us.

Exorbitant seigneurial rights (which were to be the primary cause behind a thousand years of peasant uprisings in Europe) were an undue burden upon the peasants (rustici). Tired of submissiveness, they were beginning to refuse to acknowledge those rights and made up their minds to live from then on as they deemed fit. They sought to exploit the abundant woodland for their own benefit, to harness the watercourses and to see to the organization of pasture, fisheries, and harvests (particularly of timber) for themselves. They began by overrunning every place they could. Their rebellion quickly culminated in organization along conventicle lines according to region, or else they spontaneously devised new laws together. Each conventicle then dispatched two delegates to a general assembly that could say yea or nay to the decisions made at each meeting. Their gatherings were held in the open at all times.

Duke Richard's uncle, Raoul, Count of Evreux, was dispatched with troops to crack down on them. The peasants were scattered; their delegates were taken captive and before dispatching them home, Raoul had their hands and feet chopped off. It was a harsh example. William of Jumieges, who told the tale a century later, notes with malicious glee: "Thus instructed, the peasants ceased their assemblies and returned to their carts."

Two centuries on, Robert Wace used these events as the inspiration for his *Roman de la Rou* or *The Feats of the Normans*. He has them speak glibly and these verses are probably not too far removed from what was really being said in the conventicles:

"...Why let ourselves be harmed?
Let us flee from their danger!
We are men as they are,
Our limbs are such as they possess,
And our bodies are every whit as large,
And our power to endure as great.
All we lack is courage!
So let us bind ourselves by an oath,
To defend our property and our very selves!
Let us unite one and all!
And, should they seek to make war on us,
We can pit thirty or forty peasants,
Lusty fighters,
Against their one knight.

Woe betide them, Should they come face to face
With thirty lads in the bloom of youth!
Not one of them can stand against us
If we all set about him
With clubs, great staffs,
Arrows and bludgeons,
With bows, arrows and axes,
And, for the weaponless, stones.
Then we will be able to go into the woods,
To fell trees and take what we will,
And take fish from the ponds,
And venison from the forests.
And we will have our way with everything.
With the woods, fields and meadows..."

The war of the Norman peasants was but the first in a long list of peasant revolts. The peasant world has been in constant conflict with all of the oppressor authorities for upward of a thousand years past, virtually without interruption. We may say without exaggeration that no quarter century has passed without at least a few uprisings somewhere. Most of the time, these ended in massacres. But the fact remains that for what little time their resistance lasted, complete freedom was able to prevail in the areas occupied by the rebels.

England, 1381
THE ENGLISH PEASANTS' REVOLT: THE GREAT COMPANY

> Yet, the recovery of human possessions, in short expropriation, can only be accomplished through anarchist communism: one must destroy the government, tear up its laws, repudiate its morality, ignore its agents and set to work in obedience to one's own initiative and band together according to one's preferences, one's interests, one's ideals and the nature of the task embarked upon.
>
> Elisee Reclus, foreword to Kropotkin's
> *The Conquest of Bread* (1892)

> The more broken the people, the more necessary the terror.
>
> Augustin Cochin,
> *The Revolution and Free Thought* (1916)

By the close of the 14th century, England was embroiled in the Hundred Years' War (a conflict that had erupted in 1337). It was a time of military reverses inflicted by France, and the population had wearied of the war, especially as its strongest members had been conscripted and as every village was expected to finance the equipping of "its" soldiers out of its own purse.

It was also a time of unprecedented fiscal levies. The explosion was to come in the provinces of highest population, in the ones where the relations between seigneur and serf had reached a breaking point.

As ever, the detonator was taxation. The peasants resisted the tax collectors. The government dispatched judges to punish the recalcitrant. Certain agents of the authorities were to take things a little further. To cite but one example: in certain villages, they inspected the young girls to discover if they were still virgins, and any who failed the inspection were found liable to taxation as "adults"!

The uprising came in two places simultaneously; first in Essex and Kent and, later, the East Anglian counties. In May 1381, toward the end of that month and then at the beginning of June, there was a rebellion in Fobbing, a small Essex village. The rebels dithered about which route to take. A cook by the name of Thomas Baker harangued his companions, and then each of them went off to alert his friends or relations in the surrounding villages.

The news spread quickly from village to village, everyone having his say and local "companies" were formed. On May 30, in Fobbing, there was a convention of delegates from eighteen villages. This marked the start of self-managing organization. But it ought to be pointed out that the villagers and townspeople already had their organizations in the form of the guilds (rural or artisan) and that they played their part in the manorial courts.

The local leaders were William Gildeborne, a well-to-do peasant, and Adam Michel from Colchester town. By the start of June, the unrest had spread into the neighboring county of Kent. The towns of Dartford, Maidstone, and Canterbury fell to the rebels, without resistance. At the rebels' head was a man who was to be the movement's unchallenged leader and chief spokesman, Wat Tyler. Mention was often to be made of another individual, a legend within the movement, one Jack Straw, doubtless a pseudonym, but his real identity remains unknown. It is possible that he never existed or that the name was simply an alias for Tyler himself, in that the same words and the same deeds were indiscriminately credited to both.

Attacks were made upon the property of the Knights Hospitallers of the order of Saint John of Jerusalem; their leader, Sir Robert Hales, was also the King's Treasurer. In Kent one of the leaders of operations was a John Coverhurst. Soon, by June 12, the Kentish rebels and the rebels from Essex linked forces at Blackheath. The day before, King Richard II had written to them to inquire as to the motives behind this commotion. They replied: "To rescue you from criminal advisors." As in every peasant revolt, the target was never the king, who was believed favorable to his people, but rather the advisors who were betraying him.

Also present at Blackheath was another of the great figures in the movement, the priest John Ball. A radical preacher, he already had served time in jail for illicit sermons. He was a familiar figure, and his ideas were widely known, too. He is credited with the famous saying, which he doubtless uttered, though did not devise (for it turns up at numerous times and right across Europe): "When Adam delved and Eve span, who was then the gentleman?"

Ball advocated a sort of primitive communism. Men were born equal and slavery was a subsequent invention. Froissart puts these words in his mouth and they do have the ring of credibility about them: "Good people, things cannot go well in England and shall not go well until such times as property is held in common and there are neither serfs nor gentlemen and until we are all one."

For peace, freedom, and equality to reign, there was but one thing needed: all of the great men of the kingdom had to be killed, along with the judges, the juries, and the lawmen. Moreover, the rebels' victims were drawn willy-nilly from these ranks: they were to be snuffed out just like the manorial registers (which authenticated and validated the levies and debts paid to the seigneurs); they were witnesses to the old law and had to be cut down and forgotten. The new law would be of the people's making, determined by the people. These ideas were to be taken up by Wat Tyler. They were ideas into which a hint of apocalyptic notions had intruded, as is often the case with peasant revolts.

Seeking an audience to which to spell all of this out, the rebels tried to contact the king, who was being led astray by his advisors. They attacked the archbishop of Lambeth, Treasurer Hales' manor house in Hughbury, and the prisons of Southwark, Newgate, and Fleet, and the home of the Mayor of London. At all of the prisons they attacked, they freed the inmates and sometimes wrought their revenge: at Westminster Abbey (in use as a prison) they beheaded the guard. Lord-serf relations had gone just about as far as they could bear.

They entered London, still without meeting any resistance. Meanwhile, the city's poor had risen in revolt and ransacked the Savoy Palace belonging to the Duke of Lancaster (who was a despised figure), and the explosive combination of urban proletariat and peasants was accomplished.

In contrast to the king's wishy-washy proposals, which they rejected, their demands were clear cut. The most pressing demand was that the traitors should be punished. The most revolutionary demand was that charters of manumission be issued, which is to say that serfdom be abolished.

They did not pillage London, thereby giving an earnest of their goodwill. But the meeting with the king himself had now become inevitable. It took place at Mile End on June 14. Wat Tyler spelled out the rebels' demands in the presence of Richard II. The king indicated compliance.

At the same time, in order to press their demands, the rebels burst into the Tower of London and executed Sudbury, the Archbishop of Canterbury (who had shown great hostility to them), as well as Treasurer Robert Hales and the king's physician, John Legge, who were beheaded. The looting of the property of the wealthy continued. The properties of the very unpopular John of Gaunt were an especial target. To buy time, the king had the charters of manumission drafted and this provoked the first split in the ranks of the rebels: the softer rebels, satisfied with that, returned to Essex.

On June 15 there was a further audience with the king in Smithfield. Tyler submitted further demands. The rebels refused to cease fighting until such time as they had some concrete results to show. They stood on the brink of success, on the very verge of turning everything upside down.

But disaster was quick to follow. Wat Tyler was slain by the Mayor of London. Following that, the London movement was wound up, unable to survive the loss of a strong personality like Tyler. This is a familiar scenario. One that we will meet again in subsequent upheavals.

Oddly enough, just as the revolt was petering out in London, insurrection flared elsewhere. Disturbances had broken out in Hertfordshire as early as June 14, around St. Albans, where the Lord Abbot had, under duress, been forced to concede a number of fundamental rights to the inhabitants and the neighboring peasants. The rebel leader there was William Grindecobbe.

The recently rebel counties of Surrey and Middlesex were to witness the customary burning of manorial records and attacks on property, all of it in conjunction with the troubles in the capital. But it was in East Anglia that things were to take a violent turn. In those counties of Norfolk, Suffolk, and Cambridgeshire, there was a seething anger. John Wrave, the priest of Ringfield, raised Suffolk in revolt from June 12 on. The other leaders were local men—John Michel, John Batisford (a priest), and, above all, a well-to-do peasant by the name of Thomas Sampson.

A dyer called Geoffrey Litster rebelled in Norfolk, abetted by a few noblemen who saw this as their chance to settle some personal scores; Roger Bacon was one of these. In Cambridgeshire, there was no outstanding personality: and the lesser, local leaders are less familiar. The most important of them appears to have been John Hanchache, a small-holder from Shuddy Camps. The others are known primarily from the trial they faced once the whole thing was over. They included Geoffrey Cobbe (a peasant from Wimpole), John Cook (a peasant from Barton), John Brux (from Caxton), William Bokenham (from Hinxton) and William Corre, tailor, of whom more anon.

In Suffolk, a connection was established with the drapers living in Bury St. Edmunds, where the prior perished at the hands of the rebels led by a wealthy burgess, one Thomas Halesworth, the merchant Robert Westbrom (who went on to become John Wrave's chief lieutenant), and the squire Geoffrey Denham. They had risen in revolt in response to a summons issued to the "great company" by George Dounesby. We shall speak again of this "great company," the existence of which is denied by most historians.

But first let us finish with the disturbances in East Anglia. John Wrave and his troops were ruthless: on June 14 and 15 they slew a judge, a prior, and a monk. On June 16 the charters of Cambridge University were destroyed, at the behest of Edmund Redmeadow (also called Litster, on account of his being a dyer by trade), the town's mayor, who had probably been forced. It has to be said that the maintenance of order was the responsibility of the University's censors and chancellors.

Flemings, who were numerous in the region, were very often a particular target. Not that this was indicative of any racism in the strict sense, but merely because Flemish dyers were fierce competitors of the local artisans and enjoyed privileges that the rebels found intolerable.

On June 17 the rebels captured Norwich, but the inhabitants failed to follow them. During the period between June 18 and 26, the city's bishop, Henry Despender, orchestrated the counterattack. He clashed with Litster in North Walsham where the latter was encamped. He broke through Litster's barricades and thrashed him. On June 28, the story was the same in Billericay, to where the Essex rebels had retreated. Thomas of Woodstock and Sir Henry Percy scattered them.

Right across England, there were other uprisings that were quickly snuffed out, having been launched too belatedly. News travelled slowly, transmitted by means of markets and fairs. A number of disturbances were unconnected with the peasant revolt. Others were patently supportive of the rebel peasants: in which case, the disturbances were much more serious. This linking of town and countryside moved the revolutionaries up a notch: their challenge went beyond the seigneurial system and questioned monarchy itself. And, even though there were clergy aplenty among them, they were critical of the Church.

On July 12, the king and his magistrates were finally able to restore order, tearing up all the concessions wrestled from their masters by the rebels. There was nothing now to hinder the repression.

John Ball was captured in Coventry. On July 13, he was hanged, drawn, and quartered. Grindecobbe, the rebel leader from St. Albans, suffered the same fate. Most of the leaders were condemned to death but not all by the same method. Brux was beheaded, as was Covershurst, while Gildeborne was hanged. Wrave was to denounce his colleagues, the priests, Geoffrey Parfey, the chaplain Thomas and all the others. In Essex, though, the surviving rebels pledged themselves to fight on until victory or death and to keep their demands pure and undiluted.

The nobles helped the government eradicate the rabble. William Corre, one of the Cambridgeshire leaders, was virtually alone in escaping the immediate crackdown. He left his village and became a "social bandit" along with nine companions who plundered the area. Not until October 1382 was he to be captured. But the unrest among the peasantry was to persist for 20 years.

The "rebel" organization never had the time to fully develop. Today we can cite the letters known as the "Orders of the Great Company." They are ascribed to John Ball, which seems likely, and also to Jack Mylner, Jack Carter, Jack Trewman — aliases that may well have been John Ball's aliases. The orders are highly poetic, symbolic, metaphorical, indeed, enigmatic messages.

Their meaning is not always apparent or remains very vague. Messengers roved the countryside and spread the orders, as well as more specific instructions no doubt. Troops pledged themselves to be loyal to the "grand company." In the minds of its members, that company was nothing less than the assemblage of the lower orders of society. Perhaps it never had any formal existence. But the idea was a live one for most of the rebels who understood that they were part of a broader movement. This class-consciousness, a relatively novel phenomenon for its time, was not to figure again in the minds of peasant rebels until 1789.

Some of the rebels held offices and put these to good use: Henry Bakere of Manningtree, the bailiff of Tendring (Essex) issued the mobilization order in the king's name: James of Bendingfield raised a group of ten archers from the hundred of Hoxne in Suffolk to serve with the rebels. The priests used their churches as a base from which to raise funds, issue watchwords, and mobilize the masses in the names of Tyler and Straw. All existing structures were put to use. From around the abbey in St. Albans, their power reached out to the entire lordship, which is to say, to more than 32 villages.

The rebel leaders were elected or very quickly emerged as leaders by dint of their strong personalities or long-recognized authority. Broadly speaking, the spontaneous uprising was the doing of the peasants. After which they looked for a leader better versed in military operations and coordinating activities. Wat Tyler, for instance, was contacted in the wake of his early successes by the men from St. Albans, a town that was already functioning along "soviet" lines. He was to be the unchallenged leader of the entire movement following his victory in London. This was also a weakness of the movement: when he was slain, there was no one to step into his shoes.

By the time of Tyler's death, the organization was operating fairly well. Their enemies' counterattack came too swiftly for them to be able to compose themselves in time. The cudgels were then taken up by the rebels from East Anglia (Suffolk, Norfolk, and Cambridgeshire).

Their essential demands were that serfdom be abolished and the traitors handed over. They were never to retreat from these two points. Had the first of them been accepted, the whole of English society would have been turned on its head.

But then again, what sort of a society were they after? And did they in any case have a specific vision in mind? How did they envisage their future?

One and all, they reckoned that nothing could be accomplished until the lords had been done away with. These being the roots of all their ills. But the king was spared. "With King Richard and the true commons!" was their favorite slogan. The king they saw as an authority above and beyond all squabbling and interests (it is odd to note that this monarchist view of power is still alive and well, for it is, for example, the thinking of the man who was president of the French Republic at the time of writing).

They were tremendously preoccupied with lordship but it was to be accessible to all. Tyler was to say that all men should enjoy it, which, in practice, boils down to doing away with it, but it is plain that this egalitarianism, contrary to what was to be the case frequently among the subsequent theoreticians of revolution, was to descend from above: everyone was to be equal in plenty and in happiness, and not in terms of penury.

The clergy was to possess nothing beyond what they needed to survive: their property was to be shared out among their parishioners, just like the great estates of the wealthy. They would have a single bishop or archbishop at their head and he would perform in the realm of the spiritual the very same role as the king performed in the temporal. There would be a neutral leader at the top and, moreover, "soviets" everywhere: parish councils with direct connections to the two leaders, temporal and spiritual, amounting to a virtually complete direct democracy.

(It only remained to boot out the two leaders!)

All in all, this vision was not always coherent and not systematic, not thought through. These were merely fundamental demands that, of necessity, did not have the time to be fully explored (as the rebellion lasted for only a few weeks!). But Rodney Hilton in his book *Peasant Movements in the Middle Ages*, is right to note that their thinking included an outline of a popular monarchy with a single class in control of society, administration, justice, and religion.

Some of them even went so far as to anticipate that no longer would any man work for any other man, except by his own free will or under contract. As for the rivers and forests and the game, hitherto the preserve of the gentlemen, these were to become common property.

Some of these demands were gradually to be introduced into English society. Serfdom, especially, was not to survive for much longer, having no place in the emergent modern society. Feudal dues were to be whittled away and even abolished entirely. But that would entail further campaigns. And the people who may well have set these reforms in motion had by then been six feet under for a long, long time. Such is the fate of the pioneer. We leave it to the reader to consider whether the English peasant revolt of 1381 was a victory or a defeat. Victorious for a time, a defeat for a much longer one. The path trodden by the proletariat is paved with such as these.

Catalonia, 1462-1846
LOS REMENSAS

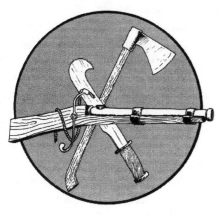

All things belong to all men, for all men have need of them, because all men have contributed what they could to the production of them, because it is not possible to assess the measure of each in the production of the world's wealth. If man and woman perform their fair share of the work, they also have an entitlement to their fair share of what is produced by all, and that share is sufficient to guarantee their well-being.

Peter Kropotkin
The Conquest of Bread (1890)

True life has not yet come to light. It sprouts from the footprints of the last incomplete men, from our footprints.

Raoul Vaneigem
The Book of Pleasures (1979)

The vast majority of Spanish peasants in the 15th century still lived under a system of serfdom. These "unfree" peasants (in Spanish, *Remensas*) found their obligations forever increasing. Added to this, especially in Catalonia, there were the *malos usos* (evil customs), five entitlements that the Catalan lords exacted from them (mainmorte, succession, adultery, arson, and mortgage—as we can see, just about anything was an excuse to fleece the peasant).

This uprising was to prove one of the longest of peasant revolts. It erupted following protracted harassment by the seigneurial lords and the feudalists' thwarting of the Catalan peasants' desires to migrate south to new lands. The Black Death had decimated the countryside. The peasants were at the end of their tether. Then along came the insatiable lords and their decision to make certain levies in kind compulsory, whereas hitherto they had been simply voluntary. The peasant, utterly determined to quit his lord's lands was now to be obliged to perform the *remensa*. As for the notorious *malos usos*, they would henceforth be applicable to all. The cup ran over and there was an uprising.

Among their basic demands, the peasants insisted upon their right to occupy and till abandoned holdings. Not that the lords were against this, but there was no meeting of minds on the size of the rents due. Whenever the peasants applied to the king to have the *malos usos* done away with, they adopted a realistic approach and offered financial compensation.

Alfonso V did not miss his chance. In 1445, he agreed. Outraged, Barcelona's nobles and wealthy landlords determined to resist, led by the Bishop of Gerona, who had a direct vested interest.

Let us look ahead to 1462 and the stirrings of the first war of the Remensas. It was to last until 1471. When the nobles did all in their power to re-impose the old order, the war erupted again in 1483, and from 1484 until 1486 and the end of the upheaval, there was fierce fighting.

A peasant by the name of Francisco Verntallat raised a peasant army, his men recruited shrewdly. He press-ganged one man out of every three in each family. That way, peasant life was not overly disrupted by the fighting and the sacrifice was borne equally by all the families. The army dug in behind its fortified positions. In engagements the soldiers took to horse, because peasants and artisans had long since been forbidden to ride on horseback by a royal edict.

To avert disaster, the king bought off Verntallat with a promotion and money. The fortifications were levelled to the ground.

At the time of the second uprising (the first was a half-victory, in that the malos usos were abolished), new leaders emerged, to organize the fight against the Catalan lords' restoration of the *malos usos*. The main leader was Father Joan Sala, along with the lawyer Tomás Mieres.

Toward the end of the fighting, Sala was displaying extremely radical tendencies, especially of the anti-clerical variety, which is rare in peasant revolts (but that could be detected earlier in the uprising in the Flemish seaboard in 1323). Mieres was an accomplished theoretician. He preached a return to natural law which states that men are born free and that it is the duty of the king to protect the peasants from the nobles (here we find the core idea in every peasant revolt: the king is a good guy, on their side, a very remote figure who affords them his peace, whereas the lords—who are close at hand and enforcing their levies—are the ones with the evil intent, straying from the straight and narrow, back to which the king must steer them). Little by little, there was a class consciousness emerging. Already the peasants were sensible of what united them and of what bound the lords together, but they had yet to make the connection with royalty. This situation was to persist virtually up until 1789 when they were to achieve complete consciousness. And then royalty was swept aside overnight.

Sala, who led the later operations, insisted upon the abolition of feudal dues, no matter what they might be. His view was that there was no question but that the ownership of the land should be vested in the peasants, which was a very revolutionary demand: for it to be put into effect, there would have to be a complete overthrow of feudal society. Not that he sought to do away with the nobility, he merely wanted to see their prerogatives reduced.

Elsewhere, other, more moderate representatives were also engaged in negotiations. Though they may have appeared more moderate, they were not any less firm: they insisted upon abolition of the *malos usos*, the abolition of serfdom, and upon the lord being banned from imposing his will by force.

The authorities were afraid to grant these demands but they were much more afraid of the group of extremists around Sala. They yielded to the demands of the "moderates". In 1486, the *Sentencia Arbitral de Guadalupe* brought the unrest and the fighting to an end. The peasants got their way and found themselves becoming small holders. For a few decades they were to enjoy an unprecedented prosperity.

This victory for the Remensas was one of the very rare instances of complete success for a peasant uprising. The rising, whilst it entailed loss of life, did not end in a bloodbath. It should be said that the Remensas were abetted by a particular historical circumstance: King Alfonso V was not afraid to lock horns with the Catalan nobility and Barcelona bourgeoisie who had been rather reluctant to recognize his authority. This tension within the ranks of the ruling class was exploited by the peasants, albeit unwittingly. The essential point is that they benefited from it.

France 1548-1574

ETIENNE DE LA BOETIE'S DISCOURSE ON VOLUNTARY SERVITUDE

> When a great idea is stumbled upon, there is always a certain time-lapse before its implications are able to assume a really practical form.
>
> Max Nettlau
> *A Short History of Anarchy* (1934)

> On what does the survival of oppression depend? On us! On whom must we depend for its demolition? On ourselves!
>
> Bertolt Brecht

Etienne de La Boétie was only 17 years old when he began to write one of the major books in the history of humanity. He was a friend of Montaigne, whose maudlin commonplaces have so enthralled the great bourgeoisie over the centuries. La Boétie had been marked by the peasant revolts in Guyenne against the gabelle, particularly the unrest in Les Piteaux (1548–1549). Constable Anne de Montmorency had crushed the rebels in Bordeaux and this had left a deep impression on the youthful La Boétie.

His book was probably completed a few years later, but it circulated in manuscript form only. Montaigne wanted to see it published. But to no avail.

La Boétie died in 1563 at the age of 33, without having seen his creation in print. Some Calvinists then got hold of the manuscript (which was finally published anonymously in 1574) and hijacked it for their own questionable cause. (At the time the Calvinists were the equivalent of today's Stalinists).

Panicking lest he be persecuted for being a Protestant, Montaigne failed to include his friend's essay among his own *Essais*, as he had planned. And it was under the title of *Contr'un* that the book was to be known for centuries, in a revamped, abridged Calvinist edition. Landauer was an admirer and Marat looted its contents unashamedly whilst narrowing its focus considerably, for his own *Chains of Slavery* in 1774.

27

It is only quite recently that La Boétie's work has been restored to its proper place: it ranks, without doubt, as the premier work among all those dealing with theories of revolt. It is a fact that its clarity, its violence, and the solid transparency of its argument make it a primary source alongside which the genteel scribblings of such as Marx, Proudhon, or Rousseau can only pale. The best proof of this is to offer a few extracts from its contents.

"But if a hundred or a thousand let themselves be oppressed by a single individual, can the argument hold, that it is cowardice that stops them from turning on him, or is it not, rather, that, prompted by scorn and disdain, they opt not to resist him? And in the end, if one finds, not a hundred nor a thousand

people but rather a hundred countries, a thousand towns, a million men refraining from attacking and crushing him who, without any pretence of diplomacy, treats them all like so many serfs and slaves: by what name shall we call that?"

"So it is people who allow, or rather, ensure their own strangulation, in that they might, by a simple refusal to serve, break their bonds. It is the people which bears the responsibility for its own subjection and cuts its own throat: and, having the choice whether to be subject or free, rejects freedom and dons the yoke, embracing its misfortune or indeed going in search of it."

"True, even as the fire from a spark grows and waxes, and, the more tinder it finds the more tinder it consumes, only to burn itself out and eventually die away when once its fuel is withheld: so, the more that tyrants loot, the more they demand; the more they ruin and destroy, the more is lavished upon them and the more they are gorged; they grow in strength and are ever better disposed to annihilate and destroy everything; but if they are denied everything and if obedience is denied them: then, without their being fought against or stricken down, they are stripped naked and undone; just as a tree receiving no more sap and nourishment at the root is soon reduced to a dried-up, dead stump."

"Poor wretched folk, demented folk, nations stubbornly clinging to your affliction and blind to your own welfare, you let the finest, brightest part of your income be wrestled from before your very eyes, your fields be pillaged, your homes laid waste and your finest heirlooms stolen! You live as if nothing is yours any more. And all of this havoc, these afflictions, in short, this ruination comes to you, not by courtesy of your enemies. But, to be sure, from the Enemy and from one who owes all that he is to you, one for whom you march so bravely off to war and for whose vanity you brave death throughout. Yet this master has but two eyes, two hands, one body and has nothing that the least of the countless inhabitants of your cities does not possess too. The thing which he has that you do not is the means which you afford him for your own destruction. Where would he come by so many hands with which to strike you down, if he could not borrow them from you?"

"Those feet with which he tramples over your cities, are they not your feet too? Has he some power over you other than that which he receives from you? You plant your fields so that he may lay them waste; you furnish and appoint your homes merely to feed his thievery, you rear your daughters so that he may indulge his lechery, you feed your children so that he may make soldiers of them (and they are only too happy to oblige!), so that he may lead them to the slaughter and make them the instruments of his avarice, the executors of his vengeance. Resolve, then, to serve no more and you will have your freedom. I do not counsel you to clash with nor to overthrow him, merely that you withhold all support from him and you will see how, like a huge colossus denied its base, his very weight will bring him tumbling down to be smashed into pieces."

"(Nature)...has shaped us all the same and, so to speak, in the same mould, in order to show us that we are all equals, or rather, all brothers. And if, in the disposition of her gifts, she has lavished a few more physical or intellectual advantages upon some than upon the rest, it was never her intention to place us in this world as if it were a jousting arena, and she did not send the strongest and shrewdest down here as armed woodland outlaws to prey upon the weakest. We should, rather, believe that, in assigning to some the larger portion and to others the lesser, her meaning was to inspire a sentiment of brotherhood in them and to equip them to act upon it; some having the might to afford assistance and others the need to avail thereof. So, since our kindly mother has given us everything, the entire earth for our dwelling-place, and lodged us all under the same roof, and kneaded us all out of the same dough, so that each of us might see himself in his neighbor like gazing into a looking-glass; if she has made us all this splendid gift of voice and speech so that we might mingle and fraternize with one another, and, through the communication and intercourse of our ideas, be led towards a commonality of ideas and intentions; if she has sought, by all manner of means, to form and to tighten the knot of our alliance, the bonds of our society; if, finally, she has demonstrated in all things her desire that we should become one, not merely united, but that we should, all together, compose, so to speak, a single entity, then, how can we for a single instant doubt that we are all naturally free, in that we are all equals, and how can anyone entertain the notion that, having placed us all in a single company, she intended some to be slaves within it?"

"Freedom is nature's way and, in my estimation, not only are we born with our freedom, but we have an innate determination to defend it."

"So, to be truthful, I can discern a difference between these tyrants, but I can detect no choice to be made between them; for, though they may ascend to their thrones by differing routes, the manner of their ruling remains pretty much the same. The people's elected leaders treat the people like a bull to be tamed; its leaders through conquest, like a prey with which they are entitled to do as they please; and those who rule by right of succession, like a troupe of slaves whose nature it is to belong to them."

"The primary reason why men serve willingly is that they are born slaves and that they are schooled to slavery. From which it follows, quite naturally; that, under tyrants, men necessarily become craven and effeminate…"

"Thus does the tyrant use some of his subjects to enslave the rest. He is guarded by those from whom he ought to need guarding, if only they had not sunk so low; but, as the saying rightly has it, in the splitting of wood, the wedges are made of that very same wood. Such are his archers, his guards, and his halberdiers. Not that the latter do not themselves, and often, groan under his oppression; but these wretches, damned of God and of men, are content to endure the affliction, in order to visit it, not upon him who afflicts them, but rather upon those like themselves who endure it and can do nothing about it. And yet, whenever I call to mind such folk, who basely lavish flattery upon the tyrant so as to make capital out of both his tyranny and the people's servitude, I am also almost taken aback by their stupidity and their malice. Because, if truth be told, what is dalliance with tyranny other than an alienation from freedom and, so to speak, an embracing, a two-handed clasping of slavishness?"

> They all sing together but each of them is
> singing a song of his own. They are masters
> of the night and each of them would be his
> own master.
>
> Pierre Clastres
> *Chronicle of the Guayaki Indians* (1972)

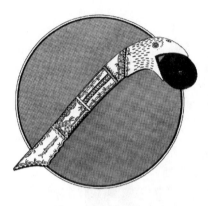

It is a known fact these days that, prior to the arrival of the white man (the French, Spanish, English, Dutch, Portuguese, etc.) on the American continent, important civilizations had evolved there and sometimes lived in concord, sometimes not. It is not a secret any more that Christopher Columbus no more "discovered" America than the man who beat him there by a few years, Amerigo Vespucci. Yet the beginning of contacts between those American civilizations and the avaricious world of the European feudalists is still dated from 1492.

That date, a crucial date in human history, marks the starting point for one of the greatest genocides in all history: the genocide of hundreds of different civilizations and peoples whose cultures may on occasion have been far ahead of the culture of the white intruders. We have a good example of this in the Iroquois civilization, which embraced several North American nations in the northeast of America, broadly overlapping with the present state of New York.

Whenever the whites ventured into this territory, the Iroquois were organized into a number of tribes, unquestionably the mightiest tribes in all the Americas. Theirs was a settled civilization. They lived in genuine villages, often located beside a river or lake. These villages were surrounded by a stockade of wooden logs, within which a permanent population of one or two hundred people resided.

They were a farming people: cereals and vegetables were raised all around the village. The men would clear virgin land and tidy up the forest in order to encourage the numbers of the game. They lived on the plains and their homes were no makeshift shelters, but well set out rectangular accommodations.

Nevertheless, they were a quite warlike people, particularly in their dealings with their neighbors, the Algonquins, to the north, or their neighbors to the south.

32

They were forever trying to absorb these into their confederation by overpowering them.

In fact, the Iroquois came in several varieties. Out to the west, there were the Oneidas with their somewhat aggressive character, and the more peaceable Onondagas. On the banks of the Hudson lived the Mohawks—a word that means simply "cannibals," which speaks volumes for their traditional ferocity. Whereas the most numerous tribe, the Senecas, lived on the banks of the Ohio. Somewhat further out lived the Cayugas.

These five groups were to band together sometime around 1570 to establish a so-called Five Nations confederation. Some 150 years later, in 1722, they were to be joined by a sixth nation, the Tuscarosas, whom the whites had recently decimated and who were in need of their protection. The Six Nation League, or, to use their own language, the Hodesaunee, was then complete. It went on to take other tribes such as the Delawares under its wing.

Tradition has it that this league had initially formed on religious grounds. A prophet by the name of Daganawidah had supposedly brought peace to these nations. His main disciple, who carried on the struggle, was a Mohawk called Hiawatha. Here we should quickly unlearn any memories we might have connected with Longfellow's legendary poem. Longfellow simply borrowed a name famous among all Indians in order to "whiten" a few Ojubway legends that had nothing to do with the historical Hiawatha. The Hiawatha in whom we are interested was alleged to have used a white canoe to visit each tribe of every nation in order to spread his ideas and had done so successfully.

The legend may very well be true, but Hiawatha's motives were undoubtedly more than merely religious (it may well be that religion was merely a pretext gilding an inexorable political imperative). The whites had come. The English and the French were at daggers drawn over the division of the spoils.

The French, moreover, were very quick to lose their temper with these Indian savages, which would cost them dearly. The Iroquois would ally themselves with the more pragmatic English who were to assume power in the region. The fellowship between Americans (by which I mean, of course the Indian, even though both words miss the mark: as these were neither peoples from the Indies nor inhabitants of a land whose name was borrowed from an Italian) was absolutely essential for their survival. It matters little whether the two prophets appreciated this fact, or that the sachems saw in the incitement to unity a resolution of this grave problem: Unity was achieved and it was to endure for more than two centuries.

For its time, the functioning of the Iroquois League was remarkable on every score and its importance will readily be grasped if we compare its civilization alongside the ones existing in Europe at the time. The whites do not emerge with great credit from the comparison.

Moreover, the celebrated constitution of the United States, when it came to be devised, was to be heavily indebted to the unwritten constitution of the Iroquois.

That had made an impression upon the more intelligent of the whites.

Above all else, it was a federation. Authority was widely distributed. These days, we should describe the arrangement as decentralization. Each individual wielded significant power over his own life. Everything related to foreign affairs, war, and peace was handled at a federal level. Decision-making power was vested in a Council of Sachems. There were around fifty of these sachems.

With regard to domestic arrangements, each nation made its own determination through a gathering of its sachems. Within each of the nations, each tribe enjoyed autonomy, each of them having its own power, its own chief. Within the tribe, each clan also enjoyed its measure of authority and its own chief. Each of them decided for herself, then they would come together with their peers and work out a binding resolution.

There was an odd and interesting manner of election. We ought to say from the outset that the Iroquois had one of the most matriarchal societies on record. Ownership of land, all assets, the home, and the children was vested in the women. Women chose their own husband and sent him packing when he was no longer wanted, even though it was the man who cleared the land and kept the tools: marriage and divorce were very straightforward.

The women would come together at clan level and they were the ones who chose the sachem (who would be the war chief and so had to be a sturdy, adult male) according to their chosen criteria. The position of sachem could be inherited, though not necessarily passed from father to son. If the chosen sachem was too young, which was sometimes the case, one of the women would act as regent.

The sachem was not elected for life. Any time that he incurred displeasure or made a mistake, the women would issue him with a warning. After a third warning, he was deposed and a replacement appointed. As we can readily appreciate, this sachem was wholly comparable with the "delegate" to a soviet, being the representative of the general consensus.

The clan sachems appointed the tribal sachems, who then appointed the sachems of the nation and so on, exactly as the council of councils is arrived at during a self-managerial revolution.

Each nation sent as many sachems/delegates as it chose to the central council of sachems: each nation had a single vote, so delegates had to come to some accommodation with one another. Then the six-member council of sachems had to come to some agreed position, because decisions had to be made unanimously. The proceedings and negotiations would last just as long as it took to win over a single dissenting opinion. Only the rather wide-ranging commonality of interests could encourage this unanimity when the time came.

Nothing was in writing. The constitution was completely an oral tradition, but everyone honored it. There were neither police nor federal taxes. Inside each of the tribes the womenfolk simply ensured order.

34

Such delegates, subject to recall at any time—which calls lots of things to mind—were not the only novelty in this arrangement. To this day, multiple elections with one vote per nation can be found in the United States, in the voting of the states in presidential elections, say. It might be said that many contemporary systems have borrowed from the Iroquois model, which was devised, let us remind ourselves, at a time when Europe was only a pitiful mosaic of poorly organized feudal fiefdoms. Marx and Engels, no less, were impressed by this, although they had access only to partial, misconstrued glimpses of it.

Among the points demonstrating the splendor of this civilization, there is one that is quite overlooked: two or three centuries ahead of Sigmund Freud, the Iroquois had dabbled in psychoanalysis and psychotherapy. In fact they analyzed their dreams in a manner none too far removed from the current practice. Questioned during the 17th century by Jesuits, who had come with the intention of colonizing their consciousness, the Iroquois explained their thinking in this sphere. Aside from its conscious wishes, the human soul had hidden desires which revealed themselves in dreams. They were the "language of desire." The essential technique employed was the "free association" so familiar to our own psycho-analysts.

It was their dreams that directed their lives and their significant actions—a frequent occurrence in many (especially ancient) civilizations, but this had nothing to do with superstition. It was, rather, a rational and scientific procedure. They had their counsellors in this, just as we have our "shrinks." And most of the time these were women.

Elsewhere, there was still another social status to be aimed at, the status of "pine" (like the tree). This was a title reflecting battle honors and indicating bravery and courage in combat. These "pines" achieved a degree of importance and sometimes they triggered frictions with the sachems. When it came to combat, the Iroquois favored hand-to-hand fighting and fought with bludgeons of the type that the Algonquins called tomahawk (not an axe but a reinforced club), sometimes with a wooden shield and a sort of plaited buckskin breast-plate. In ambushes, they, like everyone else, used bow and arrow. Captives might encounter two very different fates. If the tribe was short of man-power or had suffered heavy fatalities in need of replacement, captives were adopted as such replacements. In the absence of any such shortages, they were put to death under refined tortures.

Because the Iroquois liked torture, torture lasted a long time and the level of suffering had to be maintained right to the end. They dismembered and they roasted captives and whipped themselves into a frenzy. The Iroquois were much feared.

The strength of the Iroquois resided in their occupying quite extensive territory and in their being able to defend it. On the other hand, they were unable to extend it, and could not have enforced their authority over an unduly wide expanse. That is where they fell down in comparison to the whites. They were short of man-power. Fighting, farming, construction, clearance work—it was all down to the men and they could not do everything at once. They would take captives, seize some booty, and then flee.

The whites really arrive on their territory in any numbers around 1640. Within two centuries, their brilliant civilization was virtually extinct; their territory occupied by whites and everything had been destroyed.

The slaughter of the entire Indian nation in America by means of weapon, alcohol, and the Church, imported diseases and treachery is well known. As Elise Marienstras has it (*Cahiers Jussieu*, No. 5, Ed. 10-18): "The Amerindians were the first people without writing, the first of the so-called 'primitive' peoples with which western Christian civilization came into sustained contact. America served as a testing-ground for the theories, methods and ideology of the later colonization in Africa, Australia and Asia. It was by observing—and condemning—the cultures of the Amerindians that American and European ideologues and politicians developed the theory of the evolution of civilization, based upon a single model and pursuing a linear evolution."

The Christian faith was to do the rest, easily ensconcing itself in the already monotheistic minds of the Iroquois. They, too, believed in a Supreme Being, which speaks volumes about their alleged "savagery."

The first person to observe them in any coherent way was a rabid capitalist by the name of Morgan (it was through him that Marx and Engels heard tell of the Iroquois). Morgan made a study of them at the point when they had lost all importance, and he was to say of them that they were "a people whose sachems were without towns, whose religion was without temples and whose government was without records."

The intrusion of the whites was to put an end to the Iroquois's expansion just in time. Within just a few years, the Iroquois civilization might well have grown very powerful. And we cannot be sure that white colonization would have proceeded with such ease, had the Iroquois managed to implement their expansionist plans. The way in which elements from their civilization subsequently infiltrated their way into the mores of their conquerors offers the finest evidence of that.

THE LEAGUES AND THE CARNIVAL IN ROMANS

"If we must be prepared for anything these days, because everything is possible, it follows that we must not allow ourselves to be taken by surprise."

Gianfranco Sanguinetti
A Truthful Report on the Last Chances of Saving Capitalism in Italy (1975)

A history of the anarchist idea cannot be separated from the story of all progressive developments and aspirations to freedom.

Max Nettlau
A Short History of Anarchy (1934)

The story of the bloody carnival in Romans at the end of the 16th century has been immortalized by Emmanuel de Leroy Ladourie in his outstanding book, based upon his thesis on the *Peasants of Languedoc*. However spectacular this episode we shall be summarizing may have been, it must be viewed as part of a much broader struggle, the struggle of the peasant leagues in Dauphiné that clashed violently with the state authorities and their offshoots.

Henry III was on the throne. Catherine de Médici was all-powerful. The feudal lords were as they had always been. The bourgeoisie was slowly gaining ground, as if anticipating the blow to come in 1789-1795. In Dauphiné, Romans was a town of some importance, as well as a Huguenot stronghold.

One of the chief demands of the leagues was for peace. Since France was not at war, they asked that the troops be confined to their garrisons and that foragers refrain from looting the countryside. There was hunger all around. The wars of religion supplied the troops with a pretext upon which to swagger like conquerors. The tax collectors ground down the peasantry.

The leagues were open to all, to Catholic and Protestant alike, which is a very significant point. The movement got underway in August 1578, in Montélimar in particular. The league there was headed by Jean Barletier (real name Faure). It was primarily anti-taxation. And its ranks included peasants and artisans.

When negotiations proved fruitless, the unrest spread: to Donzère, Valence, Grenoble, and finally Romans. They modelled themselves upon the Swiss leagues. A great general assembly was held in Montélimar. There, eighty members of the leagues, Barletier at their head, exchanged views. A village union, a sort of peasant army, was already engaging the occupation troops. The assembly offered its support. The whole movement was to split into two parts—the one in the south was to remain the more moderate, while the northern faction was to see to Valence and then to Romans and was to organize a few attacks on the local seigneurs.

An ambiguous sort, one Jacques Colas, a dyed-in-the-wool Papist inclined to violence, a born orator, and a man who lived on the edges of criminality (having already killed one man and escaped imprisonment thanks only to powerful connections), was to play an important role. His connections had allowed him to become vice-seneschal of Montelimar and delegate to the States-General, which had met a short time before.

Though ambitious, he was, politically speaking, moderate. A good tactician, he threw in his lot with the leagues, having weighed up all the odds of course, and he quickly became a power within it. At the head of twelve thousand men, in March 1579 he rid the peasants of Laroche, a bandit close to the Huguenots. Laroche had previously controlled the entire area.

After that, Colas' authority was firmly established. He carried out a thorough reorganization. The nobles took a dim view of him, as did Catherine de Médici who paid a visit to the region some time before the incidents in Romans. Thanks to Colas, certain demands were to be met (that was not to be the case in Romans) and there was to be no crackdown on the movement in Montélimar. Colas himself was to intrigue his way to a title of nobility and he would end up as a member of another league, the great League of Seigneurs which is mentioned in the histories of France. That just goes to show that the responsibility for the tragedy in Romans, which might easily have been snuffed out right at the beginning, lay with the ineptitude of the powerful.

In January 1579, there was a first skirmish with the troops in Marsas. The latter, being routed, took to their heels. To the accompaniment of tolling bells and wooden trumpets, the leagues then "paid a call" on the governor of Provence, one of Henri II's bastard sons.

February 3, 1579 was the feast of St. Blaise, the patron saint of the drapers. There was a march-past by a sort of militia, captained that year by Paulmier. A burly athlete, marksman, and loudmouth, Jean Serve, known as Paulmier (because he was unbeatable at the jeu de paume), was highly respected and readily commanded obedience. He was to avail of the carnival "troop" in entrenching the power of the people.

The rebels managed to wrest the keys to the town from the notables and to admit the leagues into Romans: two thousand peasants and artisans flooded into the town hall to demand satisfaction. That was on February 10. Paulmier and his supporters forced the notables to accept a few additional town councillors drawn from their own ranks: Paulmier was one, of course, but there were also his friends, the draper Guillaume Robert (known as Brunat), the butcher Geoffroy Fleur, the shoemaker Jacques Jacques, François Robin, and Jean Jacques. With these extremists among them, the other consuls (for that was how the councillors were described at the time) were powerless to act. Allies for a time of the Huguenots who were keen to manipulate them, they were to find themselves betrayed at the earliest opportunity.

Other towns very quickly followed suit: Valence, where Paulmier was very influential, rose up on February 15 under the leadership of a miller by the name of François Chevalier, known as Bonniol, who called upon the peasants of the district to confront the soldiery. Cut off from their garrison, the troops of Maugiron and the governor of Dauphine fought their way back to Romans, which closed its gates to them. There was nothing left for them now but to be cut to pieces to the sound of the alarm bells that had been ringing out right along their route.

The authorities opened negotiations through Michel Thomé who met with Guillaume Robert (Brunat). But Thomé's overtures failed and he withdrew. It was also at this point that the Huguenots approached the leagues through their leader Lesdiguières who controlled a district near the Alps.

The complexity of the situation and of the competing authorities dissolved into utter confusion when on to the scene came another felon, a genuine bandit this time, a Captain Laprade (real name Antoine de Lavalle). He was close to Lesdiguières and he held the Chateaudouble fortress from where he launched his sorties. Unfortunately the formidable alliance of peasantry, Huguenots and highwaymen, was not to be, and this was to be sorely regretted later on, for nothing could have stood against it. Negotiations in the little village of Charpey came to nothing. Laprade was furious at this failure and thereafter he butchered any peasants whose path crossed his.

The peasants' league by then numbered fourteen thousand men armed with arquebuses. A campaign was launched against Laprade, although Paulmier did not have much stomach for it. The bourgeois reluctantly backed this operation. They sent two captains, one of them an old friend of Paulmier's, a league moderate by the name of Laroche, who had come to despise his former comrade. In spite of that, they joined forces and even joined forces with the leaders of the king's army to put paid to the "redundant player," Laprade. Chateaudouble was captured and razed to the ground in March 1579. Laprade sought refuge among his Huguenot friends but it was not long before he was murdered at their hands.

All of this was happening at the same time as the events in Montélimar mentioned earlier. There was a curious parallel between these episodes. In Romans, there was henceforth a dual authority: the popular authorities (with Paulmier's supporters) and the bourgeois authorities. The latter had a peerless leader who fascinated Leroy-Ladurie who paints an arresting picture of him—the royal magistrate Antoine Guérin. Guérin held virtually all of the formal powers: the governor, the consuls, and various councillors obeyed him. This caste had long since arrogated all power to itself: for additional security, they had co-opted one another. The battle against Laprade had enabled them to get their breath back in Romans, to arm the non-Paulmierist population and to cope without the soldiery.

In Romans proper, 750 out of the adult population of two thousand belonged to the league. They were armed and had two cannons. In April, they slew the seigneur d'Orbain with a shot from an arquebus, torching and looting his castle because he had had numerous peasants murdered. Others, too, were to suffer reprisals.

That summer, Guérin laid his plans for the bourgeois response. He sowed dissension between Paulmier and Laroche, the two leaders of the league, by winning round the moderate Laroche who switched camps. Lesdiguières took great care not to rally to Paulmier's aid, lest Paulmier become a more powerful leader than himself.

Catherine de Médici, the queen mother, arrived in Montélimar in July, there to meet Jacques Colas, whom she despised, before moving on to Valence and finally to Romans where Paulmier presented her with his grievances, referring to the long-established books of grievance and declined to kneel in front of her. In spite of his insolence, he agreed to hand over the keys to the town and surrendered the cannons to Guérin. Which was a mistake.

At the same time, three thousand peasants entered the city. Robert (Brunat), the League's chief delegate (he was its chancellor) persuaded the Parlement in Grenoble to concede certain demands. It went through the motions but was to honor none of its promises.

The rebels' "extra-ordinary advisors" were eventually accepted onto the town council. Paulmier, Robert (Brunat) and François Robin were to represent the league right up until the end of that year. At the general assembly of the town (the most broadly based leadership body), they numbered six out of the 68: those named above, plus Geoffroy Fleur, Jacques Jacques, and Jean Jacques. They were to hand over to others, rotating their delegates in accordance with the ancient "soviet" traditions. Among them we will find the blacksmith Antoine Nicodel. This was to last right up until the eve of the next carnival, at which point everything went to pot.

The butchers, led by Fleur (the League's president) had been on strike since the summer. The bakers had followed suit that autumn under the leadership of Antoine Fresne, known as "Pain-blanc," and Mathelin des Mures, a potter who used his pots for baking bread. The tax revenue had stopped coming into the municipal treasury. A delegation from the strikers was called at the town hall in January 1580.

There was growing excitement right throughout the Rhone valley as the carnival approached. In Montelimar, power appeared to have slipped through the fingers of Colas, who thereafter kept a low profile. Bonniol tried to get the leagues to enter Valence, but the moderates had thwarted him in this: Valence witnessed a replay of the Paulmier-Laroche conflict in Romans.

The carnival in Romans was in fact two successive feasts: Candlemas (February

2) and then the feast of St. Blaise; the latter was the feast day of the drapers, who, as we have seen, were an important group. Every year at this point the nobility were overshadowed and replaced by the artisans who dressed themselves up like the nobles, and paraded on horseback to the sound of drums, everyone bearing arms. In grotesque pantomime shows, the common folk depicted their grievances against the rich and powerful. With bells at their toes, carrying tambourines, wearing shrouds, swords, and carrying rakes, brooms and flails in lieu of scepters, they struck terror into the bourgeois by calling out "Before three days have passed, Christian flesh will be on sale at sixpence a pound." The bourgeois accounted for only three hundred out of the seven thousand inhabitants of the town.

Paulmier was dressed up in the bearskin that he never left off, not even when he attended council meetings and took his seat as consul. Everyone was dancing in step and revelling in their mourning dress. The carnival phenomenon is a familiar one: everything is reversed and, to borrow Christopher Hill's expression, becomes "a world turned upside down." The rich man becomes the poor man, the poor man the rich one, the serf his lord, the ugly man becomes handsome, the cheap becomes dear and vice versa. Poor quality wine was sold at premium prices and delicacies allowed to go for next to nothing. The rich would dress in rags, as poor unfortunates strutted around dressed up as archbishops, Turks, kings, etc.

The two parades did not mix with each other, but hurled abuse at each other when their paths crossed. Jokes were taken to heart by the powerful and maybe they were right to do so. That was to prove what sparked the drama.

People constructed reynages—folklore kingdoms over which an animal totem presided. In essence this consisted of an impressive parade followed by a banquet and a foot race. The winner won a prize and was crowned "king." But the threats uttered during these were not simply folklore. Both sides had it in mind to eliminate the enemy physically. Leroy Ladurie astutely notes that this was a capital combination of the sacred, the warlike, and the peasant. In his memorandum on events, Guérin was to state "None of these dances had any object other than to let it be known that the dancers wanted to see them all dead."

The rebels' reynage was the reynage of the Sheep, an unsettling emblem, an unmanly and surprising one. Four days later, the moderate members of the league established their own reynage. They selected the Cockerel, a more aggressive symbol. At the same time, the Huguenots were mounting a push in Grenoble.

A third reynage was established by the bourgeois themselves, some sixty people centered around Guerin. Their emblem was the Partridge. To help them recognize one another, they pinned to their hats a scrap of paper bearing their handwritten symbol. The letters meant nothing to the illiterates who made up the bulk of the kingdom of the Sheep.

Thus, the whole struggle for power was to be played out through and by means of the carnival. This folklore was lethal. The followers were in place. In the bourgeois camp, the Partridge kingdom, there were women, whereas the Leaguers were exclusively male. The Partridge kingdom was doctored. It was contrived to have Laroche as the winner and consequently he became the Partridge King. Paulmier had spotted the threat behind this contrivance and he hinted heavily to the bourgeois that he might bring his people, which is to say, the peasant Leaguers, into the town.

On February 9, Laroche announced himself the "King of Romans." His "joke" program was in fact a specific plot in which the hand of the magistrate Guerin could be discerned. Moreover, it had been Guérin's idea to reverse everything at that point, including food prices. He thought of this as a way of poking fun at these serfs posing as masters. This was something that the people concerned may not have appreciated. Laroche sat on his throne in the Cordeliers monastery. Bourgeois dressed up as flunkies or officials served him. To make an impression on the populace, a "sham" army stood by, made up of archers who were anything but "sham." Their every move, and they made plenty of moves, was followed by the populace. All of the protocols of royalty were scrupulously observed.

The Partridge feast started on the Monday. Laroche attended Mass with all due pomp and circumstance, along with his guard, forty helmeted men bearing arquebuses and five-meter long pikes, plus twenty splendidly uniformed Swiss. "Sham" envoys arrived to genuflect in front of him.

Paulmier had whipped up two other, lesser reynages, those of the Huguenot artisans (the Hare) and the peasants' reynage (the Capon). Those emblems were poor omens: one creature noted for running away and the other for being eaten. Everyone paraded.

The processions bumped into each other. Laroche invited Paulmier to attend his feast. Paulmier declined the bait. "Never will I go where my enemy is triumphant…"

The following day, the Tuesday, they bumped into each other again. It was then that they traded the harshest insults, such as "Christian flesh at four pence a pound!" (Note that the price had fallen by two pence!) Paulmier, mounted on a donkey, was wearing the red and blue robes of an undertaker. A feast had been scheduled for that afternoon.

Naturally, the Cockerel threw in its lot with the Partridge. The fighting was to break out that evening at a masquerade (a masked procession) attended by the entire town. The Capon's peasant supporters were slaughtered in a surprise attack by the bourgeois and the moderates of whom they trusted too much. The latter had switched straight over from carnival procession to systematic beating. The whole thing had started with the women who had taken fright at the people's reynages or who had feigned their fright so as to supply a pretext. Guérin was at the back of the whole business.

Then a band headed by Laroche forced its way into Paulmier's place. The latter, alerted by the noise, came rushing out, halberd at the ready. He knew nothing

42

about his allies' having been slaughtered. Before he had time to size up the situation, he was stabbed with pikes and finished off with a shot from a pistol. His supporters who showed up at the scene were killed on the spot. There was a rout, even before there had been a proper fight. Some escaped from the town by leaping from the walls or swimming the Isere River.

Paulmier's corpse was tossed onto a dung-heap. His effigy was to be hanged by the feet, his body, disinterred after a few days, creating too great a stink to be hanged in person.

His supporters in the town were massacred. A few threw up barricades that were quickly overcome. One of those who resisted, Sibeuf, escaped although wounded and raised the alarm in the nearest village, Saint-Paul. "The bigwigs in Romans have butchered the people." Fifteen hundred male peasants gathered outside the town. At that point, the town gates were still under the control of Roux, a Paulmierist known as Leguire. But the peasants were not to rescue him. And they did not dare venture more than thirty meters inside the town. When all they needed to do was to press on and claim the victory. Fear of fighting held them back. The fact that there was no one there to greet them made them uneasy: after all, they had no way of knowing what had just happened.

The massacre was to last for three full days. Had effective liaison between the peasants and the town's artisans been established during the fighting, everything might have gone the other way. Neither of the two social groups was to escape the repression. Guérin had outwitted them: the danger implicit in their alliance had not eluded him.

With the slaughter in Romans finished, the scene now switched to Moirans where two thousand peasants had dug in. They were crushed within six weeks. The last district of Romans to fall, Clérieu, was the district occupied by the well-to-do artisans and was strategically significant. The supporters of Capon, led by Roux, had dug in there, after their withdrawal. Their barricades were solid. Rather than risk a fight where the outcome was uncertain (and rather than risk a linking-up with the outside), Guérin negotiated with them, promising them impunity, and he brought it off.

Inside the town, the rebels had suffered only around thirty fatalities. As ever, the peasants were to account for the bulk of the victims. The town was taken under control, and all the town gates save two were bricked up. Councillors were chosen and installed by Guérin.

The rebels were brought to trial: Robert (Brunat) and Fleur were tortured, hanged and put on display at the town gates after having been dragged out on a grille to Paulmier's effigy in March, 1580. Under torture, Robert had denounced his comrades. Several others were hanged also, Mathelin des Mures among them. Others such as Robin or Jean Jacques, found their assets seized and heavy fines imposed. Antoine Nicodel was also hanged, along with "Pain-blanc" who had handed over his keys to the town to the rebels. Thirty-three of those sentenced to death were sentenced in their absence.

43

Jacques Jacques was to be sentenced to ten years' imprisonment and to be flogged.

The assets seized were added to the wealth of the victors: Guérin blithely helped himself to what he wanted of Paulmier's belongings. Later, he would be ennobled and was to inscribe a stolen apple tree upon his coat of arms.

Beyond the city walls, the bourgeois and the nobility crushed the leagues. Some resisters lived off the land while others threw in their lot with the Huguenots. One minor noble, a Huguenot captain and semi-bandit, André de Bouvier, led four thousand peasants ensconced in the Beauvoir fort. Previously, Bouvier had been hostile to them. The massacre in Moirans on March 26 sounded the death knell for the peasants. Their leader, Lapierre, was hanged. Nine hundred men were killed or summarily executed and two hundred were taken as prisoners. The survivors held out for awhile longer in the mountains with support from Lesdiguieres. But Lesdiguières was just biding his time before disposing of them and did just that. When the massacre came he never lifted a finger to help them. Beauvoir's fort fell in September 1580. The captain of the fort, Ferrant, was to be spared for surrendering the fort. Somewhat later, Bouvier and another Huguenot captain by the name of Dallières were to give themselves up at the castle in Pont-en-Royans and in the village of Saint-Quentin, which they still held. Both were to be spared as a result.

Among those summarily executed in this affair was Sibeuf who had escaped the butchery in Romans to alert the peasants. We should note that the womenfolk accompanying the defeated peasants were to escape being raped. That was a rare enough occurrence to merit mention. In Romans the hangings were to continue into May 1581.

In Dauphiné, everything was restored to "normal." The originality of this episode is that it was played out as a symbolic psycho-drama, where theater took the place of sociopolitical or military action. Not for nothing does Leroy-Ladurie speak of the carnival in Romans at the core of the struggle of the peasants' League as a "work of art," of "body art" in a sense.

England, 1647-1650
LEVELLERS, DIGGERS, AND RANTERS—
THE ENGLISH REVOLUTION

Liberty is the ultimate goal of all
human development.

Bakunin
Œuvres

Every worker is entitled to sabotage
whatsoever conspires to destroy him.

Ratgeb
*From Wildcat Strike to Widespread
Self-Management* (1974)

The turning of the world upside down
is effected by the shortest distance
between one delight and another.

Raoul Vaneigem
The Book of Pleasures (1979)

Seventeenth century England displayed the usual features of pre-revolutionary times: the powerful Church was utterly corrupt. It was in the throes of crisis to boot: there was a universal sentiment that it stood in need of reformation, a thorough one this time. The

bourgeoisie was buying up land and titles and slowly acquiring real power. The gentry was dabbling in commerce: this was the beginning of a great intermingling at the top.

Puritanism was fashionable, but the righteous were split into numerous rival sects gutting one another intellectually. The most radical elements, the Independents, sought wholesale self-management of communities (the spiritual leader of each community was its real social and political "chief"), with each individual group empowered to speak for itself. This egalitarianism gradually eclipsed temporal concerns. Religious demands became social ones, initially among the peasants and artisans and later the other sectors. We might invoke the memory of the Lollards, these popular preachers outside of the hierarchical structure who roamed the countryside.

There had long since been a campaign underway against enclosures (fences). The aim was to prevent by fair means or foul, the brutal expropriation of the peasants by grasping business interests. The breaking down of enclosures had become a symbol. In 1607, some Diggers—ancestors of the ones of which more anon—led by a cabinet-maker by the name of Steer had tried to wipe out the nobility. In doing so they had taken their inspiration from the Comuneros in Valencia, whose leader, during the reign of Charles V, had been another carpenter.

Ever since 1625, England had been ruled by Charles I, a Stuart, a liar, and wily despot. In 1629 he had dissolved Parliament and introduced a personal rule that lasted until 1640. Among his opponents was a draper by the name of John Lilburne who was sentenced to be flogged for the dissemination of seditious writings. A mystic, Lilburne relished the torture and upbraided onlookers for their cowardice, while scattering tracts he had been carrying hidden in his pockets.

In April 1640, a new Parliament asserted itself, with lawyer John Pym the "star" of the opposition. Within a month the king had dismissed this assembly. Hence its description as the Short Parliament. After a redrawing of the constituency boundaries, Charles agreed to a new Parliament, which was to be known as the Long Parliament, in that it was to last somewhat longer.

In November 1641, Pym had drawn up a Long Remonstrance indicting the king's rule. It was passed and read out by Pym: that triggered the troubles.

Denied the chance to replace Pym and his supporters, a humiliated Charles I withdrew to Oxford along with the royalist parliamentarians. The ones who stayed behind came to be called the "Westminster rebels."

There were preachers all over the country. The famous slogan "When Adam delved and Eve span, who was then the gentleman?" (a relic from the revolt of 1381) had reappeared as early as 1642. Materialism and anti-clericalism were spreading.

If the rich were the source of all ills, salvation was to come through the poor man: such was the underlying message of the popular philosophy of the time. Because they lacked land, drifters were forever on the move. This mobility was to prove their strength and survived into the Restoration period.

Troops were raised and money collected. One Oliver Cromwell, MP for Cambridge, appeared on the scene. A small holder, (who had been a member of the 1628 Parliament) he drew his recruits from his own county, paying for their mounts and equipment, and gradually he built up his own regiment. In August 1642 this was to become the famous Ironsides.

For the time being (January 1643) he was a colonel. He commanded one squadron while those close to him commanded the rest. He selected his civilian officers from among the humble religious folk and never on the basis of their military talents.

There were many radicals who joined this army, quite often as its chaplains. This was the case with William Erbery or with Henry Dell who was to write: "Power resides within you, the people: hold on to it and take good care lest you be stripped of it."

Lord Manchester commanded the army of Parliament. Cromwell became its lieutenant-general. The first significant engagement came at Marston Moor: this was a victory for the parliamentarian forces, a success that might have proved final, had Lord Manchester not dragged his feet: this aristocrat who seemed to have turned traitor against his own class was in fact trying to save the king.

London erected fortifications on its outskirts, with the entire population—women and nobles included - working upon the construction.

In February 1645, a twenty-two thousand-strong parliamentary army was under the command of thirty-three-year-old Thomas Fairfax, one of the finest fighters. In actual fact, his cavalry commander, Cromwell, was the real commander of it.

On June 14, 1645 at Naseby the royalist forces were routed (five thousand dead, all of Charles I's personal papers - papers testifying to his misappropriation of funds—seized). The king fled into Scotland and tried to bargain his way out of trouble. But the Scots could not come to an accommodation with him and they handed him over to London in the winter of 1646-1647.

At the same time, the situation took a seriously revolutionary turn. The troops were demobilized (the war being over), but for months they had received no pay. The first soldiers' soviets emerged in eight cavalry regiments in April 1647. In a show of fellowship, they wore red cloth armbands. Each squadron elected two delegates. There was absolute equality between men and NCOs. The delegates then elected two "agitators" to act as spokesmen for the entire regiment. Non-compliant officers were simply bypassed.

The inventor of this system of direct democracy was a common private, Edward Sexby. The ferment originated among the regiments of Cromwell and those of Colonels Warwick and Ireton (the latter, thirty-six years old at the time, was to become Cromwell's son-in-law).

Sexby and two other privates, William Allen and Thomas Shepherd, presented the resisters' petition, in which the parliamentarians were described as "tyrants" eager to be rid of the revolutionary army. The term "presbyterian" was used at the time to indicate the moderate elements.

The officers followed suit: they elected two delegates per regiment and all of these delegates together made up the Army General Council.

On June 5, 1647, they held their general assembly near Newmarket. A manifesto at this point described them as "a union of free men of the people of England," gathered together to "champion the liberties and fundamental rights of the people."

A printer called John Harris placed his workshop at their disposal and he was to act as go-between in dealings between the soldiers and the civilian revolutionaries who were frantically agitating. Especially Lilburne.

At this point, on June 3, Cornel George Joyce, acting for the Army Cavalry Committee, abducted the king with a detachment of men and brought him to Army headquarters. Fairfax was not pleased with this, but Ireton let it go. Cromwell who was afraid that Parliament might beat them to it, approved.

Parliament was unhappy but was forced to capitulate when Cromwell, Fairfax and eleven colonels insisted that the army's demands be met. The king, who was very well treated, promised favors to Cromwell and to the colonels. The soldiers were none too pleased.

There were inflammatory tracts in circulation from the pen of Lilburne (who had risen to the rank of captain in the army, then become a staff lieutenant-colonel). The more violent of the rebels even denounced certain "agitators" who had let themselves be corrupted. These rebels became known as the Levellers. What was meant by "levelling" (and Michelet says that the levelling instinct is timeless) was absolute egalitarianism, before the law, in electoral terms and in terms of the rights of the individual. The Levellers had their "social contract" that they called the Agreement of the People. This was put to the army soviets in October 1647 at the Putney Conference. This agreement was circulated for endorsement. Everyone was entitled to vote, except the womenfolk (things had not gone that far just yet), beggars, and servants. The movement's moderates, such as Wildmann disbarred the latter, whereas the more radical elements (Sexby and Rainsborough) had been prepared to grant them the vote.

Numerous other documents were also to be circulated and these included an out-and-out draft Constitution. Submitted to Cromwell, this draft pointed out that the army was there to defend the people's rights, that there was to be only a single chamber (the Lords being redundant), that the franchise was open to all (except women), that no one could dissolve Parliament, that the enclosed lands were to be returned to the peasants, that the assets of the bishops would be used to cover back pay, and that all clergy should be elected by their parishioners.

Cromwell was outraged. It took some persuasion to deter him from exterminating the rebels. In the end he entered into negotiations with them at the Putney conference in October 1647. They insisted upon the abolition of monarchy. One colonel, Thomas Rainsborough, sided with them.

Cromwell's spokesman, Ireton, opposed such abolition and also opposed universal suffrage. Rainsborough stood his ground. Sexby declared: "We were called up into the service of the kingdom. We have risked our lives for the restoration of our innate rights. Several thousand of us soldiers perished for that. And here we are being told now that a man of no property has no rights in this kingdom. I am amazed that we have been so deceived," then, pointing to Cromwell and Ireton: "But we enjoy the very same birthrights as that pair who pose as law-makers."

There was plainly a gulf between the revolutionaries who were keen to carry on the struggle and those who wanted to harness it for their own purposes. Lilburne ensured that the wavering agitators were replaced. This was a tactical error, for the radicals were moving too quickly for many of the soldiers who could not quite keep up.

The army was called upon to arbitrate in the dispute. But Cromwell and Ireton ensured that the regiments assembled in a number of locations rather than all together. Lilburne and Thomas Harrison defied him and brought their troops to Ware to join up with some others who had received the summons (and who failed to turn up). They wore on their hats green ribbons emblazoned with the words "For England's liberty and the rights of the soldier." They also wore some leaflets pinned to their hats.

They were reviewed by Cromwell, who was booed. In a fury, he tore off their ribbons. Scuffles broke out and the ringleaders were arrested (they included William Everard) and hauled before the court martial. Fourteen of them were convicted and three were sentenced to death. One (private Richard Arnold) was executed after the drawing of lots. He was shot in front of his comrades. The agreement was not even to receive a reading.

In spite of this, certain demands of the Levellers' were taken up: the House of Lords was abolished and a republic proclaimed. But these reforms had been drained of their essential content. Ireton turned the soldiers' texts to his own ends. A provocation was contrived and it sparked a mutiny in Burford (May 1649). This mutiny furnished the pretext for dealing with the Levellers. Their leaders were arrested, their supporters scattered. Democracy vanished from the army ranks along with them. Several of them were executed and one of the ringleaders, Henry Denne, saved his skin by turning renegade. Another, Robert Lockier was shot and his funeral was a splendid affair, showing just how popular they were. They had failed to take power inside the army. If they had, revolution would have erupted across the country.

The king who escaped and finally came to an accommodation with the Scots salvaged the situation. The war flared again. Cromwell set off on an offensive, Ireton opened a second front in Kent, and Fairfax held London. Victory was quickly secured (in September 1648) but Cromwell had in the interim discovered Charles I's true plans for him (he meant to see him hanged).

Ireton then purged Parliament: 47 MPs were placed under arrest and 96 barred. Charles I was brought to trial and sentenced to death by the High Court (44 votes in favor, 20 opposed, and 65 abstentions!). In January 1649 he was executed in front of Whitehall. The executioner who beheaded him with an axe held up his severed head with the words: "Behold the head of a traitor!"

A Council of State assumed control of the country. It was made up of 41 members, including the commanders of the army and magistrates. The Levellers, or what was left of them, had their misgivings, although it had always been their view that the king's death would usher in a new era of Christ. Lilburne talked about "new fetters." His chief lieutenants were Richard Overton, Thomas Prince, and William Walwyn. Lilburne gave a public reading of a pamphlet entitled Part Second of England's New Fetters (a sequel) to the House of Commons. There was a huge audience. The MPs were damned as cowards and the army plot (against the revolutionaries) denounced. The next day (this was in March 1649) all four of them were arrested.

They officially repudiated the designation Levellers, for significant dissension had emerged within the movement. Acquitted in October, they were released. Whereupon Lilburne was elected to the City Council (an election annulled by the government).

We should mention one Leveller of growing significance: William Everard. An agitator, he was implicated, as we have seen, in the mutiny in 1647. He was a visionary and prophet, one of the many at the time. He had been a member of a farming commune in Buckinghamshire and had written a pamphlet about this: The Light Shining in Buckinghamshire.

He was, without question, an important theoretician: an advocate of strict egalitarianism. A communist, he talked in terms of mankind at large and not just about the situation in England. "All men, possessed of the same privilege of arriving in this world, should enjoy in equal measure the privilege of enjoying its blessings. Which means that no one has any right to seize another man's land."

He and his followers welcomed the description Levellers. Lilburne drew a clear distinction between them. The Levellers wanted just laws (like the laws of the Bible) and supported equal shares in property, equal rights, and directly elected governments—in short, the republic. They practiced the "clearing of estates," which is to say they laid claimed to lands left idle.

At the same time, along came the most extraordinary figure of his day, a man in his forties, by the name of Gerrard Winstanley. A former clothier, Winstanley was another driven man who had published lots of texts since 1643. He had had a vision on his farm near the Thames. Everard and Winstanley met each other and saw eye to eye.

Winstanley then wrote The New Law of Justice, a blend of new religious arrangements and new social arrangements. The land, he claimed, belonged to him that worked it and should be amalgamated with the land belonging to others, with the fallow lands being worked by the community. Laws would not be repressive but rather educative. He anticipated a corps of elected officials including planners who would oversee production. These would be rotated every year in order to avert bureaucratization (which is a remarkable insight because bureaucratization had yet to put in an appearance and was not really to exist for another several centuries!)

Lawyers and prisons were to be abolished and compulsory labor would take the place of incarceration. The death penalty would be retained only for very grave crimes. Marriage would be solely civil (marriage for love). Work was not an evil in itself, but exploitation was. By doing away with wages, work could be set free and thus become a pleasure. As we can see, Winstanley is an essential political theorist of the seventeenth century, a startling forerunner of 18th, 19th, and even 20th century European thought! Marx borrowed heavily from him but gave him little credit.

The State was to be headed by a Supreme Court of Justice, and MPs would be elected annually. Foreign trade was to be a state monopoly (Christopher Hill, one of the great historians of this period, and a Leninist, points out that this was one of the first measures adopted by the Bolsheviks in 1917!). Health care was to be free and education accessible to all, women included (a real novelty, that!) and teachers were to be elected and would teach philosophy, politics, and sciences. In addition there were to be some schools of this sort in Wales.

A materialist and pantheist, Winstanley was the leading theorist of the English revolution. He was the only one to have taken his ideas so far as to dream of the operations of an alternative society. Had the abolition of private property been implemented as he had advocated, it would have implied a radical upheaval and the collapse of the whole of English society. Winstanley wished to live in accordance with the laws of nature, in concord with the planet: that, to him, was what the social revolution was all about.

He was one of the rare "feminists" of his day. He saw men and women as virtually equal, in rights at any rate: as he saw it, women should have the ability to preach.

But to return to our account of events: Everard and Winstanley hooked up with each other and on April 1, 1649, with thirteen men, they settled in Walton, Surrey, on the common by St. George's Hill. They set about breaking up the fallow land. Soon their numbers had swelled to forty. They were to reclaim the name of Diggers, by way of paying homage to the Diggers of 1607. (In 1966, the San Francisco Diggers gave the name a fresh currency.)

It was around this time that other politico-religious factions emerged, some of which hitched their stars to the revolutionary wagon of the Levellers and Diggers. The Ranters, for example, who were even more hard-line, and more "outspoken," although essentially less adventurous in practice. They got their name from the fact that they allowed themselves to speak their minds, used puns, and "got high" (on tobacco, an effective new drug, which sent them into ecstasy), drank beer, were licentious, sang and danced, when not launching into interminable speechifying. Abiezer Coppe, one of their leaders, was notorious for his swearing. He cursed the Puritans (the Ranters did not recognize the Bible, so there was no such thing as blasphemy as far as they were concerned).

Scarcely organized, they had no "leaders," merely forceful personalities. They arose out of the failure of the Levellers (between 1649 and 1651). Like Winstanley, they were pantheists and materialists, but they never managed to come together, which was a great pity. They criticized the Levellers and Diggers, accusing them of betrayal.

Coppe was a fine writer, one of whose works was sentenced to be burned (1650). He had faced prison without backing down and he had won popularity by scattering fruit all around the courtroom to feign madness.

Coppe saw adultery as no sin (another novelty). Nor was fornication. Women belonged to everyone (and, vice versa, we can only suppose). He praised all this, often living with two women simultaneously, just as Albert Libertad was to do much later on. Ah, that's anarchists for you…

As dyed-in-the-wool pacifists, the Ranters, rather than the Diggers, were the fore-runners of the Hippies of 1965-68: they had no love of work but a fondness for pleasure, food and drink and were to scandalize the Digger community. Winstanley was to write scathingly about them. Their "leaders" were people like Lawrence Clarkson, who had turned preacher after quitting the army. It was said that he had availed of a "baptism" (in the days when he was a baptist) to get two "sisters" into his bed. He was an advocate of free love. A one-time Seeker (see below) he had turned Ranter after release from prison in 1650. He went on to become a Muggletonian. Then there was Jacob Bauthumley who was to have his tongue spiked for blaspheming.

Come the Restoration, Coppe was to change his name and died in 1672 as a doctor. Scrutiny of these people puts one in mind of Rabelais and his Abbey of Theleme.

The Quakers who were to flourish after all these sects failed were to turn their ideas to use, recasting them in a sense of austerity and Puritanism. The religious side was to eclipse the social message. That they should sever all links with the Ranters is understandable: one London woman at a Quaker meeting stood up, lifted her skirts and displayed her backside: she was promptly denounced as a "Ranter!" Lilburne who was not a joker like Coppe or Clarkson, was to become a Quaker.

Another sect was the Seekers and there were the Shakers, too. All of these folk were lumped together as "Roundheads," a description employed these days to mean Cromwell's supporters, he being crop-haired. But none of these factions was set in concrete, and the personnel were open to change, too. They frequently flitted from one sect to another (as we saw with Clarkson). William Erbery, one of the Seeker leaders, is also regarded as a Ranter: a one-time army chaplain, he died in 1654. They were very like-minded, Protestants in the process of shrugging off their faith and English bourgeois society. During this period, by the way, they called everything into question: economics, politics, society, religion, philosophy, mores, ideas, customs, fundamental thinking...

It is true that, as Hill states in his book, they wanted to see the "world turned upside down." That was what they had in common.

Winstanley, a great agrarian theorist, was eager above all else to clear the land as a remedy against endemic poverty. The agrarian communes that he started to establish were, in his mind, to be the beginning of a complete transformation of society. The vegetables he planted and had others plant were, a short while later, to become the springboard to agrarian reform in England: this new method of fertilization offered a solution to the country's farming difficulties, and Winstanley was clear-sighted. He was not just a visionary, but in his own way, a scientist, a sage, capable of blending knowledge and ethics, expertise and inspiration.

The Digger adventure was short-lived. The nation's wealthy, outraged, plotted against them. Led by Pastor Platt, they brought them to the attention of the courts, had them shunned, and then alerted the Council of State. Fairfax sent in the cavalry against these vagabonds. The hatred against them is understandable: they had barricaded the local vicar out of his church, dismissed him, and abolished tithes.

They responded to Fairfax's summons, declining to doff their hats in his presence (he being their equal): Everard delivered a lengthy Biblical harangue. In the end, they were not personally punished but moved home to Cobham Heath, where they began all over again.

Winstanley published The Standard Unfurled by the True Levellers (which is how they styled themselves, differentiating themselves from Lilburne's Levellers). The Leveller-in-chief was none other than Christ himself.

But the boycotts and the arson attacks were to grind them down. In April 1650, they disbanded. William Everard vanishes from the historical record after that. Information about these people is meager. The supposition is that he was the same person as John Everard (1575–1650?) who was regularly jailed for his eccentric religious notions, a translator of mystical books, a pantheist who reckoned that God could be found in man and in nature and that he was behind miraculous apparitions. This fanatic had been incarcerated on a number of occasions. There were other Everards and it is possible that in memory they became a single, composite personage. It is also feasible that he was involved in the Burford mutiny.

In the end, the army was to erase all of their influence. The Diggers, Levellers, and Ranters did not have enough of a foothold in the population.

In February 1649, the Scots had proclaimed the Stuart heir king as Charles II. The war resumed in July 1650, but once again, Cromwell swept all before him. The army was demobbed once and for all: Parliament had a real fear of it. At the same time (September 1651) the soviets were liquidated. Winstanley also bowed out with a plot of land and entered the service of Lady Eleanor Davies.

Like the rest, the Levellers were never to amount to a homogeneous, properly constituted political grouping. The entire far left of the revolution was fragmented into different tendencies that could never see eye to eye. Wildman and Lilburne stood for the moderates, whereas Walwyn and Overton were the radicals of the London group, the equivalent of the Diggers out in the country.

Inside the army a similar situation occurred. One William Jackson, a lieutenant, supported wholesale communism, including common ownership of women (1650). Where they all fell out was over the issue of property (we will find the same rifts in 1792–1796). The moderates did not want it touched (Lilburne opposed Winstanley on this point). Cromwell was to play upon these differences and the repression was to batten upon the Digger communities as the movement grew.

To conclude our history, we should say that Parliament next tried to outflank Cromwell. He thwarted this maneuver by interrupting a sitting and upbraiding them. His lieutenant after that was Thomas Harrison, Ireton having passed away in 1651.

Parliament was brought to heel, overhauled and kept under the dictator's thumb. Its "deputies" were often drawn from the ranks of the "Fifth Monarchy Men," hand picked by Harrison. These were a sect that took over some of the ideas of the Levellers and Diggers, ideas that still held some sway.

This was a time of significant legislative efforts, in which we can identify the influences at work; tithes were abolished, a civil code introduced, and civil marriage instituted. The debt had now been paid.

Cromwell queried all this in 1653. He wanted no one around him except his trusted cronies. Even Harrison retired. His new right hand, John Lambert, lined his own pockets and was corrupted. The last of the Levellers disappeared.

Sexby tried to mount one last international plot against the dictator. It ended in failure. He fled to France. A year later, he returned to England, only to be caught. He died in prison, without ever standing trial.

Cromwell allowed himself to be half-persuaded into being proclaimed king. He backed away from this but was awarded the right to choose his successor. He restored the House of Lords. In September 1658, he died, bearing the title of Lord Protector.

His inept son, Richard Cromwell was a royalist (what a let-down!). He was to meet the end he deserved: the army rebelled and he was overthrown. In December 1659, General Monck wound up the Security Committee installed after the abdication of the younger Cromwell. Charles II ascended the throne in May 1660. This was the Restoration. Everything returned to the way it had been.

The trial of the "regicides" was implacable: Thomas Harrison was hanged, his genitals ripped off, and his entrails removed while he was still living, the whole lot being burned before his very eyes. Then he was decapitated and quartered. Two others suffered the same fate. John Lambert was to rot in prison for twenty three-years. In January 1661, to mark the anniversary of the death of Charles I, Cromwell's and Ireton's corpses were disinterred for hanging!

The influence of the Diggers and Levellers was to be discernible in the Ormee in Bordeaux (see below), but they themselves were the heirs of Munzer and his peasants. It was the Diggers, too, who were the first to show the connections between land ownership and the oppressive structures of society. This was something that Marx was to keep in mind. Their "world turned upside down" is, moreover, reminiscent of Marx overthrowing the theory of Hegel who, he contended, "walked on his head." Their sole failing was the sectarianism that barred them from achieving the unity they needed to succeed.

This is a familiar phenomenon and one that was to recur much later on, during the Paris Commune or the 1789 French Revolution, or, indeed, in May 1968. And all these Diggers, Levellers, Ranters and the like—don't they remind you of the countless leftist sects of the 1968–1972 period?

Bordeaux, 1649-1653
THE ORMEE

I see in this combination nothing more than a multiplication of my strengths and I give my consent to it only for as long as such multiplication is forthcoming. That, then, is association.

Max Stirner
The Ego and His Own (1844)

In the eyes of historians, the Fronde was merely a rebellion of discontented aristocrats against encroaching central authorities. Less well known is that the aristocrats' revolt was very late in starting, beginning only toward the end of the uprising, and that the Fronde was a broad popular movement (there were nearly eight thousand different pamphlets and handbills called mazarinades, lashing out at Mazarin and the burning issues of taxation, religion, feudalism, and monarchy alike). Mazarin, the outsider who ruled France, was the favorite target of all these attacks, but the tyranny had originated with his predecessor, Richelieu, and it is equally certain that the king, who was not equal to his obligations, had his own shortcomings.

The pamphleteers articulated a number of overlapping policies: equal taxation for all, complete abolition of privileges, etc. One of them urges in tones reminiscent of La Boétie: "The great are only great because we carry them upon our shoulders: if we were only to shrug them off, they would cover the Earth."

We need to be clear that in 1648, when the Fronde erupted, the aristocracy was incapable of unleashing anything at all by itself. In spite of that, their relentless movement is used today to disguise the considerable challenge posed to monarchy at the time, a challenge in which a number of shrewd historians have seen a widespread re-enactment of 1789.

By contrast, we will find the rising bourgeoisie articulating demands close to those of the people and showing no bashfulness about hijacking their arguments. In the political program of the Paris Parliament, we can detect a desire to curtail the king's powers; to transfer these gradually to the Parliaments; to do away with monopolies, tax-farming, and the intendant system; to ensure that people thrown in prison were speedily brought to trial; and to adopt protectionist economic measures. As we can see, a mightily ambitious program.

In Paris the telling catch phrase was "Long live the Republic!", and it has to be said that they came within an ace of proclaiming one.

As early as during the revolt of August 26–28, 1648, the Parliament of Paris became, de facto, a revolutionary club along the lines of the future Cordeliers or Jacobin club. Its first pronouncement sought the amalgamation of all upper chambers, a scheme for a parliament-government destined to take over the reins from the king and his minister. For the first time, the Court panicked and fled to Rueil. In 1649, it was to flee a second time, this time to Saint-Germain. The leaders of this Fronde of the people and bourgeoisie were Broussel, Beaufort, and a very popular lawyer and superb public speaker, Boile. Mention should also be made of an aristocrat, the veteran plotter, Prince de Gondi, who was keen to get his feet wet, but only if there was a real prospect of success (he had declined to participate in many half-baked plots, except for the plot of the Comte de Soissons in 1640–1641) and whose brazen ambition was to become first minister and cardinal like all the rest. In spite of this somewhat wishy-washy ambition, he wanted to wield power without turning into a tyrant like these wretches Richelieu and Mazarin who had proved incapable of this. We should point out that Condi entertained pretty much the same ambitions, and we shall see this alliance of aristocrats with the restless third estate coming through—an alliance of interested parties!

Although it erupted spontaneously, the movement was headed by bourgeois who were always to the fore in this pre-capitalist age when, in concert with the common folk, they opposed the feudalists, Mazarin, and his Intendant of Finances, Hemery.

The pretext upon which the bourgeois revolted was to be a measure adopted by the government, prescribing that the Officers of the Parliament would henceforth have to pay in advance for a right known as the "paulette," The backlash was immediate.

It was in Bordeaux that the most interesting incidents came to pass. There, the Fronde occurred in three stages. The first two are of no great interest, but the third is.

In August 1648, the bourgeoisie threw its support behind a popular demonstration for the first time. It was threatened with troops. The Parliament of Bordeaux, supported by the populace, established a finance council to raise money for a police council to defend the city, and an army some twenty thousand strong. Libourne was attacked: but the attack foundered upon the fortress there. Three thousand people perished. Parliament members who backed Mazarin were driven out.

Mazarin who was busy fighting the Fronde in Paris put an offer to the rebels in Bordeaux: he offered an amnesty, the abolition of certain taxes, and undertook to tear down the Libourne fortifications. The rebels agreed in January 1650. This victory was a considerable fillip to the Parliament of Bordeaux. So ended act one.

But in Paris the Fronde was a failure. Its leaders—Conti, Condé, and Longueville—were arrested (January 1650). The nobles rose in revolt. Their supporters fell back toward Bordeaux, where Condé's wife, the Duc de la Rochefoucauld, and Bouillon sued for protection. The Parliaments turned down their suit but an outraged populace rose up and ushered them inside the city. This was the first indication of divorce between the bourgeois and the people.

Two months later, the king's supporters launched an attack: they numbered seventeen thousand against eight thousand peasant and artisan Frondeurs. So violent were the clashes that thousands perished, but the royal army (nine thousand fatalities) was beaten.

Further negotiations ensued: another amnesty and governor d'Epernon, the bete noire of the revolutionaries from Guyenne, was driven out and Condé's supporters were permitted to leave. That was the end of act two.

From then on, the Fronde was split into two: the Little Fronde (supportive of the king, but opposed to Mazarin), and the Great Fronde (which backed the Princes). In Bordeaux the Parliament could not quite manage to run the city it had captured and found itself obliged to enact the very measures against which it had fought, such as imposing a tax on wine. People were furious. The Parliament was accused of corruption and high-handedness. Especially in one document called *Apology from the Ormée*. That signaled the opening of the final act, the real story.

The origins of the Ormée are not certain. There are a number of theories. Let us suppose that they complement one another. The Ormée began in June 1651, following a rumor to the effect that d'Epernon was to be re-appointed as governor in Guyenne. Three thousand residents of Bordeaux assembled in the Ormière, a square surrounded by ormeaux, elm trees, and featuring a tower. The talk was of putting paid once and for all to the Mazarins (the supporters of the all-powerful minister). But the likelihood is that the widespread discontent was considerable and that d'Epernon's appointment was merely the spark that ignited the social conflagration.

The influence of England's Leveller movement on the Ormistes was considerable. Bordeaux was always more au fait with events across the Channel than the rest of the country was.

It was the Fronde's first truly revolutionary gathering. The Ormée was sometimes spelt as Ormaie, Hormée or Hourmée. Condé seized his chance. He wrote to them and arrived to join them and was to remain there from September 1651 until March 1652. It was on the latter date that his troops were defeated at Agen by the king's forces.

The deliberations of the Ormée took place beneath the trees, this being an ancient democratic tradition. The participants threatened to drive their adversaries out of the city. Every action was determined at a grassroots level, in the square. The first skirmish of any note occurred on May 15, 1652, when a notice was posted everywhere reading: "For the attention of the bourgeois gentlemen of Bordeaux." It denounced the

Mazarins, and the armed members of the Ormée burst into the Parliament.

Prince de Conti, Condé's brother, was governor of Guyenne and did his best to arrange reconciliation between the sides. Suspect Parliament members were expelled from the city.

The Ormée's main leaders were Christophe Dureteste, a court solicitor who presided over it, and his assistant, the lawyer Pierre Villars.

Soon there would be no more than about ten nonsuspect parliamentaires left. Condé himself took fright, tried to bring them to heel and was soon put in his place.

There was a battle with the bourgeois, led by a jurat (the Jurade, another of the city's leadership bodies, was the supreme authority in matters of justice), Fontenelle, and a councilor called Thibauld. The Ormée sustained eight fatalities, including two of its leading lights—Jacques Monleau (an attorney with the Parliament) and François Lafitte (a merchant). The Ormistes threatened to torch the city in retaliation, but things calmed down.

No longer trusting Condé, they were keen to take matters into their own hands now. The Jurade and the Parliament (traditionally, rivals—after all, the Parliament had made its revolution) came to an accommodation with each other against the Ormistes. In June, the banished returned to the city, which re-ignited the fighting.

On June 25, 1652, the Ormée seized the town hall as the tocsin was ringing. Four thousand Ormistes took to the streets. Three thousand attacked the Parliament, brandishing axes and mallets, trundling three cannons before them and using cartloads of firewood to burn down houses. Fifty-two people were killed and something like sixty injured, but the Ormée won the day. A quarter of the population of the city (numbering around twelve thousand) was in on it.

The probability is that they were drawn essentially from the populace, but the leaders were petty bourgeois, artisans, and businessmen, the odd court official and the occasional noble who went over to them after their victory.

Anti-statists, they had an acute class-consciousness (the dispossessed) and a sense that they, the common people, would save the country. They wanted to do away with corrupt officials and to change the judges (whom they would choose for themselves) and they dismissed the Parliament and sped up the courts (bringing suspects to trial in twenty-four hours, dispensing with lawyer, prosecutor, and bureaucracy).

The Ormée was one huge soviet. Henceforth, there was to be work for all. They voted for assistance to the indigent, widows, and orphans, and rents were reduced.

The Assembly, the "Company of the Ormée" claimed all the old powers (formerly held by Parliament, Jurade, etc). Their slogan was "Vox Populi, Vox Dei." Their government was to be "democratic" (a rather uncommon notion at the time). But they were still loyal to their king.

Edward Sexby, the English leftist leader, passed through Bordeaux as an exile in 1651 and left behind Lilburne's Agreement of the People. The Leveller struggle was to make a deep impression on the Ormistes. They were, in fact, to establish contact with the Levellers.

The moment that they realized that the monarchy was in cahoots with their adversaries, the Ormistes turned republicans. There were two schools of thought inside the Ormée. One school, the majority, supported the proclamation of an independent government, but they were at no time to proclaim that republic, for time slipped through their hands and maybe they lacked the boldness to do so.

Their program was to be an almost verbatim reproduction of the Leveller program. That program was very ambitious, very revolutionary: it was against the monarchy, which was something of an oddity at that time. Individuals were believed to be equal by birth and all privileges had to be abolished. The people's wretchedness was implacably denounced. Ormée members sought to build a democratic republic in every land, with a national assembly (remember that in those days these words had not yet been drained of all meaning and that these ideas in fact represented the bridge to universal happiness) and a parliament elected annually by all adult electors (except for servants, enemies of the Republic, and beggars).

But parliamentary authority was not the whole story. It was not immune from usurpation. Consequently, there had to be checks and balances, and these guys were perceptive. Everyone was to be equal before the law, there was to be freedom of religion, slavery was to be abolished, magistrates were to be elected by the people, and everybody was to share the burden of taxation (except the poor).

Now they went into action. At the outset, there was an Ormée Chamber, a general assembly of five hundred members, the grand soviet of direct democracy. The president, as we have seen, was Dureteste. But now they changed this into a Chamber of Thirty, which, little by little, whittled away the powers of the five hundred-man Chamber. It was an effective executive organ. The Chamber of Thirty, which emerged on June 27 as the Ormée's political agency, at first changed its line-up every fortnight! Later, this was to be slowed somewhat. Its first task was purely legislative, but those in charge very quickly took control of everything. They drew up a charter, elected new jurats of their own, and looked after the military side of their revolution. The leaders were Dureteste and Villars, whom we have met already, plus the lawyer Jean Pontellier, the squire Daniel de Tustal, and police commissars Pierre Guirault and Guillaume Crozillac.

They led the fighting, saw to the erection of fortifications, raised a fleet, and even issued an appeal to England (promising a port and a wine monopoly in return). Their meetings were held in public.

Another assembly, the Chamber of Twelve was to oversee private suits and act as an appeals court. Dureteste was on this as well. Dureteste had his standing bodyguard (so did Villars). One anecdote will give some idea of what he was like: Dureteste set off with his squadron to do battle with the enemy bourgeois. He arrived in the presence of one of them along with his men and announced to him: "Having learned of your illness, I bring you a prescription to go and take some air, and if, after tomorrow, you are not outside of the city, you are to be stabbed or thrown into the river…" In this way, he struck terror into the wealthy bourgeois. Dureteste was also secretary of the Leadership Chamber. He was a busy boy.

The others played multiple roles, too: Villars was commander of the guard and a member of the Thirty; Crozillac was one of the Thirty as well as judge at the Bourse; lawyer Pierre Robert was also one of the new jurats. Some of them even lined their own pockets this way.

Again they banished the outlawed parliamentaires. The city was now in their hands. It was under the military jurisdiction of the captains—Dureteste, Pontellier, Tustal, Guirault, Crozillac, Jannet the hermit, and the squire Henry Du Puy. (Conti was powerless.) Moneys seized from those banished were used to compensate their victims. They abolished neither the Parliament, the Jurade, nor the Bourse: they did change their personnel. That was all. They supervised tax collection. In the end, they were not able to level the fortifications (such as the La Brède castle). All in all, this amounted to a range of quite moderate measures.

They were scarcely to venture outside of the city. Nevertheless, they did dispatch envoys to La Réole, Vayres (where the garrison sided with them) and Libourne (where they supervised the taxes).

Having seen off Condé, the royal army might have seized Bordeaux but it was an army in the throes of disintegration. There had been desertions aplenty and incessant looting, while at the same time, the French fleet had been defeated by the English. Thus the Ormée was to know a few months of peace, during which it introduced Bordeaux to a democratic regime quite close to self-managing communes, in that the rebels arrived at all their decisions for themselves.

Cromwell sent them twelve hundred Irish mercenaries but would help them no more than that. He had his misgivings about them. No doubt they were too much the Levellers for his taste.

No one was more taken aback by their success than the Ormistes themselves, hence their hesitancy in proclaiming their independent republic. The most conservative tendency had been eliminated politically and the radicals were now all-powerful. A mini-terror had even resulted in a few foot-draggers winding up behind bars. The notorious and sinister Ha fort was partly demolished.

Several plots were hatched against them, and failed. One plot, led by the priest Ithier, was exposed by Villars whom they had attempted to bribe along with six other Ormistes (including Crozillac and Guirault). Ithier was paraded with a rope about his neck, bearing a placard that read "A traitor to the homeland," and was defrocked. He escaped a lynching by the skin of his teeth and his accomplices were rounded up.

As we have seen, the Ormistes helped improve the living conditions for Bordeaux's proletariat. They were less "solicitous" of the peasants. Initially greeted with enthusiasm, the peasants were eventually barred from entering the city: it has to be said that the main support for the Ormée came from the city's "proles," without whom none of this would have been possible. The rest were of no use, especially when the military position started to deteriorate.

Because, little by little, the Ormistes found themselves out on a limb. The bourgeois raised their heads again. The royal army was overhauled and recaptured several adjacent towns, one after another, and the rebels were not strong enough to withstand it.

The Ormistes had run out of money, run short of grain, and were drained by conspiracies. Even so, they declined an amnesty offered them if they would only surrender.

Inside the city, conspiracy was afoot. An anti-Ormee attack began in July 1653. The Ormée had lost some of its power to mobilize. The tide was turning. Conti entered into a compact with their adversaries.

In fact, the situation had altered all over. The bourgeoisie never remains allied with the proletariat for long. In Paris, the Parliament was afraid of revolution. It sought power and a restoration of order, rather than to see society destroyed. So it vowed to rein in the insurrection that was irritating it. Pamphlets were banned! (By a coincidence, some mazarinades had begun to upbraid the Parliament for its soft line.)

It was around this time that the nobility's Fronde started. A nobility-bourgeoisie alliance was the only remedy against revolution. The Parisian army would thereafter be under the command of nobles. The Princes de Condé and de Conti, and the Duc d'Elbeuf came to the fore. Louis de Condé, who the Ormistes had mistrusted, was the most moderate among these Frondeurs. He certainly wanted power but had no desire to see the monarchy toppled. He was well aware that his authority would be stronger under a monarch whom he could control than surrounded by a restless populace. He simply wanted to supplant Mazarin, nothing more.

The Fronde was over by 1649, in reality. After that it was merely the creature of the nobles, the bourgeois having allied themselves (the Parliament led the way here) with the king against the nobles. They had chosen their side. The fighting would peter out by itself.

There was one last popular uprising in 1652, in the wake of a provocation by Condé. It was to cost him whatever chances he had left of winning. In view of which it is understandable that Condé should have parted company with the Ormée the following year.

Such then was the inevitable fate of the Ormée. The reactionaries tore down the red flags that the Ormistes had posted everywhere and replaced them with white flags. The town hall was recaptured. The Ormée was overthrown.

For once, though, there was to be no bloodbath. The repression was severe, but most of the Ormistes were to be banished or imprisoned (about three hundred in all). The nobles were simply confined to their estates. A few people were sentenced to death (Villars was one) but they were spared in the end (1658). Robert recanted in public. Dureteste at first went into hiding but was captured in January 1654. He was to be executed: he was broken on the wheel, beheaded, and his head placed on a pitchfork on top of the Ormée tower. In March 1655, another Ormiste, charged with theft and murder, was executed in the same manner: this was Beaulieu. One way or another, by August 1653 it was all over. Bordeaux became the king's territory once again.

The Ormistes' lack of daring, the difficulty they had in conceiving of a thoroughly alternative society, and the fact that they were swimming against the tide of history (which had France evolving into a capitalist society and nation-state, the precise opposite of what they sought) all conspired to ensure that they failed.

Their struggle is particularly unfamiliar to the French, especially to the citizens of Bordeaux. It has to be said that Louis XIV, with an eye to the future, had all records of this crisis of his reign destroyed- with some effect.

Heirs to the Levellers, the Ormistes were the direct ancestors of the revolutionaries of 1789. But not until 1789 did another upheaval cause turmoil in the region. It is not a good idea to miscarry revolutions, especially if one outlives them.

France, 1789-1796
THE FRENCH REVOLUTION

Law without reason is not law, but perversity.
St. Thomas

A tragic paradox: freedom, the very symbol of life, is won through the taking of life.
Ricardo Flores Magon,
Regeneración (1910)

Were I a subject, I should revolt for sure.
Louis XIV

What is the French revolution? Open warfare between the patricians and the plebeians, between rich and poor.

Babeuf

Few events in human history have inspired so much writing and comment as the French Revolution, an event that, for all its twists and turns, occupied only six years. And yet, that period indicates its full term, not taking into consideration the many interruptions suffered by people's power, which never really grasped its freedom with a sure enough hand to savor it in peace.

There is no way that the years between 1789 and 1796 can be condensed into a few pages. Michelet himself, who stopped at 1794, filled twelve stirring volumes: biased and crammed with mistakes though they may be, they remain an unparalleled model of comprehensive and scrupulous research. Even so, he is foremost among a handful of historians of the proletariat who are all too overshadowed by academic mandarins—historians ranging from Nettlau to Dommanget, who have made this book possible.

We shall make do with a resume of events. Forgive me if I do not expand upon many points. To be honest, soviets often operate along similar lines and repetition is not always of service.

Like many a proletarian revolution, the one in 1789 opened as a bourgeois revolution and closed on the same note. The orgasm came in between: dancing the night away does not rule out a return to the factory come the morning, just like the day before.

Louis XIV's summoning of the Estate-General and the drawing up of the cahiers de doléances (registers of grievances) was all the beginning of a process over which, to be honest, no one was to have any control right up until Bonaparte's dictatorship.

In April 1789, just prior to the Estates-General, the Breton Club was established. Within a short time it was to become the celebrated Jacobin Club. Bourgeois historians generally look upon it as the seat of the revolution's far left, when it was to be only the home of Robespierrism (named after its leading politician), which is to say, roughly speaking, the center-left of the parliamentary current, or even the Montagnard left. For a time Barnave or Alexandre de Lameth dominated it, both of them right-wing bourgeois. The club, founded by a nobleman, Adrien Duport, was to be resolutely closed to the populace, if only by dint of its costly membership fees.

July saw the proclamation of a National Constituent Assembly, the speaker of which, a right-wing academic and astronomer by the name of Jean-Sylvain Bailly, was one of the leading lights. His role was an important one at the outset, notably in the Tennis Court Oath episode, when the deputies pledged not to be separated until such time as they had devised a constitution for the country. Mirabeau made his famous wisecrack about the power of bayonets and the king was forced into a corner.

Among the deputies, young and not so young men, who were to make a name for themselves, there were: Jérome Pétion, a lawyer; Robespierre, another lawyer; Siéyès, a priest; Barnave, a lawyer, and the doctor Guillotin who had the brainstorm of retreating into the Tennis Court, pending the arrival of other eccentric brainstorms at a later date.

The people were no fools: they had realized that there was no way that the weakness of the regime could be remedied. In recent months, hunger riots had multiplied. On July 12 the people revolted, and the beginning of the revolution can be dated from then. A stammering young journalist, Camille Desmoulins, was one of the agitators. He clambered onto a table, pistol and sword in his hands, and shrieked "To arms!" Apparently it was his idea that as an identifying sign they should wear a cocarde made of some foliage from a tree, the green being the color of the popular Jacques Necker, one of the few ministers of whom the people did not take too dim a view.

Up to that point, the reforms proposed by the Assembly had not posed too serious a challenge to the regime. That challenge had to be made through actions. And only the people of Paris could do that. So, as Michelet says, "With the rising sun, an idea dawned over Paris and everyone saw things in the same light. It shone in every mind and in every heart there was one voice: get on with it, seize the Bastille!" This would be believed, but there was nothing but crude symbolism in this phrase.

The movement's leader was Jacques Thuriot, of whom more later, a lawyer who always seemed to be on hand for crucial moments ("He put paid to the Bastille, and he did for Robespierre," as Michelet puts it). There were numerous women involved, so this was serious business. Thuriot called upon the Bastille's governor to surrender, a wheelwright was to cut through the chains holding the drawbridge, one man rushed forward, fell, and was killed. He was followed by a second who gained entry: such is fate! This man was Stanislas Maillard, a court usher still wearing his black robes, probably one of the more attractive personalities in the revolution thus launched. The French guards threw in their lot with the rebels who were led by a lieutenant and a NCO. The Bastille fell, Governor de Launay and the quartermaster Flesselles were lynched and their severed heads were to be carried around on pikes, the first in a long series of severed heads.

By the following day, Paris had a mayor, Bailly, whom Le Chapelier replaced as speaker of the Assembly. La Fayette, the popular adventurer famous from the American Revolution became military commander of the city.

On July 17, there was a meeting with the King who could avoid the issue no longer. Bailly offered him the keys to the city, while La Fayette proffered the new blue, white, and red cocarde, which was assured of a certain future.

The whole of France succumbed to the "great fear" made up of rumor and paranoia. It originated among the peasants, who anticipated the arrival of 'brigands'. When these brigands failed to materialize, then, lest they might appear to have panicked and armed themselves to no purpose, they burned and looted the chateaux of their oppressors, who then started to succumb to a "great fear" of their very own. We ought to note that a certain former parish priest by the name of Jacques Roux was to be involved in one such instance of looting, thereby acting out his favorite theories.

But other leaders of this revolution emerged. These were the ones from the Cordeliers convent who were to offer serious competition to the Jacobins—the likes of Camille Desmoulins, Georges Danton, and, shortly Jean-Paul Marat, Legendre, Santerre, and so on. The Cordeliers club was a lot more open to the proletarians and would quickly turn into the stomping ground of a heterogeneous far left.

For the time being, there was a three-pronged revolution underway: the parliamentary revolution in the Assembly, the anarchist revolution on the streets, and a proprietorial revolution out in the countryside where the feudalists where taking to their heels.

On August 4, there was a monumental incident. Possessed by an astonishing fervor, in a single night, the Constituent Assembly witnessed its members abolishing the ancient regime and its privileges root and branch: even the horrified nobility repudiated these. Even so, it was to be remarked that most of the bigwig leaders of the Assembly—Mirabeau, Bailly, La Fayette, and Siéyès—had not been present at the time. Everything was in need of reorganization. They set to work. For the moment, the peasants seemed to be benefiting the most, since they were the ones most burdened by feudalism: they had to be calmed down. Appeasing them was also the only way of preventing them from making undue trespasses against the sacrosanct rights of property.

Freedom of the press encouraged the flourishing of hundreds of new newspapers, the propaganda implications of which were enormous: there was Loustalot's *Les Révolutions de Paris* (Loustalot was a non-entity who died in 1790 and was replaced by Sylvain Maréchal); Marat's *L'Ami du Peuple*; Desmoulins's *France Libre*, which was replaced by his *Vieux Cordelier* (in 1793). The Jacobins had the *Journal des Amis de la Constitution*, written by their secretary, a writer by the name of P.A.F. Choderlos de Laclos who was in fact an agent of the Duc d'Orléans (leader of the "constitutional monarchist" branch of the royal family). Only later would Fréron's *L'Orateur du Peuple* and Hebert's *Père Duchesne* see the light of day.

Caught up in the frenzy, they passed the Declaration of the Rights of Man and the Citizen on August 26.

By early October, people were finding the king's indifference intolerable. The womenfolk, more aware perhaps than their menfolk to the problems of food shortages, decided to seek out the "baker" (whose duty it was to provide them with the bread they expected) in his chateau in Versailles. The leading light was a flower seller by the name of Madeleine Chabry, known as Louison, but the eight thousand women chose a "captain" who undertook to lead them. This was Maillard, of Bastille fame. The volunteers from July 14 were on hand: they even brought their cannons with them.

First, they went to the Constituent Assembly, where Maillard expounded upon the wretchedness of those perishing of hunger. A deputy for whom this was his real debut supported him in this: one Maximilien Robespierre. Proclaiming themselves citizens, the deputies accompanied the women to the king's residence.

On sighting the king, Louison fainted with a cry of "Bread!" Louis XVI, overcome, clasped her in his arms. As she came to, she called out "Long live the king!" and came within an ace of being lynched for it. The women mingled with the Guards who would not disperse them. They handed over their cartridges to the National Guards. Théroigne de Méricourt was beside herself, haranguing her companions in her red frock coat and riding hat.

One soldier who fired a shot was spared, but his horse was eaten raw. The king appended his signature to the Declaration of Rights presented to him. The next day, the mob swarmed over the chateau. It took the cool head of Sergeant Hoche (of the National Guard) and then the arrival of La Fayette to avert further incident. Everyone was to return to Paris along with the king, the queen, their son (to enthusiastic chants of, "Baker, baker's, wife and baker's boy"), and La Fayette leading the way. It was on this day that this whimsical officer, who was just a glory-hunting imbecile, was to become a royalist (not that anyone ever found this out until he turned traitor).

It was he, La Fayette, along with Mirabeau, Siéyès, and Talleyrand who was to launch a royalist club, the '89 Club. They might have seized power at this point, but they were prevented from doing so by their political insignificance. It was at around this time that Guillotine proposed a machine that would speed the punishment of those under sentence of death and that the assignats first appeared.

The end of that year saw the counter-revolution beginning to stir itself, through the clergy on the one hand, through the emigrés (the Comte d'Artois) on the other, and finally through Marie-Antoinette who was in cahoots with her family in Austria.

In April 1790, the 48 sans-culotte sections that were to make up the General

Assembly of the Paris Commune were set up. These were the revolution's first soviets. The sovereign people in action. The general assembly of each section held all the power. The poor were compensated so that they could attend. Chairmen and delegates were elected and subject to recall, as were the commanders of their armed forces (sixty battalions strong). Within a short space of time, they had adopted the use of familiar forms of address, the title "Citizen," and a sans-culotte form of dress, with red bonnet, carmagnole (short jacket) and striped trousers, not to mention the pike that was the symbol of their power, just as the scepter symbolized that of their aristocrat foes. Universal suffrage was an absolute must at every level. As yet this was not described as direct democracy or generalized self-management, but that is what it was, in embryo at least.

Seigniorial rights were "redeemable" (and consequently not abolished, a sure sign that the bourgeoisie controlled the Assembly) at great cost. The assets of the clergy, too, could be traded. The big landlords and the rich had a field day. The peasants had torched the registers (as usual) and had started to farmland left idle. In the Midi, the counter-revolution was rampant and there were a number of bloody clashes between the two camps.

Everywhere, without prompting, people were reorganizing themselves. One million, three hundred thousand new civil servants and magistrates whose education was going to be crucial, were to be recruited. Civic spirit was to arise often out of public accountability, but that, too, was to prove a defect in the system (since most people did not have the training for it).

For the first time, perhaps, this was an internationalist revolution: Anacharsis Cloots, a one-time German baron, introduced the "deputies of the human race," drawn from every nation and wearing national costume: they had come together into a federation for the occasion.

Incidents in Nancy in August 1790 sparked a massacre of the Swiss, who were all laudable patriots, after the Assembly misinterpreted events. La Fayette pressed for the restoration of order. The people's sense of outrage was considerable. By now the Jacobins were blatantly opposing the Constitutionalists, who were mostly royalists, although they were all involved in the struggle against the existing monarchy.

The previously well liked Necker, fell from favor, was brought down and fled. Phase one was at an end. Three separate camps had emerged, each of them embodied by the three main clubs. Let us take our bearings at this point:

—The Jacobins who rallied all the intellectuals (Sedaine, Chamfort, David, H. Vernet, Talma, Laclos) were represented well throughout France. At this point, they were divided into three schools of thought: the Orleanists (Laclos being one), the royalists (like Lameth) who backed Louis XIV and a constitution, and finally, the bourgeois tendency represented by Robespierre, who was club chairman for a month.

—The more "popular" Cordeliers, who had a foothold only in Paris, included all the journalists (Marat, Desmoulins, Fréron, Hébert, and Fabre d'Eglantine) as well as the revolution's great public speakers, like Danton, or the illiterate butcher, Legendre. From their ranks would come the far left tendencies like the Enragés or the Hébertistes and the likes of Billaud-Varennes, Collot d'Herbois and Chaumette.

—The Feuillants, which is to say, the far right, non-forward-looking royalists, like Barnave, Bailly, Siéyès or La Fayette.

Mirabeau died in April 1791, just in time: his corruption had yet to come to light. In June, Louis XIV fled. The story is well known: in Varennes he was spotted by a post-master, Jean-Baptiste Drouet, making his way home. Drouet was another remarkable figure from these times. Fetched back to Paris, Louis XIV was discredited and was never able to regain his former favor: it was plain that he had been engaged in treasonable action.

No one, though, was for a republic at that point. Marat's dreams were of a dictator (himself!). So were Freron's (he saw Danton in the part). La Fayette might even become that dictator. Republicanism was to make headway after Varennes.

A word about some of the exemplary females of the period: Olympe de Gouges, a republican at this point, was to turn royalist once the king was in jeopardy and this was to cost her her head. But she had time to lobby for women's rights. With the backing of Condorcet, Madame Palm-Aelder was demanding political equality for women. Many women were swept up in the emotion of the revolution and many a politician's speeches were written by his wife or mistress, unable to issue appeals on their own behalf. We shall soon be looking at the role of Madame Roland, who was the Gironde all by herself.

In July came the massacres of the Champ de Mars, when Cordeliers supporters carrying a petition drafted by Brissot and Laclos calling for a republic, clashed with La Fayette's troops.

The incident had been predictable. And more cautious souls had gone to ground: Danton, Legendre, Freron, and Desmoulins were away, campaigning. The second stringers were on hand and this was their big chance: the publicist Jacques-René Hébert and the student Chaumette were to give a lead. People like Momoro, a printer, and Maillard, who was still around, mingled with thousands of the common folk and with the National Guards. The sans-culotte constituency had taken to the streets.

For the first time, the Assembly took fright at their strength. Bailly attempted to calm the mob, but a shot was fired and the massacre ensued. La Fayette could have prevented the troops from opening fire, but he failed to do so, being content to see the mob being taught a lesson. The firing came from the soldiers, not from the volunteers of the National Guard.

Robespierre, who almost died of fright that day, was nonetheless feted by the mob which looked upon him as another sans-culotte (something that he never was to be). He sought refuge in the home of a master-carpenter by the name of Duplay, with whom he was to find lodgings, something that worked wonders for his street credibility.

The Jacobins capitalized upon the royalists' hesitancy. Pétion had the Club purged: from now on, all moderates were to flock to the Feuillants, while the radicals stayed behind. Power lay in the hands of Robespierre and Pétion. They had the support of the Cordeliers.

War erupted with Prussia and Austria—the allies of the émigrés. At the same time, the Constitution was ready. It only remained for the Constituent Assembly, its job finished now, to dissolve itself. That it did, in September, at the end of its colossal legislative undertaking.

The new assembly was inaugurated on October 1, 1791. This was the Legislative Assembly. Robespierre had been very insistent that there should be a complete change of personnel from the deputies who had belonged to the Constituent Assembly. The king lost all of his privileges into the bargain. He was merely the equal of the Assembly's speaker. Royalists and Constitutionalists were thrown into panic. La Fayette had fallen out of favor. He was only military commander now and had failed to win a seat in the municipal elections. (In order to finish him off, the royalists had voted against him). Pétion was returned as Paris's new mayor.

There was yet another massacre: in Avignon, which had just been reclaimed from the Papacy, bloody revenge was taken after a magistrate was murdered. Many innocent people were slain, especially females. Harsh decrees were passed against the emigrés, the king, and the priests. Vergniaud (a Bordeaux lawyer) and Isnard made a name for themselves. Isnard was on the Watch Committee that had been set up. Other members included Antonelle (of whom more anon) and some Jacobins.

Meanwhile, in the Paris Commune, or, rather, among the sans-culottes, a prosecutor, Manuel, had been appointed. Dantom was his deputy. The problem of the war loomed large. Everyone was for war: the royalists in hope of killing off the revolution, the deputies in order to consolidate it. Only Robespierre was against it: as far as he and his supporters were concerned, the real enemy was the enemy within.

Besides Vergniaud and Isnard, others were coming to prominence—people such as the lawyer Jean-Jacques Brissot, and Condorcet, a marquis and renowned philosopher. They all belonged to the new intake of deputies who were to make up the Assembly. They were in favor of the war. This is when the frictions with the Robespierrists began.

In March, they became the ministers upon whom the Court was obliged to call. Their supporters included Dumouriez (in reality, a closet royalist who also had links to the Duc d'Orléans) who was in charge of Foreign Affairs, Roland (Jean-Marie Roland de la Platière, erstwhile mayor of Lyon) in charge of the Interior ministry, and Clavières at the Finance ministry.

They came to be known as the Brissotins or Girondins (just as the Robespierrists were henceforth to be known as the Montagnards). Their leaders did not hold ministerial office: they preferred the Assembly. War had been declared.

It was at this stage that the Marseillaise—in which the watchword of "Liberty, Equality and Fraternity," coined by Momoro—was adopted and the address "Citizen" came into vogue.

Among the Jacobins, Robespierre had the upper hand. He never tired of making all sorts of allegations against the Girondins. In June, some ministers were sacked while Dumouriez threw himself into the arms of the Feuillants. On June 20 the mob forced the issue and invaded the Tuileries to urge the return of patriotic ministers. This uprising was led by the Dantonist, Legendre, and by a brewer called Santerre, who was the real leader in the "Faubourg" at the heart of the sans-culotte constituency. Danton was pulling the strings in this episode which was well managed.

Legendre showered abuse upon the king. Twice cornered, Louis XIV donned a red bonnet and cocarde and back-peddled to court a populace that was still naive and romantic. Pétion turned up to smooth things over.

Even so, the sans-culottes sections were to pass a resolution calling for the king to be deposed. A Committee of Insurrection was set up and it included Santerre and two Girondin journalists, Gorsas and Carra. Robespierre who could gauge the tension in the air, said nothing. The plan for the insurrection of August 10 was drawn up by Carra and Barbaroux (another Girondin) and encouraged by such as Danton, Manuel, Pétion, Thuriot, and Sergent (who, along with Manuel, represented the Commune). The Tuileries were taken by storm.

The Commune's Council-General was replaced by the sans-culottes. This new Commune was to be truly revolutionary. It would accept men and women alike. It adopted the red flag. Direct democracy was fully operational and from now on they would oversee everything: they were armed and in the insurrection proper had acted without leaders: Pétion had taken himself off and just let things take their own course. The royal family fled, and what toadies stayed behind were butchered. Théroigne de Méricourt was in the tick of the fighting. This girl of "easy virtue" (meaning that she had had lots of lovers, rather than that she was a prostitute: her lovers included Siéyès, Pétion, and Romme) was rabidly anti-Robespierrist and found herself being flogged in the streets a short while later by some Montagnard "bucks."

Santerre became commander of the National Guard. The Girondin ministers returned to office, with Danton as well at the Justice ministry. But real power lay with the sans-culottes. This was to last up until September 2, or for around a month. A number of remarkable personalities came to the fore: there was Chaumette, a cleric who had changed his forename to Anaxagoras, one of the Cordeliers' best orators, Jacques-René Hébert, and Marat (who, while not joining the Commune, attended its proceedings in his journalistic capacity). And there was Robespierre who had backed them in his speeches without, however, getting his hands dirty.

Also to the fore were Collot d'Herbois, a former actor, and Jean-Lambert Tallien, a cleric: for them, this was their debut. Louis XIV was imprisoned in the

71

Temple. Panicking, La Fayette fled the country and defected to the enemy.

The army was under the control of Dumouriez. A Revolutionary Tribunal was established to reassure the sans-culottes, who had been pressing for one. The elected judges were to dispatch their first suspects to the guillotine. The first victim was a confidant of the king. His head was displayed to the people. Such was the emotional charge of the moment that the executioner collapsed, having dropped dead of a heart attack!

As a result of treachery, the enemy entered French territory after the capture of Longwy.

Chaumette became prosecutor for the Commune, the dictatorship of which was now established fact. The Commune oversaw the organization of everything. Self-management (if we may use that term) was a frequent phenomenon. Tallien, a supporter of Danton, was the Commune's secretary. All of this was awash in a demented romanticism: people were driven by sentiment alone, cried their eyes out (like Collot, Hébert, or Panis), or embraced one another at the drop of a hat. Cochin too was a good example of the extent to which the leaders of the day were mediocrities or wastrels who had finally and clumsily come into their own.

The September Massacres occupied the period from September 2 to 5, one of the Revolution's most violent episodes and which radicals have found hardest to bear and most controversial. Robespierre was to use his authority to excuse them, although he had had no hand in them. Journalists like Fréron and Marat had whipped the mob into a frenzy. It was common knowledge in advance that bloodshed would follow. The people had had their fill of perishing of hunger while imprisoned royalists glutted themselves in the prison cells and received visits from their mistresses (corruption was a real problem). Two out of the forty-eight sections were to vote for the massacres. Marat, primarily, and Panis (who with Sergent held sway on the Watch Committee) were the chief instigators of events, having had the prisoners paraded through the streets. They were then massacred The blood-crazed sans-culottes toured all the prisons to slaughter indiscriminately. Their victims were often innocent common criminals.

Robespierre and Billaud-Varenne were exultant. Danton went into hiding. Prior to the killing, everyone had rescued somebody (Manuel, for example, had hidden Bueaumarchais, an enemy of his, lest it appear that he had had a hand in his being killed). During the episode, Maillard was magnificent: he had set up a makeshift tribunal to try suspects: and thereby saved innocent lives, even at the risk of his own. Maillard was passionate about legality and justice. He was to express a view that the people's justice "was punishing deeds and not thoughts."

Inside the Watch Committee, Panis (Santerre's brother-in-law) was a Robespierrist, Sergent (Marceau's brother-in-law) was opposed to Robespierre, and Marat was, even though not an elected member, in the Robespierre camp: it was Robespierre and Panis who had allowed the "graft" to proceed. Marat was in his element. Those who had carried out the massacres had not been numerous, numbering around four hundred. Many had not been sans-culottes at all. They found themselves being disowned. The army was demoralized and shunned the septembriseurs.

In the elections, Robespierre, Panis, Marat, Sergent, Danton, Desmoulins, Saint-Just, Collot, and so on, were returned as deputies. The Legislative Assembly gave way to a National Convention.

That very day, a handful of people, barefoot and in rags, with no uniform but their working clothes, bootless and poorly armed, routed the Prussians at Valmy. Dumouriez was at the head of this sans-culote band, with Kellerman as his aide. To a cry of "long live the Nation!" from thirty thousand throats, the enemy had cut and run. But Dumouriez was not to press home the advantage, and was only there because Couthon (a Robespierrist) and others had forced his hand. The sans-culottes and the Republic had known success on the same day: they had never before been so powerful but this was the last time.

Elsewhere, there was royalist unrest in the Vendée.

In the Convention, the factions were in place. The majority said nothing. The talking was done by the moderates, the right if you will, known as the Marais (and accounting for about half the deputies). There were some striking personalities among them, although they occasionally voted with the left: people like Barère (Bertrand Barère de Vieuzac, lawyer, and the greatest turncoat in all French history), Siéyès, and Cambon (who was to do a U-turn and become a Montagnard).

On the revolutionary side, we ought to draw a distinction between proletarians and bourgeois. The bourgeois were deputies, whereas this was only rarely the case with the "proles." But there was a right wing, the Girondins, with folk whom we have already encountered like Brissot, Vergniaud, Condorcet, Roland, Isnard, Carra, Pétion, Barbaroux, Clavières, etc. and others whom we shall be meeting like Buzot, Gaudet, Ducos, Fonfrede, Gensonne, Louvet, Rabault Saint-Etienne (the list is provided for the reader's reference later). They were moderate republicans, most of them well-to-do bourgeois. Their soul, their inspiration was Madame Roland, the erstwhile Manon Philipon.

Further to the left stood the Montagnards. To be honest, they were already split into two factions themselves: in simplistic terms, into a left and a center-left. The latter were the Indulgents, sometimes also described as the Dantonists, from the name of their chief member. The faction also included Fabre d'Egalantine and Desmoulins, but also Thuriot and Hérault de Sechelles. The genuine left were the Jacobins proper, the Robespierrists, if you like. Marat was one, as were Couthon, Saint-Just, Lebas, Collot, Billaud-Varennes, Lindet and Pache. By this point the Robespierre-Danton-Marat triumvirate was at the helm.

But the Mountain (Montagne) also had an ultra-left! Who were not deputies. These were the Mountain's proletariat. Even then, they were described as

Hebertistes, from the name of the popular editor of the *Père Duchesne* (with its print run of six thousand copies). Their leaders we have met already: Chaumette, Nicolas Vincent, Antoine Momoro, and Charles Ronsin. Along with other sans-culottes who were not Montagnards but stood further to the left, they made up the Cordeliers. They were the anarchists of their day. They were dubbed the Enrages. The best known of them was Jacques Roux, a peerless public speaker who preached in the churches, galvanizing the womenfolk, and who was to be one of the most interesting revolutionaries of his day, as well as among the most violent and maybe the most intelligent. There was another working man, Jean Varlet, and we might mention as well Anacharsis Cloots, the "orator of mankind." In Lyon, there was Leclerc, the lover of the actress Rose Lacombe, herself the leading light of the Societe des Femmes, the revolution's great feminist organization.

The characters were in place. Try not to get lost along the way, in the midst of all the fuss and confusion.

Already, the Girondins were accusing the Montagnards of having been behind the September massacres (which, in the case of anyone but Marat, was untrue). The Montagnards were levelling accusations of royalist at the Girondins (which were untrue). The Gironde attacked Danton for having embezzled Commune funds (not until the twentieth century was the proof of Danton's corruption produced).

One Girondin who swung to the left was Cambon. He was in charge of Finance. His pet hate was Dumouriez who had just scored the victory of Jemappes. The war was under the control of Pache (another Gorondin convert to the Mountain) who was out of his depth but was installing sans-culottes here, there, and everywhere- to the detriment of the speculators surrounding Dumouriez.

Robespierre told the Jacobins that he did not belong to the Commune, that he had not called on it prior to the massacres (these were all lies, he explained to the deputies). Barère salvaged the situation for him.

The Girondins' mistake was their failure to join forces with Dantonists, thereby putting the Jacobins in a corner. Madame Roland was at no time in favor of this and that was to cost them their heads.

The people were quite weary and attendance at assemblies were falling. Danton himself was washed out, and had come down in the world considerably, his companions now being utterly corrupt people like Fabre d'Eglantine. The death of his wife was almost to push him into madness. (He was to disinter her body after a week in order to hold her in his arms.)

Through the good offices of Clavières, a banker who had become Minister of Finance and who had devised the assignat, the ascendant bourgeoisie had its finger on the purse-strings. They, too, quickly disintegrated upon contact with power. Some were already flaunting their opulence.

These shortcomings account for the void into which the Jacobins were to fall. Collot was chairman of the Commune, with Robespierre as his lieutenant. So they had the sans-culottes behind them. They purged the club, expelling Brissot and the other Girondins. Cloots became club chairman. In this way, the violence-prone hotheads from the Cordeliers were contained. Robespierre was right to take this action, for they were powerful people. Varlet, although only twenty years old, was a street orator with a following in Robespierre's own section, the chairman of which, the Spaniard Guzman, was another Enragé.

The king's trial opened. Saint-Just pressed for the death sentence. Outside the country, no one leapt to the king's defense with undue vigor, for the emigré community had need of a martyr.

A new Commune was installed. It was very Jacobin in complexion, with Hébert (prosecutor), Chaumette (deputy prosecutor), and Lhuillier (Robespierre's agent). Only the mayor of Paris, Chambon, was a Girondin. In the Convention there was heated debate about the revocability of deputies, with the sans-culottes insisting that they must be so. Vergniaud was in the chair. All of the secretaries were Girondins. Thus, there was a dual power situation, with the Gironde prevailing inside the Assembly but the Mountain holding the upper hand in the Commune.

In the end, Louis XIV was sentenced to death and executed in January 1793. The Commune had selected Jacques Roux, the apostle of pillage and number one foe of the hoarders of every description, to accompany him to the scaffold.

Representatives were also dispatched to all parts on mission. Their powers were boundless. Dictatorship was not far away now. The war mobilized volunteers: these could elect their officers and overhaul disciplinary arrangements. Dumouriez turned traitor and his troops mutinied.

In Lyon, the counter-revolution succeeded. A Revolutionary Tribunal was set up to deal with suspects. The Terror was raging. Danton shrieked: "Let us be terrible so as to spare the people the need to be so!"

In March, the Enrages rioted. The sans-culottes rifled the bakeries. Hébert and Pache (Paris's new mayor) kept Roux, Varlet, and Leclerc in check, because their extremism was dividing the sans-culottes against themselves.

April 6 saw the launching of the Committee of Public Safety. Its nine members could expedite or delay a warrant, but they were to be subject to recall at any moment. Barère, Cambon, and five others represented the non-Mantagnard left, while Danton and one other represented the Mountain. There were no Girondins on the Committee. Even the Jacobins had no representation other than the lawyer Robert Lindet, who was to prove one of the revolution's honest administrators.

Furious with the selection, the Jacobins, whose chairman by then was Marat, threw themselves into the arms of the anarchists whom they had hitherto been denouncing.

Desmoulins, whose spirits were still high, wrote his *History of the Brissotins*, an implacable indictment. Marat charged twenty-two named deputies with treason.

He had the sans-culottes behind him. The success of the Vendée rebels drove the Jacobins on. They took up all important administrative and judicial posts. Antonelle and Fouquier-Tinville (the public prosecutor) were effective on the Revolutionary Tribunal. Guadet had Marat arrested, but the Commune brought him back in triumph: he was untouchable.

In the army, Adam de Custine, an aristocrat like all of the leaders thus far, had taken over from Dumouriez and was behaving just like him. He lost his head that July. Isnard, the most violence-prone of the Girondins, was speaker of the Convention. The Convention carried out an investigation of the Commune and Varlet and Hébert were even under arrest for a time. But Isnard's clumsiness provoked revolts in May and June. The Enragés, Rose Lacombe, Roux, Varlet, Maillard, not to mention a mysterious Committee of Six led by an engineer by the name of Dufourny, directed operations. Reluctantly, the Jacobins played along and called an insurrection which had started without them. Robespierre delivered the coup de grace to the Girondins. Twenty-nine of them were arrested along with two of their ministerial colleagues. Politically, the Gironde was finished. The arrests had been carried out when the Convention was under siege from the sans-culottes. Just to be on the safe side, they had even voted with the deputies.

The Gironde was not guilty of the allegations mooted against it, but its political mistakes had been dangerous and things took a turn for the worse. Its handling of things had been a disaster. Yet again, the sans-culottes had pushed History down the course the revolution needed. "The sans-culottes represent the force that allows the most conscious faction of the bourgeoisie to crush the aristocracy and its allies," wrote Albert Soboul.

The 1793 Constitution, the most radical one, was voted through. It introduced public education, paved the way for a civil code, carried out the division of communal assets at last, and thanks to Leclerc and the Enragés, a revolutionary army was established. Even Hébert was left with the wind taken out of his sails.

The Committee of Public Safety underwent a change of personnel. In May, Couthon, Saint-Just, and Hérault de Séchelles joined its ranks, followed in July by Robespierre (Danton dropped out). Lazare Carnot and Prieur de la Cote d'Or joined in August, followed by Thuriot and Prieur de la Marne. Robespierre had inserted "the Supreme Being" into the Constitution. He took measures that favored the wealthy bourgeois. He was taking a turn for the worst.

The Enrages were seething. Roux and Robespierre hated each other. On June 25, Roux articulated his utter hostility in his extremely radical *Manifesto of the Enragés*, in that he raged against the very same sacrosanct rights of ownership that Robespierre was championing. Roux's address read: "Liberty is but an empty sham when one class of man may starve the other with impunity. Equality is only an empty sham when the rich man, by dint of his monopoly, wields the right of life or death over his fellows. The republic is only an empty sham when the counter-revolution is daily at work on the prices of produce which three-quarters of the population cannot obtain without shedding tears."

Behind him, Roux had the sans-culottes, the Commune, and the Cordeliers. The time had come for the Jacobins to give him his come-uppance. Robespierre schemed. He who never set foot inside the Cordeliers Club showed up there with Collot and Hebert who had also had a bellyful of Roux for overtaking them on their left. They contrived to have Roux and Leclerc expelled. The campaign against Roux left no stone unturned.

In the War ministry, the Hebertistes were "kings": Ronsin was the minister-general, Vincent was secretary-general. Momoro was on their side. Marat railed against Roux, his sole competitor. All of these people entered into an alliance with Robespierre.

In Nantes, the Vendée rebels were driven out and Cathelineau was killed. Danton married for a second time... in a religious ceremony! How far he had fallen. Ronsin disgraced himself in the West (with executions, rapes, and murders of patriots).

On July 17, Charlotte Corday assassinated Marat and in Lyon the royalists executed Chalier, one of the Enrages. The local Girondins obliged them in this.

Robespierre was speaker of the Convention. Carnot and Prieur de la Cote d'Or were reorganizing the army. Military success led to the Hebertistes being eliminated from that service (as they had not done a thing to win the war).

In September, there was further Enragé unrest which benefited the Commune. Pache supported them. But Hébert and Chaumette did not see eye to eye anymore. Collot and Billaud, who had also supported the Enragés, joined the Committee of Public Safety, just as Thuriot dropped out of it. Danton had no desire ever to rejoin it. But the divided Enrages were eliminated anyway. Roux and Varlet were arrested. Leclerc managed to go underground (and would keep out of sight for a long time) and Claire Lacombe's Société des Femmes was disbanded.

Year two opened with in-fighting at the top, to determine who would be guillotined by whom. No need to worry: they would all get their come-uppances, except the reactionaries who were proliferating like rabbits. The terror was at its height. Couthon neutralized Lyon with the help of some peasants. This success played into the hands of the Robespierrists. The Queen was executed. Kléber smashed the Chouans. Then came victories over the Prussians: all of which boosted the power of the Jacobin victors.

Now the time had come to dispose of the Girondins physically. This was Brumaire: out of the twenty-nine Girondins convicted, twenty managed to escape in time. One of them, Buzot, raised a rebellion in the West. This time there was real collusion with the enemy. Fresh names were added to the list for good measure this time. On October 31, these people were executed. The victims included Vergniaud, Brissot, Balazé (who cheated the executioner by committing suicide), Fonfrède, and Ducos (who had often voted against the Gironde). Madame Roland followed soon after, as did Rabaud Saint Etienne and the Feuillants, Barnave, Bailly (the former mayor) and, Gorsas.

The fugitive Roland took his own life when he learned of his wife's fate. By the beginning of 1794, several more would follow suit in the Gironde: Pétion and Buzot committed suicide in the countryside whilst Barbaroux bungled his attempt and was to be executed. The arrested Condorcet also shot himself. Others were to make good their escape: Isnard and Guadet slipped over the border.

The Girondins had been in power and yet had failed to make revolution. Even so, they had tried to put the brakes on what the sans-culottes were doing. The Jacobins stepped into their shoes. They were to pursue the same policy, albeit with a touch more bloodshed. Though more effective, they had not invented anything. Their sole legacy to us is parliamentarism, for which they had a real talent. As for the Enrages, they would doubtless have come up with something, except that they were opposed by two, much too well-organized parties. Among their interesting proposals was "Tax the rich," a sans-culotte demand.

They operated through soviets: direct democracy at every level, self-management within their sections, elected officers subject to recall, rabid anti-capitalism (which was something new because capitalism was only in the process of being born at the time). But they were still captives of the old structures and of their political immaturity. Atheism was insufficiently widespread, except in Cloots (who would talk about "Our Lord Mankind").

Chaumette ran the Commune's General Council virtually single-handedly. He was to do sterling work unaided, which makes him a character a thousand times more interesting than a Robespierre or a Danton. But, to tell the truth, the sans-culottes had run out of steam, having lived on their nerves since 1789. Sans-culotte activity, carried out by Chaumette and others, had a low profile but consumed a lot of energy: the measures taken on behalf of women (even though Chaumette himself was a misogynist and male chauvinist), the sick, the mad, the poor, children, and libraries were remarkable.

The planting of vegetables in public parks is still cited as an act of lunacy! However, in a time of famine, Chaumette, one might think, had been well advised. It was he, too, who had the archives preserved for historians, who organized celebrations for the people, who set up hospices, founded the Conservatory of Music and found homes for the children of the condemned (which was quite an innovation, the sins of the fathers having previously fallen upon the children), and it was he who taxed the rich and dispensed these funds to those in most need. Thanks to Chaumette, the Commune enjoyed boundless popularity: married couples came forward to be remarried before him so that their union might be a real one! And all of this was going on in the autumn of 1793.

Meanwhile, what were the Jacobins doing? They were talking and keeping the guillotine well fed. They ranted against Cloots, who was the Club chairman, for a month, and really irritated him. Romme was speaker of the Convention, to the great annoyance of Robespierre who was agitating against everybody. The Feast of Reason, organized by Chaumette, drove Robespierre crazy. This Enrage was shoving a secular, atheistic, pacifist feast down the throat of Robespierre who dreamed of the Supreme Being, and that feast was a great success.

He acted. He manipulated the weakened Danton (who was even heard to speak of the Supreme Being!) and used him to bring down the Commune. H'ebert dumped Chaumette just at the right time. Cloots was expelled from the Jacobins and demolished by Desmoulins. Robespierre had freedom of religion voted through (with the cult of Reason being swept aside). Antonelle, too, was dropped from his position as chairman of the jury which dispatched people to the guillotine (the chairman of the tribunal, Herman, was a dyed-in-the-wool Robespierrist).

This was dictatorship, enforced by the Robespierre-Couthon-Saint Juste trio. At the War ministry, H'ebert had been replaced by Carnot, Prieur, and Lindet who amended a few shortcomings. In fact, the real power was shared between the Committee of Public Safety, which oversaw the war effort and politics, and the Committee of General Security which ran the political police and the revolutionary committees.

In December, in Toulon, the young Robespierre made a convert of an officer who had hitherto been a supporter of the Dantonists Fréron and Barras. That officer's name was Napoléon Bonaparte. It was he who recaptured the city which royalists had surrendered to the British. At the same time, Saint-Just was in Strasbourg with Lebas. There he wrought miracles. The army of the Rhine followed him with enthusiasm. On his arrival, and without spilling any blood (except for that of Schneider, the local dictator), he started to backslide: "Ten thousand men in this army go barefoot. You must tear the shoes off all Strasbourg's aristocrats within the day, and by ten o' clock tomorrow morning there will be ten thousand pairs of shoes marching on headquarters." It was done.

There were other methods, too. Fouche in Lyon, Collot and Fréron, and especially Carrier in Nantes blithely slaughtered the often innocent population (mass drowning, use of artillery). The ghastly accounts of what was done are authentic and reflect no credit on those responsible: more of the mediocrities that Cochin and Michelet alike have pointed out.

In Bordeaux, Tallien, who was without doubt one of the greatest low-lifes of the age, went one better: he lined his own pockets by auctioning his grace and favors. In Provence, Barras and Fréron were to do likewise. Yet they were the ones to outlive the Terror, not the others. They became the future conquerors of the French Revolution. And their regime survives to this day.

However, there were other, honest revolutionaries among the envoys on mission. Aside from Lebas and Saint-Just, we might cite Robert Lindet. In the West, Lindet matched the results produced by the others. But he had no need of any death sentence to bring this off!

But the Cordeliers were not dead. Robespierre was even obliged to seek alliance with Hébert and Collot (there were still enemies on the right in need of liquidating!). The terror was escalated in order to put paid to the Dantonists. Vincent, the leader of the Cordeliers after that, was set free after having been rounded up along with Ronsin and Maillard. They were still the untouchables.

In January, Desmoulins was expelled from the Jacobins. He had let himself be manipulated by Fabre d'Eglantine who was arrested for forgery (which he had committed, but this particular forgery was not a forgery!). The dictatorship closed in. Saint-Just pushed through the Ventose Laws setting up the popular commissions charged with trying suspects. The Cordeliers draped the Declaration of Rights in mourning weeds by way of a protest against the dictatorship.

Seeing that he was bound to be executed, Jacques Roux took his own life in prison. He was the only possible leader of a great alternative movement that might have averted Jacobin dictatorship. The other Cordelier leaders were too dubious (Hébert) or had been eliminated already (Chaumette). Not until Babeuf came along would there appear a personality and theoretician of his stature. And the fate he was to meet was to be the same.

Hebert was very powerful by this point and henceforth he was the ultra-left. But he clung to his alliance with the Jacobins, which is tantamount to saying that he was next in line. Robespierre really was the ancestor of the Stalinists of every hue (Lenin, Trotsky, Stalin). His tactics were to rely upon the revolutionaries to bring down authorities against which he could not achieve anything unaided, then to liquidate each tendency, one after another, while invoking the support of the others, until only one was left.

Desmoulins attacked Robespierre, who took fright and recalled Saint-Just. A war of words ensued. At the same time, the Cordeliers fell out with one another. Hébert was disowned by the rank and file who had had enough of his chicanery. An insurrection was in the offing, but this time they were stopped good and proper: Ronsin, Hébert, Vincent, and Momoro were even charged with "royalism!" On March 24, they and their supporters were executed. Cloots was tossed into the same batch for good measure. This time the genuine left was liquidated.

The Hébertistes, too, might have played a significant revolutionary role but they still had too many ties to the bourgeoisie. They were only left-wing Jacobins.

Chaumette was arrested, but politically, he had died long since. The Dantonists panicked. Rightly so. They bungled their coup in the Convention designed to regain power. Everyone warned Danton that his turn was next but he stood his ground. Robespierre lacked the courage to point an accusing finger at his old partner: but Saint-Just would do it. Danton was reluctantly found guilty.

Danton was arrested along with Desmoulins and their case also involved Phelippeaux, Hérault de Séchelles, Chabot, General Westermann, and the Enragé Guzman. They were all guillotined. The following month it was the turn of

Chaumette (executed as a "Hébertiste"!). The Commune no longer existed. The Jacobins stood alone. Robespierre's last declared enemy was Cambon, the financial expert, and inflation was raging.

The bourgeoisie lorded it over everyone: the literate folk had taken advantage of the starving illiterates in this revolution. The cult of the Supreme Being had official approval, even if everybody found it ridiculous. From then on, they schemed against the "tyrant" Robespierre. Carnot was elected speaker of the Convention, in defiance of Robespierre. Fouche became chairman of the Jacobins, for the same reasons. The last remaining "Dantonists" allied themselves with the faction of the corrupt: Tallien, Barras, and Fréron, who were just waiting for their chance.

The Feast of the Supreme Being in June 1794 demolished any lingering resistance. A furious Collot and Billaud joined in the plot. The Prairial Laws set the official seal on a dictatorship unparalleled in France before or since. No more defense counsel, no more witnesses, no more investigation: instead, every suspect was to simply be executed. Couthon introduced the draft legislation on Robespierre's behalf without consulting the other members of the Committee of Public Safety; they gave way, but it was the last straw.

Only two more months remained of the Great Terror. Things seemed to be going swimmingly: Saint-Just and Jourdan scored a victory over the enemy at Fleurus. Robespierre made mistakes: he had Fouche expelled from the Jacobins and Barere took his place as chairman, whilst Collot was speaker of the Assembly.

On Thermidor 8 (July 26) the Convention opposed Robespierre and refused to endorse his speech of indictment (he was ranting against everybody, but there was no one left to succumb to his paranoia). Barère turned traitor at the optimum moment, as ever, and Cambon stole his thunder.

But the following day, Thermidor 9, was when the scene was acted out. Legendre and Thuriot also deserted him. Tallien interrupted Saint-Just in mid-speech, then launched into a violent attack on Robespierre. Robespierre made to speak but was howled down to cries of "Down with the tyrant!" The speaker, Colot, used his hand-bell to drown him out. Thuriot put his charges to a vote. The game was up. His friend Coffinhal took Robespierre out, along with his supporters—Saint-Just and Couthon, who stood accused along with him, his brother and Lebas who walked out in sympathy. They fled to the town hall.

The next day, the Jacobins never stirred: they had lost all credibility. The last remaining Enrages were in prison (Varlet) or on the run (Leclerc). Soldiers arrived to take them unawares and arrest them. A gendarme called Merda fired his gun at Robespierre and smashed his jaw. Lebas tried to shot himself in the head, while Augustin Robespierre threw himself from a window and broke both legs. The others— Saint-Just, Couthon, Dumas, mayor Lescot-Fleuriot, and Payan—were arrested. Barras had prevented their supporters from approaching. Only Coffinhal managed to escape.

The reaction had succeeded; there were general celebrations on the street, and

81

steam was let off. The tension had been too high and the terror had hung heavily on many a mind. Just about anything would be acceptable as long as it was a change.

Robespierre's twenty-one supporters were executed the following day without benefit of trial (which was something new and demonstrated that dictatorship had not ceased when the dictators disappeared). They were soon followed by their friends, including Coffinhal, who was tracked down.

Tallioen joined the Committee of Public Safety which virtually ceased to exist. The Convention had been in existence for around fifteen months. The bigwigs in power came to be described as the Thermidoreans. Theirs was a stop-gap government, the sole merit of which was that it had stopped the terror. The rejoicing was a touch premature. These were the days of the gilded youth (Jeunesse dorée) who indulged themselves in homosexual orgies and sinister celebrations. Barras, Fréron, Legendre, and Tallien found that every cloud has a silver lining, as did Tallien's mistress, Thérésa Cabarrus, a demi-mondaine recently discharged from jail.

The people who had toppled the Jacobins fell into four categories:

—those who had formerly been their accomplices in all the outrages of the terror and who had capitalized upon that in order to line their own pockets: people like Fouché, Freron, Barras, and Tallien—the butchers, if you like.

—the left-wing of the Committee of Public Safety, Jacobins grown weary of Robespierre but who were up to their necks in his dictatorship: people like Barère, Collot, or Billaud.

—members of the Committee of Security (at odds with the Committee of Public Safety, which had stifled it): people like Vadier (its chairman) or Amar, who had also played their part.

—finally, the moderates from the Committee of Public Safety who had let the Robespierrists have their way. These were the "technicians", the technocrats avant la lettre: people like Carnot, Prieur, or Lindet.

At the same time, right-wingers like Cambacérès, who had long kept mum, were beginning to rear their heads again. The reaction even enjoyed applause from the anti-Jacobin ultra-left such as Babeuf or Varlet, momentarily blinded by their hatred of the tyrant.

Early in September, Collot, Billaud, and Barère resigned from the Committee, as did Tallien. Anti-revolutionary hysteria began. It made no distinction between moderates and extremists: everything going by the name of Revolution was vilified and those furthest to the right encouraged this blanket condemnation.

Under the auspices of Cabarrus and the singer Garat, balls were organized at which precious youngsters would appear in very exclusive haunts (entry was not allowed unless one had had a family member guillotined) with the backs of their necks shaved—guillotine-style—and would offer one another a "victim-style" greeting, dropping the head as if guillotined. All monuments reminiscent of a "mountain" (!) were demolished and they even went so far as to ban pronunciation of the letter "R" (for revolution), which gave rise to exchanges in gibberish.

Revolutionaries were hunted down. Dragnet searches and executions proliferated. Carrier was executed at the end of a sensational trial. The "terrorists," Billaud, Collot, Barère, and Vadier (the latter a fugitive) were also accused and sentenced, before it was the turn of Thuriot and Cambon (who went on the run).

These convicts were deported to Guyana where Collot d'Herbois, the old alcoholic, died a ghastly death in 1796: suffering from a fever, he helped himself to some alcohol—fuel alcohol. Billaud-Varennes was rescued from deportation come the Brumaire events and was to go into retirement (dying in 1819). Thuriot managed to escape in time and was to finish up as a lawyer in Napoleonic times, passing away in 1829. Vadier and Barère were also to make good their escape and lived on until 1841. Cambon who was to make a comeback and would even become a deputy, was exiled after 1815, and died five years after that. These were a few of the survivors of the Great Terror. There were not many.

While they were on trial, there were a number of revolts, like the Germinal revolt (April 1795) into which the women dragged the last of the sans-culottes. They were to be led by a certain Van Eck. After shouting "Bread!" at the Convention, they were assuaged by a few fine phrases. The sans-culottes now were only a shadow of their former selves. Previously, they had been the embodiment of popular sovereignty. That sovereignty had been inalienable and not subject to delegation. Every usurper of it was a tyrant. Everybody participated and everything was self-managed: they had burst in upon every assembly. Laws had required their sanction. The "blessed pike" had been the very symbol of the people armed.

Now here they were submitting to disarmament at the hands of reactionaries. Here they were agreeing to the exclusion of women from assemblies and letting the Thermidoreans getaway with rejecting the notion of "popular sovereignty."

There was another attempted revolt in Prairial (May 1795) when the rebels even succeeded in killing a deputy. Prieur de la Marne was arrested, as was Romme (who committed suicide). The National Guard was overhauled: no more poor people would be accepted into it. The Constitution was completely amended.

In Vendimiaire, there was even a counter-revolt: the bourgeois booted out the remaining revolutionary deputies. Barras was behind this and Bonaparte became chief of staff (he, too, having switched sides).

In October, the Convention was wound up. It was to be replaced by an arrangement comprising an Assembly, the Five Hundred, and a Directory, the chief members of which would be Barras and Carnot.

Babeuf had revised his opinion of Thermidor. He had understood now. Corruption, venality, and debauchery—the regime's rottenness was patent. His conspiracy was underway.

The final revolutionary spasm opened with discussions surrounding a group known as the Pantheon Club, from the winter of 1795 to 1796. Its members included: Lebois, a printer supporter of Marat: Michelangelo Buonarrotti, an amazing character and a forerunner of communism: Jean-François Baby, a bourgeois; Amar, formerly of the Security Committee, an anti-Robespierrist who was now rubbing shoulders with Robespierrists, Hébertistes, and Enragés: they were all bound together into a sacred union in opposition to the reactionaries. Most of them had served time in prison.

They then joined forces with Gracchus Babeuf, a communist theorist fascinated by agrarian issues. A journalist, he was publisher of the *Tribun du Peuple*, attacking property and dreaming of phalansteries (this before the word was ever devised) in which the soil would be farmed by small communities. He, too, was no stranger to prison.

Along with these people, who should pop up but Antonelle and Drouet (who was still a deputy, a member of the Five Hundred); the banker Félix le Peletier (brother of the revolutionary martyr), who would provide the funding; the writer Sylvain Maréchal; Simon Duplay (Robespierre's landlord), whose family had been massacred; plus others such as the student Augustin Darthe, one of those who had stormed the Bastille, the industrialist Antoine-Marie Bertrand, former officer Charles Germain, and Clemence and Didier and Debon.

The two leaders, Babeuf and Buonarrotti, were fine theorists. Their researches complemented and enhanced each other. Extremely egalitarian types, they were pre-Leninists: they believed in the success of a revolutionary minority, in dictatorship of the proletariat (this separating them clearly from the sans-culottes and Enrages), in putsch tactics (for which they were laying the groundwork). They favored a return to rural life (not for nothing was Maréchal one of their number) and they reckoned that the most taxing tasks should be rotated and that property should be abolished and taken into common ownership. The appropriate structures, they reckoned, were collective farms of between twenty and fifty people. As we can see; theirs was a hodge-podge of communist, socialist, and anarchist notions, purpose-built for others to stake their claim to such ancestry. Today Babeuf is claimed as a forebear by the Socialist Party and Communist Party alike, as well as by politicians with Libertarian tendencies.

Their Club was shut down in February 1796, whereupon they went underground and set up a well thought-out Secret Directory made up of the communists Babeuf, Debon, Maréchal, plus the Robespierrists Darthe, Le Peletier, and Antonelle, plus the hybrid Buonarrotti. Every arrondissement in Paris was to have its agent, as would every troop of soldiers. No detail had been overlooked!

Seventeen thousand men were to participate in their putsch! The bakeries would be commandeered, the bread distributed free of charge, and the homeless would be moved into the dwellings of the rich. Along with some other former Montagnards, Lindet joined them. Barras took fright and placed himself in their service!

All in all, they were also great feminists. Their propaganda was significant. They would probably have struck a chord with the populace.

But they were betrayed by an informer (or coward who panicked at the eleventh hour) by the name of Grisel, one of their military agents. Carnot, who had been in the know right from the outset, blew the whole affair out of all proportion ("a devotee of law and order, the man in charge of the nation's defense, he was outraged at the intensity of the Babouvist propaganda inside the army and looked upon these new Levellers with horror," say Furet and Richet). He had them all rounded up in May. Barras switched sides again, just in the nick of time: he had not had any inkling that things were about to go pear-shaped!

A provocation contrived by Carnot triggered a shoot-out with the last of the Babouvists. Thirty lives were lost. Baby, arrested on the word of an informer, was executed in October 1796.

The demise of Drouet, Lindet, Vadier, and Amar spelled the end for the last "terrorist" faction. Only the last of the Jacobins, Pasche, was to leap to their defense. Though arrested, he saved his skin by pledging to be done with politics. He kept his word and died in 1823.

Oddly enough, Carnot's intelligence was incomplete: Maréchal and Debon had not been denounced and were not troubled. Buonarrotti and Germain were deported along with some others. Buonarrotti was to have further exploits in Italy after that (dying in 1837). Le Peletier, Clemence, Marchand, and Lindet managed to escape. Le Peletier was to be acquitted in any case: so was Drouet, who became a deputy again, then a lawyer under Napoléon (dying in 1825). Varlet escaped yet again. Drouet had escaped with the connivance of Barras and went on later to become a sub-prefect under the Empire.

Of the forty-seven people indicted in the case, only two were sentenced to death: Darthe and Babeuf. They were dying when they were executed in May 1797: they had stabbed themselves while waiting for the verdict. Babeuf was 36 years old, Darthe 27. They were the last of the revolutionaries of 1789–1796. For the dispossessed, nothing had changed and hunger was an enduring problem. Babeuf's own 7-year-old daughter perished of hunger just prior to her father's execution.

According to Michelet "Babeuf's Terror was the making of Bonaparte." Curt but true. It provided the pretext for Brumaire. But that is another story. One that has nothing to do with revolution, nor with freedom.

We shall merely note the extent to which the happenings during these years have left their mark upon our lives. The fundamental divisions and differences over competing ideas about life, liberty and happiness are the same today as they were two centuries ago. Our political life is divided along the same lines. It is merely less bloody these days. The more mischievous among us might well deplore that. Blues in the night, that's how I see things.

France, 1870-1871
THE PARIS COMMUNE

"The deeper one goes into political life, the more noticeable it is that France has only ever had one honest government: the government of the Commune."

Henri Rochefort, on the twenty-sixth anniversary of the Commune in 1897

"The first great "defeat" of proletarian power, the Paris Commune, was in point of fact its first great success, because, for the first time, the primitive Proletariat asserted its historic capability of directing every aspect of the life of society in a free way."

Mustapha Khayati
On the Poverty of the Student Milieu (1966)

Between the revolution of 1789 and that of 1871, there are many points of comparison. But there are also many points where they are radically different. The advances made by the proletariat over the space of a century were immense. In certain members of the Commune, we will discover the direct heirs to the sans-culottes, as well as the most dismal Jacobins.

Moreover, in the intervening period, some important theorists had passed that way, leaving enduring traces behind them: Fourier (and his disciples such as Victor Considérant), Proudhon (who was very influential at the time) and indeed, Bakunin and Marx.

What connects all these strands, is that they were all patriots (war with the neighbor across the Rhine galvanized every mind), albeit that they subscribed to a less simple-minded patriotism than in 1789–1794. If we are to get our bearing in what follows, we must first specify the tendencies and their representatives before we place them in context in the thick of the action.

The International had a substantial French section, a blithe mixture of anarchists and Marxists, the former plainly enjoying the greater influence at the time. Prestigious and feared by the powerful, the International had been flattened and its action took place in the minds of men rather than on the streets or in the factories. The personnel of the I.W.M.A., pacifists, were opposed to property: they were

86

internationalists and favored a federal system.

Their leaders were: a working man turned deputy, Tolain, an anarchist of the Proudhonist school; and Benoit Malon, soon to become mayor of Paris. To these we might add Eugene Varlin, an anarchist bookbinder. Among the noteworthy members of the International were the mechanic Adolphe Vassi (who had organized significant strikes in Le Creusot), who was to pass for the "leader" of the Commune because his name was always printed at the top of the list (they had, democratically, opted for alphabetical order!): the teacher and Proudhonist Gustave Lefrançais (a regular visitor to jail); the carpenter Jean-Louis Pindy; the spiritualist parfumier Babick (a unique eccentric); the engraver Theisz; the mechanic Augustin Avrial; the Hungarian Léo Frankel, who was indisputably the only true Marxist of the lot of them and whom we shall find later setting up the revolutionary party in his homeland; the Proudhonist Charles Longuet, renowned primarily for being the son-in-law of Karl Marx; the cook Victor-Elie Grelier; the old Proudhonist Charles Beslay, surrounded by an aura of great prestige; and, indeed, Camélinat, who was to wind up a Communist by 1920.

Then there were the Blanquists. Incontrovertibly the Jacobins of their day. Their chief—and that he was—Louis-Auguste Blanqui, theoretician of the revolutionary minority (every generation has its own) was to bungle the chance of his lifetime: arrested on the eve of the uprising, he was never to be released nor exchanged and was to deprive his party of the only leader that it had. Among his followers were the 24-year-old student Raoul Rigault; Théophile Ferré, Louise Michel's great love; the painter Gabriel Ranvier; Gustave Flourens; the foundry worker Emile Duval; the journalist Emile Eudes; the physician Edouard Vaillant; Amilcare Cipriani; the lawyer Protot; and Blanqui's second-in-command, the bourgeois Gustave Tridon, who was sickly and no replacement for his leader.

Mostly intellectuals, the Blanquists were connected with the Carbonari, were putschists, terrorists if need be, and revelled in clandestine activity and conspiracy, claiming to be the heirs of Chaumette and Hébert (when in fact they were closer to a Robespierre or a Saint-Just) and they had no real program for "afterward."

The third faction on the ground was the Republican Alliance, an umbrella group covering all sorts. They were the ones dubbed "Jacobins" at the time, but it is hard to tell why: they were left-wing republicans, opposed to the traditional "decent left" of the Louis Blanc or Ledru-Rollin variety. Most of them were quite well up in years and had "done" 1848. The great figure among them was Charles Delescluze, who had a string of convictions, was a deputy, and was highly regarded; then there was Arthur Arnould, a queer fish, in that he was an anarchist and a member of the I.W.M.A. and a journalist to boot; there was the deputy Millière, director of the newspaper *La Commune*; former naval officer Charles Lullier; and second-raters like Peyrouton, Razoua, Floquet, Gambon, Jules Miot, and lastly, the dead loss of all dead losses, the old deputy Félix Pyat, director of Le Vengeur, a comic opera character, as yellow as he was loud-mouthed.

LOUISE MICHEL

ROSSEL

J. VALLES

The Blanquists, being centralists, were all for the dictatorship of the proletariat. The Proudhonists were against the State, decentralists, autonomists, and federalists. Yet for a time they were to come to an accommodation. Ah, but that is one of the delights of these orgiastic times when one can join forces against dictatorships!

By way of a prelude to events and in order to give some flavor of the Napoléon III regime, let us call to mind the Victor Noir affair. The emperor's brother, Prince Pierre Bonaparte, a less than glittering personality, deeming himself to have been defamed by Rochefort, the then director of the *Marseillaise* newspaper, challenged him to a duel. Rochefort sent along his seconds, Millière and Arnould. But one of his reporters, Paschal Grousset, had also taken up the challenge and sent along his second, Victor Noir. Pierre Bonaparte, in his wrath, could find nothing better to do than to murder the young Victor Noir. This caused a real sensation and Noir's funeral procession was enormous.

The war of 1870 brought about the collapse of the Empire. The defeat at Sedan finished off the regime. On September 4, the legislature was invaded, but moderates like Jules Favre intervened in time and a republic was not proclaimed (a republic would doubtless have averted the Commune).

A government of National Defence embraced the Parisian deputies along with the military governor of Paris, General Trochu. This was a victory for the social-democrats, the non-revolutionary left. But at the same time there appeared a pre-Commune in the shape of the Committee of the Twenty Arrondissements, a federation of twenty watch committees monitoring the mayors of each arrondissement. This Committee, more radical than the organizations themselves, sought "to have done with wage slavery once and for all." Which was a comparatively novel slogan. Its members included Blanquists (Ranvier, Flourens, Duval, Ferré, Tridon), Internationalists (Lefrançais, Malon, Pindy, Avrial, Beslay, Camélinat, Frankel, Longuet, Theisz, and Varlin, who was shortly to quit the Committee), and elements that defied classification, like the writer Jules Vallès. Their program was centered above all upon national Defence and some rather liberal political reforms. They pressed the government to give way to a government of the left: "Give way to the Commune!" was the cry. This was in January 1871.

A word about Thiers, a name that is hard to utter without feelings of profound disgust. This venal, unscrupulous politician, a by-word for runaway ambition, was the very embodiment of the villainous upstart. It was he who was to do all in his power, deliberately to ensure a general bloodbath, so as to be rid once and for all of the plebes who had been a hindrance to him for nigh on forty years. There was not one shameful act in the history of those forty years in which Thiers had not been plunged up to his neck. The non-Communard, social-democratic left was to back him to the hilt. Foremost among them was Louis Blanc, but there were also Arago, Henri Martin (who, once the Commune had been crushed, would drag the massacred victims through the mud: often resorting to the same terms as the right had deployed against the left back in 1848, which is to say, against the likes of Arago, Martin, Blanc, and the rest). Thiers and all these folk today have streets called after them (!) in France and in Navarre.

On October 31, 1870, the cry of "Long live the Commune!" echoed through the streets. On this occasion, the rioters were Blanquists. Their putsch failed and the mob failed to follow their lead. Blanqui fled. Flourens was arrested. In November in Paris the municipal elections saw

ASSI

COURBET

R. RIGAULT

lots of revolutionaries returned to official positions: Ranvier, Flourens (who was in jail), Lefrançais, Millière, Malon, and Tolain, not to mention people such as Clémenceau, were elected mayors or deputy mayors. Some of them had been involved in the revolt in October.

In January 1871, there were further disturbances created by the republicans this time. Flourens was freed by force, at the instigation of Cipriani. Trochu was replaced by Vinoy as commander of the army in Paris.

The Assembly was removed to Bordeaux. Its membership was drawn primarily from the right, and Delescluze, along with Garibaldi (the Italian revolutionary and Italian deputy), was booed when first he appeared. They tendered their resignations, as did Pyat, Victor Hugo, Rochefort, Malon, Tridon, Ranc, and Clémenceau, all of them deputies at that point.

Capitulation by France followed and the Prussians occupied Paris which they quit two days later (on March 3).

On March 13, the National Guard constituted itself as a federation with a Central Committee—nothing short of a soviet. Its leaders were elected and there were to be three representatives from each arrondissement. The former commander of the (pre-Soviet) National Guard, General Clément Thomas, was dismissed by his men.

The Paris Commune came into existence on March 18. On that date, troops tried to remove cannons from Montmartre (for fear of insurrection). The National Guard mingled with the troops and turned them away: they reversed their rifles. Clément Thomas (of whom we ought to know, he was one of the butchers in 1848) and General Lecomte were arrested then massacred by the mob of mutineer soldiers.

Vinoy's troops withdrew. Thiers, as head of the provisional government, was terror-stricken: one can be a big fan of massacres and yet be the worst of cowards. He fled to Versailles. The civil service followed suit: the capital was left without any authority. Power was there for the taking.

The revolution had been a spontaneous thing: the work of the troops. Only after the event did the Central Committee discover what had happened. Command was assumed by Varlin, Georges Arnold (an architect), and Jules Bergeret (bookseller).

The National Guard set up shop in the Town Hall. Its proceedings were chaired by Edouard Moreau, an outstanding figure in the Commune, who, according to his biographer, Marcel Cerf, was to be the "soul" of the Commune and was to draft most of its documents.

Reconciliation with the government proved impossible as Jules Favre was labelling them as murderers.

So the Central Committee took power. This was, to borrow Elisée Reclus' phrase (Reclus played his obscure part in the Commune as a soldier) "universal suffrage armed."

In its ranks were to be found the cream of the revolutionaries of the day: members of the International, like Assi, Varlin, Babick, Pindy, Grelier; Blanquists like Protot, Duval, Eudes, Rigault, Ranvier; Republicans like Lullier; and "miscellaneous others" like Moreau, Bergeret, Faltot, the musician Billioray, Francis Jourde, H. Geresme, Arnold, Maxime Lisbonne (actor).

Tasks were shared out. It was a real government. Assi ran the Town Hall. Varlin and Jourde looked after Finance. Moreau saw to the printworks and to the *Journal Officiel* (gazette). Duval and Rigault looked after the prefecture of police. Eudes was in charge of the War department. Bergeret was in charge of the Paris garrison and staff. Garibaldi was made general-in-chief of the National Guard, but in the end he declined the appointment. Lullier was in charge of the artillery, Combatz of telegraph services and Grelier and Antoine Arnaud of the department of the Interior.

Lullier was to inherit Garibaldi's post. The appointment of Lullier, a loud-mouthed, pretentious alcoholic, was only the first of a long list of mistakes which were to cost the Communards their lives. Lullier had the forts surrounding the capital occupied but he overlooked (!) the Mont Valérien fort which Vonoy wasted no time in seizing. Throughout the life of the Commune, that fort was to pose a threat to the rebels. Given to inconsistency, Lullier was to refuse to advance, became half a traitor, and—once stood down, drunk, and almost crazy—was to take to his heels. His replacements were three generals, Brunel, Duval, and Eudes.

On the day after the uprising, Bergeret proved unable to prevent the National Guard from opening fire on some pro-Versailles counter-demonstrators.

The mayors of Paris were divided. There were some Communards among them, to be sure, but some of them had already fled to Versailles, like Louis Blanc. Others, such as Vautrin or Tirard, were hostile to the Commune but would do nothing until the troops arrived. Clémenceau was torn—to be honest, he was hostile to both camps, tried to reconcile them, and was regarded askance by them all.

Instead of dismissing them, the Communards gave in to them: the mayors would have their mansions and the Town Hall. This surrender was granted in return for vague promises of speechifying in the Assembly. The Committee of the Twenty Arrondissements, being more radical, was openly hostile to all of this. Under pressure from it, the Central Committee disowned the delegates it had sent to the negotiations and held on to the Town Hall. The Bordeaux Assembly deserted the mayors. Their fate was sealed.

Elections to the Paris Commune, which was to become the provisional government, took place on March 26. They were organized by the Committee of the Twenty Arrondissements. An election manifesto was submitted by Vallès and Pierre Denis (its author). It mooted the idea of communalism at every level, with officials being elected and subject to recall, districts to be re-organized, judges and officers likewise to be elected, the police abolished and replaced by the National Guard. Education was to be secular: there would be a social insurance provision, a commission of inquiry into the preceding government, and the decision was made to work toward the abolition of wage slavery. Denis, as a consistent Proudhonist, was also to draw up the Program of the Commune, but his style would be cramped somewhat by the Jacobin, Delescluze. Broadly speaking, that Program was to be implemented during the few weeks when the Communards were in effective authority.

It was Ranvier who made the announcement that "The Commune is hereby proclaimed." The Central Committee devolved power to it. Which was a tactical error: the urgent necessity was to attack Versailles while there was yet time. The Central Committee was a power to be reckoned with and it was to take the Commune some time to become as much—enough time for Versailles to recover.

There were ninety elected representatives, of whom only thirteen belonged to the Central Committee. Among those elected, there were twenty-five working men, but the majority were petty bourgeois. There were moderates—like Arthur Ranc, Méline, and Tirard. However, the revolutionaries were in the majority. We might cite, in no particular order, Arnaud, Pindy, Theisz, Billioray, Assi, Malon, Verlin, Lefrançais, Frankel, Babick, Avrial, Rigault, Ferré, Eudes, Duval, Ranvier, Delescluze, Pyat, Flourens, Trison, Vallès, Miot, Jourde, Arnould, Beslay, Brunel, Vaillant, Gambon, Protot, Geresme, Beregeret, Blanqui (in prison), and Grousset, whom we have met already. And there were others, too: Vermorel, Jean-Baptiste Vlément (whose song le temps des cerises became the Commune's anthem), Clemence, Jules Allix (a madman who was to be committed), and Ostyn (another crackpot) and soon Beslay was the Commune's first chairman. They did not all see eye to eye and there would be many frictions between them.

They established Delegations which were nothing short of ministries. Thus, Duval was Delegate for Police and was military commander, Vaillant was Delegate for Education, Protot Delegate for Justice, Jourde was Delegate for Finance, Bergeret commanded the Paris garrison, Frankel looked after Labor and Trade, Eudes looked after War. Elsewhere, each of them was assigned a particular sphere of economic and social activity: Theisz took charge of the Post Office (so judicious were the reforms he introduced that they were to be retained afterward); the bronze-smith Camélinat reformed the money and stamps; Vallès looked after the Supply Corps for a short while, before Varlin and the Moreau took over from him; Longuet looked after publication of l'Officiel for a short while; Treilhard looked after Public Assistance where he was to do outstanding work; Razoua was governor of the Military Academy; Viard was in charge of Provisions and Grousset of External Relations, while Andrieu took charge of Public Services.

By the way, we ought to point out that Garibaldi declined to take part while Tirard and other moderates were to pull out later. A supplementary election brought in Cluseret, Eugène Pottier (author of The Internationale), Longuet, Arnold, and the celebrated painter Gustave Courbet.

Within weeks, the Commune was to introduce more reforms than all the other governments of the previous two centuries together. Judge for yourself:

—Night-time working was done away with.

—Empty workshops were made over to produce cooperatives that were set up.

—Vacant accommodation was commandeered.

—A placement office was established in each mayoral mansion.

—Sales to pawnshops, fines and deductions from wages were suspended.

—Working hours were reduced. Frankel even came up with a proposal for an eight-hour day.

—The trade unions were re-established.

—Equality of the sexes was enforced.

—A project for self-management in factories was drawn up: Avrial took a particular interest in this but circumstances were scarcely favorable.

—Lawyers' monopoly, the judicial oath, and trafficking in fees were abolished.

—Wills, adoptions, and powers of attorney were arranged free of charge.

—Marriage was free and the formalities were simplified.

—The death penalty was abolished.

—Judges would henceforth have to be elected.

—The revolutionary calendar was re-introduced.

—Church and State were proclaimed separate: the funding set aside for religion was abolished and mainmorte assets confiscated.

—Education was free of charge, secular, and compulsory. Evening classes were introduced.

—Religious bric-a-brac and tawdry gods were melted down, and debating societies set up in the churches.

—The Brea church, erected in memory of one of the men who had mown down the workers in 1848, was demolished. The confessional chapel of Louis XVI and the Vendome Column.

—The red flag was adopted as the symbol of the Federal Unity of Humankind.

—Internationalism was put into effect: the Commune's ranks included Frankel, Dombrowski, Wrobleski, Okolowicz, and Kiensel: in all, they included 1,725 foreigners (Belgians, Italians, Poles, Hungarians, etc.).

—There was a centralized press office to handle information (this was Moreau's brainchild).

—An appeal was issued to the International.

—Conscription was abolished, as was the standing army.

—Money was re-organized, as were public assistance, postal services, telegraphs, the national printing works, taxation, and departmental remits. Finance, in particular, was brilliantly revamped by Jourde who had no equal for his accounting skills.

—There was a draft plan for labor exchanges.

—Moreau considered establishing a national administrative college, of which the present-day ENA is only a copy.

—On the artistic side of things, there were many artists in the Communard ranks (Courbet, Corot, Daumier, Manet, Milet, Flameng, Gill, and so on): actors ran theaters for themselves; artists had a completely free hand and were to create magnificent posters all over the place.

As we can see, there was a lot to do. They got by with little sleep and wound up exhausted and worn out. The establishment officials and underlings withheld their cooperation and actively obstructed the implementation of reforms. Everyone was paid just fifteen francs per day.

By contrast, teachers' pay was doubled. At the department of Finance, Jourde was to decline his three billion francs (and, just for the record, he claimed his fifteen francs a day). The scrupulously honest Jourde was the very model of the Communard: revolutionary, but respectful of the public interest to the point of absurdity. In all, the Commune was to spend 46 million francs, raised through levies, taxation, and a supplementary Banque de France loan issue (the bank was only too happy to have the business). In the same period, Thiers was to spend 260 million francs! Jourde and Varlin, who made sure than this simple honesty was adhered to, were to die—in Jourde's case, penniless, and the Varlin's with 300 francs in his pocket (this money was rifled by the officer who killed him).

The great and corrupt banker Jecker, wanted to charge an employee (on 30 sous a day) 100,000 francs for an ordinary passport. The employee declined the offer and had Jecker arrested. At the end of the insurrection, Jecker was to be shot.

Exemplary women organized ambulances and cared for the children. Aside from the celebrated Louise Michel, we ought to mention the wealthy beauty Elisabeth Dimitrieff, a friend of Marx, as well as Andrée Léo and Nathalie Le Mel, a member of the I.W.M.A..

The Communards' direct democracy system was to prove very influential, more importantly, it proved that it was feasible. Anarchists found confirmation in it and the Marxists chewed it over for a long time (until such time as they were to come to power somewhere). The Luxemburgists were later to embrace it as their own. Communards also practiced rotation of offices and this, taken together with the revocability of elected persons, represents the best guarantee against the recurrence of any sort of bureaucracy. Marx, who did not for one second believe in it at the time, was to sing the praises of the Commune afterward, after due consideration.

A new *Père Duchesne* appeared and a revolutionary tribunal, both of them survivors from the past along with the revolutionary calendar: these Communards were not, sad to relate, sufficiently freed of the old outlooks. Their lack of parliamentary skills were also to count against them.

By the time that the Central Committee came up for re-election, there were only twelve old hands left on it, the remainder being newcomers. Moreau was no longer a member.

On April 2, the Versaillese mounted a surprise attack. Beregeret spotted them while on a reconnaissance trip. Thiers had overhauled his army. That he had been able to bring this off quickly was due to the German occupiers. In fact, Bismarck had realized that war was merely a joke when set alongside an insurrection. War between powerful capitalists has to come to a halt when faced with serious matters such as a revolution. Had that revolution succeeded, it would probably have spread through a number of other countries, especially Germany. Priority had therefore to be given to dealing with the trouble makers: there would be plenty of time for making mincemeat out of each other later on.

So the war was suspended lest it hamper Thiers in the crushing of his rabble. He was allowed to make more recruits than surrender would have made possible— he was allowed to recruit released prisoners of war into his forces! Bismarck was also to blockade the Communards on the one hand but granted the Versaillese free passage. The Germans were not to intervene directly in the fighting (leaving that to their enemies was the safest course).

The Communards were caught on the hop by the attack. Duval, who refused to give ground, found himself captured. Vinoy had him shot out of hand. Flourens, who was in command of another unit, was also captured and cut down on the spot by a saber-wielding officer: he, too, had refused to turn back and had taken cover along with his adjutant, Cipriani, who was wounded.

The Commune renamed the Place d'Italie the Place Duval (it has since reverted to the old name). The delegate second in command of the war department, Cluseret, took over from Duval. This was to prove yet another of the colossal mistakes in the Commune's choice of men. Cluseret was completely out of his depth in the post. He was an ambiguous character: in 1848, he had been on the side of the butchers. Then he had changed tack, travelled widely and fought alongside Garibaldi and then in the War of Secession, then served with the Irish Fenians. He was to be a weak link in the Commune, not lifting a finger to thwart the advance of the Versaillese.

The Communards, whose morale had been badly dented by the onslaught and by their comrades' deaths, retreated on all sides, in spite of the sterling work of a remarkable Polish officer, a revolutionary who would have been the ideal military leader for the Commune (although that was out of the question, he being a foreigner): Jaroslaw Dombrowski. He had played a part in the Polish Uprising of 1863 and gone on to escape from Siberia.

Once the Communards caught on to the danger posed by Cluseret's incompetence, they dismissed him and placed him under arrest. But by then it was too late. This "exotic charlatan and dilettante" as Talès calls him, had done his damage.

Louis-Nathaniel Rossel, graduate of the Polytechnic and an officer who had defected to the Communards was appointed to replace him. To be honest, one wonders exactly what he was doing there. He owed his appointment to the fact that he had been an officer under Bazaine, whom he had refused to follow in his treachery, as a result of which he had been cashiered. He was no Communard but he was a patriot and that was the only connection between them.

Rossel was to reinstate discipline, which may well have been needed, but was to prove rather ineffective. The Central Committee was a constant hindrance to him. He was not always heeded by his troops, who were commanded by Generals Dombrowski and (another Pole!) Wrobleski, La Cecilia, Eudes, and Bergeret.

May 4 saw the capture of the Issy fort. It was at this point that Rossel realized that he could mount a putsch of his own and thereby rescue the insurgent authorities which were falling apart. He was, perhaps, the only one with enough authority to impose his will. But he lacked conviction and resigned, while publicly accusing the Central Committee and the Commune of having tied his hands (the accusation was not a very clever move in the circumstances and one that led to his being accused of treason). He himself asked that he be placed under arrest, but escaped the very next day with the connivance of Charles Gérardin, a Commune deputy, who had had him in his custody and who fled with him.

The brouhaha created by this falling-out was a serious contribution to the troops' loss of morale. It was the last thing they needed. Such prima donna tantrums were out of place in the circumstances. But they say a lot about Rossel's hubris. It comes as no surprise that this two-faced military man should be so admired today by the Commune's class enemies, who have striven to justify his actions, even though they would have had him shot on the spot at the time: he was one of their own, after all.

Rossel's experience extended only to regular armies and he had found much of the Commune's innovation incomprehensible. But the man chosen to replace him could not take in anything at all, for he was a civilian, the aged Delescluze. Of Duval's three replacements, there was not one who was really followed by his troops. These soldiers were incompetent, their officers inefficient nonentities. Only 320 of their 1,140 cannons ever saw use, the quarter-master corps was a shambles and, to cap it all, the Communard forces were outnumbered, less than 15,000 facing 100,000 Versaillese.

The Communards were to be driven by ongoing conflict. The Central Committee (which exercised authority over the National Guard) and the elected Commune each refused to defer to the other. This quickly resulted in duplication of all posts and thus to proliferation of conflicts of authority.

To begin with, an executive commission was established to oversee implementation of decisions reached by the nine delegations (Tridon, Eudes, Vaillant, Duval—all of them Blanquists—and a republican, Pyat, Bergeret and Lefrançais).

On May 1, it was the turn of the Committee of Public Safety (another echo of the previous century), charged with overseeing pretty well everything. Its membership included: Ranvier, Antoine Arnaud, Léo Meillet, Charles Girardin (before he fled) and Pyat. Here again the Committee could well have established a dictatorship or at any rate its authority. But there was to be nothing of the sort.

After the capture of the Issy fort, Delescluze gave them a dressing down for talking instead of fighting. They made do with a reshuffle—Meillet, Pyat, and Girardin being replaced by Gambon, Eudes, and, Delescluze. The new line-up was to be no improvement on the previous one.

As far as the old Empire's structures were concerned, there was to be little change. Often, the Communards were very good administrators but that very fact stopped them being good militants. The food shortages persisted as Bismarck thwarted all attempts to obtain fresh victuals. Come the arrests, they would realize that they had been wholly infiltrated by numerous traitors. On the other hand, Europe was enthralled by what was going on. There were high hopes riding on this experiment that was unparalleled in History.

Out in the provinces, there were faint-hearted attempts to set up Communes in Lyon, Saint-Etienne, Le Creusot, Toulouse, Narbonne (where Digeon pulled it off almost single-handedly), and in Marseilles (the work of moderates like Gaston Crémieux or Landeck).

Garibaldi, who had himself declined the leadership of the National Guard, advised the Communards to appoint themselves a dictator. The Blanquists agreed, but they were feeling the loss of Blanqui. Rossel, as we have seen, after having seemed poised to become one, was to drop the idea, in spite of support from the generals (especially the Poles). Dombrowski was commander-in-chief of the city, too.

But the fighting continued. On May 21, the Versaillese entered Paris via the Porte de Saint-Cloud, in spite of Dombrowski's efforts. On learning the news, the Commune, which was chaired that day by Vallès, made do wit bringing its proceedings to a conclusion! There would not be any more.

Similarly, Delescluze resigned his post. He simply dispatched everyone to man the barricades. He was a great believer in the "bare arms" of the populace. From that point on, there was no leadership. It was a case of everyone left to his own devices. It was scarcely the time for that, what with the super-organized armies facing them. A compromise between a traditionally-organized army and an army bereft of any rational structure was never devised. That would have to wait until the 20th century. They even neglected to destroy the Commune's paperwork: this was subsequently produced as evidence in trials.

Thiers had the option of a very quick victory. But he was to resort deliberately to delaying tactics, at the risk of losing it all: he wanted to squeeze every drop of glory from his victory and create the impression that he was the great heroic figure. This merely dragged out the slaughter.

The Town Hall was captured in spite of resistance put up by La Cecilia whose orders were ignored. Seeing that their cause was lost, a bitter Dombrowski deliberately sought death.

On May 23, the Communards torched the great symbols of the Empire—the administration buildings, the Tuileries, the ministries. On May 24, they executed their hostages, notably the clergy (the Archbishop of Paris whom Thiers opted to sacrifice rather than see Blanqui freed), the policemen, and the judges. Rigault and Ferré, Blanquists, headed the list of those who had taken the decision.

As a final proof of the military incompetence of the Commune, the barricades upon which they had expended so much effort turned out to be useless.

There was ferocious resistance in Montmartre, thanks primarily to Wrobleski, just as there was in the Chateau d'Eau district where the resisters were led by Lisbonne. Lisbonne was wounded, as were Vermorel, Brunel and, Protot.

Not wishing to survive this latest failure, Delescluze set out, dressed all in black, walking stick at the ready, to seek death in the Place du Chateau d'Eau. The initial executions carried out by the Communards were small recompense for the outrages perpetrated by the Versaillese. Thiers' troops were doped with alcohol and had the help of the Germans who delivered Communards into their clutches.

In all, the Commune shot a hundred people and killed around nine hundred in the fighting. There is no comparison with the fifty to eighty thousand Communards who were killed and executed over a period of weeks. For the carnage was now underway.

In addition, there were to be upward of forty thousand arrests. People were shot or killed on the flimsiest pretext. Lots of innocents were to be cut down. There are examples aplenty of this and they are common knowledge. The myth that Thiers peddled regarding the pétroleuses was to cost many a wretch her life. There was neither rhyme nor reason to the Versaillese forces' paranoia. One after another, they mowed down a Vallès, a Billioray, a Cluseret, a Ferrê, a Longuet, a Brunel, a Gambon, a Lefrançais—every one of them a case of mistaken identity!

On the other hand, they did shoot the right Raoul Rigault and Jacques Durand.

By May 28, it was all over. Léveque, Varlin, Moreau, Millière (a moderate who had taken no part in the Commune even though he was a deputy) were shot or killed in atrocious circumstances.

The executions carried on into June. The only thing that halted the massacre was fear of an epidemic on account of the excessive numbers of corpses.

Conveyor-belt courts offered the future victims summary trial, though often they got no trial at all. A hysterical mob turned out to purge its fear, to wallow in the blood and to touch the mangled flesh and brain tissue. Dead or alive, the victims were subjected to vituperation and beaten. Bodies were stripped of spoils. Revellers and whores attended the celebrations. Some were to be caught up among the shiploads of prisoners.

We all know about the Marquis de Gallifet who hand-picked batches of victims with the words "I am Gallifet." Prisoners were taken to Versailles and humiliated by a howling mob. There were to be plenty of instances of personal scores being settled. During this period no less than 400,000 denunciations were made! The Communards had systematically declined to pay any heed to narcs.

Fifty court-martials were to be commissioned to act out sham trials. They would hand down 35,000 sentences—93 of them death sentences, of which twenty-three would be carried out. The first to be tried were the members of the Central Committee: Lullier (who cried out that he had betrayed the Commune—which was the truth—was nevertheless to be sentenced to death), Ferré, Trinquet (two of the few people who owned up loud and clear to what they had done), Assi, Jourde, Grousset, Billioray, and Courbet. Ferré was sentenced to death; Trinquet was deported for life; Courbet to six months in prison and to rebuild the Vendome Column; the others were sentenced to deportation.

Aside from the twenty-two members of the Commune, there were others. Rossel was sentenced to death, so were Lisbonne and Gaston Crémieux. Rochefort (who had been merely a sympathizer), Louise Michel, Cipriani, Amouroux were banished to the penal colonies. Some people debased themselves at their trial, secondary figures mostly.

Vermorel died in prison in Versailles of his wounds. An exhausted Tridon, although he escaped, died a little later. Forty-eight Commune members managed to escape to England, Belgium, or Switzerland. The populace in Paris and in the provinces displayed tremendous ingenuity in hiding them, helping them, and looking after their upkeep.

A wounded Frankel crossed into Switzerland. His homeland was not to extradite him and he went on to become an agitator of some note. Brunel, who had been wounded, also went into exile. Vallès, Lefrançais, Theisz, Ranvier, Ostyn, Longuet, Protot, Meillet, La Cecilia, Pindy, Clémence, Malon, Arnould, Ranc, Vaillant, Razoua, etc., also made good their escapes. Beslay was brought to trial and acquitted: it has to be said that he had protected the Banque de France! Elisée Reclus, was to be spared due to an international campaign by scientists (he being a world-renowned geographer).

On November 28, Rossel and Ferré were shot along with a sergeant charged with having deserted the army for the Commune. The executions of the twenty-two others were to drag on into 1872.

The newspaper and literary hysteria whipped up against them was to be frightening. Lidsky's book *Writers versus the Commune* testifies to that. Théophile Gautier, George Sand, the repulsive Dumas Fils, Alphonse Daudet, Edmond About, Barbey d'Aurevilly, and (to a lesser extent, as might be expected of a reputed "people's" writer) Emile Zola, were to be the chief peddlers of calumnies on these dregs of society.

The deportees were shipped out to New Caledonia. There was to be a Kanak uprising there and to be honest it has to be said that, just like the other white convicts, some of them leapt at the chance to come down hard on the Kanaks in return for remission of sentence! There was one extraordinary exception to this sordidness: Louise Michel, who tended and educated the young Kanaks (when she left it was in a mixture of triumph and tears). This exemplary woman enthralled all who had any dealings with her, including her enemies.

There were some escapes: Jourde and Rochefort and Grousset and three others escaped in 1874. They capitalized upon the opportunity to kick up a stink by disclosing the conditions in which they had had to live out there.

Trinquet, by contrast, was recaptured. Others drowned. Some perished out there, like Billioray. As for Lullier, whose sentence had been commuted, he carried on with his dismal career by denouncing certain of his comrades.

Although the International was, inevitably, broken by 1872, at least a republic emerged from the whole business, after Thiers was sent packing in 1873. But the republic was a bourgeois republic and it is still with us. 50 percent of Parisian industry was wiped out, for the massacre victims were primarily workers.

While Marx belatedly hailed the Commune, Bakunin, although he had never had any illusions that it might succeed (he was very quick to spot its shortcomings), was to be an enthusiast right from the outset. Although it was scarcely revolutionary in its aspirations (leaving both property and capital untouched), it proved revolutionary in its actions and in its very existence.

Its military reverses were very grave ones. Louise Michel was astutely to observe: "What was needed was an army possessed both of the revolutionary zeal injected by Delescluze and the strict discipline upon which Rossel insisted."

Antoine Arnould commented that the communalist idea, which had shaped the movement's basic thinking, had started to go into decline the day that the Commune was proclaimed!

In spite of such criticisms, the Paris Commune remains as one of the proletariat's great "victories," the last of a great era, or the first of a new age which was to last right up until the Spanish Civil War. A fine orgasm, at any event.

If children are capable of shifting for themselves and of being autonomous, why wouldn't adults be so too? Every human aspires to be free, to be the master of his own life, without having to submit to the oversight or authority of anyone or anything.

J.M. Raynaud and C. Ambauves
Libertarian Education (1978)

To be free men. To live as comrades in the here and now, not after the revolution.

Albert Libertad's motto

These days one could expound upon the educational advances of Freinet, or the Nouvelle Ecole, or upon experiments like Decroly or others that have become famous more through their wrangles with the authorities than for their achievements, but we ought to be clear that this strand of alternative education is as old as Charlemagne. In every age, in every civilization where education has been subject to the iron rule of an authoritarian agent or church, schemes and attempts devised to let children live their natural lives, are thrown up and survive the storms for a time. There are examples galore of this.

The trend was very strong in the years between 1880 and 1921. World War, Stalinism, and Nazism were to overwhelm this enthusiasm. As was to come to light, the hostility of the Catholic Church was to prove relentless, and the standard-bearers of the compulsory catechism were not to shrink even from murder just as long as they could impose their own unhealthy obsessions. To misrepresentation and denunciation, Spanish Catholics were to add political conspiracy, capitalizing upon the man's absence in order to have the outstanding educator Francisco Ferrer, creator of the Escuela Moderna (Modern School) — the forerunner of all the modern schools, including the Freinet schools — arrested on a phony pretext. Ferrer, who was to be represented as a terrorist, was to be shot to widespread outrage in 1909.

Paul Robin too was to fall victim to the Church, but it would not cost him his life. Born in 1837, Robin was a teacher frequently in hot water with the greatly bureaucratized educational administration, most often over his peccadilloes.

Robin was a socialist. He spent time in Belgium (where he married the daughter of a famous revolutionary, Delesalle) before being deported for his ideas. He then turned up in Switzerland where he met Bakunin. This started his drift toward libertarian ideas. He ended up in London where he joined the International (and in 1866 he was even on its General Council), before being expelled by Marx when that great ancestor of Stalin realized that he was harboring a Bakuninist in the bosom of "his" International.

Robin was a university lecturer and struck up a friendship with Elisée Reclus and Kropotkin. He became a liberalizing influence on education in the Blois district when he joined the inspectorate (at the time, under Jules Ferry, the director of primary education was a former Communard, Fernand Buisson).

Robin's great achievements started in 1880, when he was entrusted with the governorship of the Cempuis orphanage in the Oise department. The position was less attractive than the inspectorate. "Afford me in freedom whatever it may lack in majesty," was Robin's response to those who harped on this comedown. And Robin proceeded to implement ideas that he had been entertaining for some time past.

His pupils were all orphans, varying in number from 130 to 180 and in age between 6 and 16 years, and at that latter age they were left to fend for themselves, that is, to earn a living. Among them there were a few boys and girls who were slightly mentally handicapped and they were watched over by twenty teaching staff chosen by the school inspectorate and this would occasionally create methodological problems since not everybody was convinced about Robin's "integral education."

Boys and girls followed the same courses. One-third of their time was given over to physical education, which was a great innovation. The children engaged in all sorts of sports, including horse riding, and play was given great priority. Everyone, staff and pupils, ate the same meals, essentially vegetarian fare.

All activities were offered to the children, not foisted upon them. Numerous vocational courses were on offer in the workshops and the pupils could choose whatever took their fancy. Pupils were able to venture out into the adjoining fields and meadows, to engage in all sorts of creative and artistic pursuits, and to have their lessons in the open air (following up questions which they had posed). Freinet was to borrow heavily from the Robin method.

At the age of 12, the child selected a trade that he then set about mastering. Morally, the emphasis was on the notion of freedom and brotherhood.

The orphans had their choir and a brass band and they sang or played only pacifist tunes and workers' songs. In 1883, Robin set up his first holiday camp and took the children away to Mers-les-Bains.

All problems and frictions were settled by discussion between those concerned. The children all bathed together (in the swimsuits of the day), which created a great scandal among the clergy and respectable bourgeois. In addition, Robin was one of the pioneers of sex education and his pupils learned, in mixed-sex classes, whatever they needed to know about the subject.

A press campaign targeted Cempuis and it focused particularly upon the fact that the classes there were mixed sex! This was from 1891 onward. The climate was not propitious, for this was when the great anarchist outrages were at their height. The fascists of the day, such as Drumont, the famous anti-Semite, made a special target of them.

Robin carried on, regardless of the climate of hostility, to teach the history of civilizations (rather than the history of great battles), educating his children to the horrors of warfare and he carried on combating the chauvinism of history teaching. He took as his basic motto "No handless minds and no mindless hands." Happy enough to put certain results (which, it has to be said, were astonishing) to the outside world, certain staff members prevented Robin from achieving all that he wanted: having no time for paper qualifications and streaming, he gave in to custom and practice.

There was no punishment, but there were rewards: most often, rewards took the form of useful items. One day Robin was asked by a journalist: "Can you get their attention in the absence of punishment? By what miracle?" To which Robin had blithely replied, "Simply by ensuring that the children are happy."

Francisco Ferrer visited Cempuis to borrow ideas for his own scheme. Robin, a regular writer for the press, especially *L'Internationale* or the Proudhonist *La Liberté* was renowned as one of the leaders of the neo-Malthusian movement, Neo-Malthusianism meaning birth control. An ecologist before the time was invented, Robin, like lots of others, had spotted the dangers implicit in population growth. He campaigned for contraception, which in those days was code for sex education for adults, especially for women, and he published dozens of pamphlets explaining how to avoid pregnancy when one already had too many.

Such beliefs only fed the hostility he encountered. Casimir Périer was the president at the time and his devout wife wielded great influence. The Church peddled the most ridiculous slanders about Cempuis which its newspapers depicted as an out and out bordello.

On August 31, 1894, Robin was dismissed. The orphanage was taken in hand by his former student , chief collaborator and disciple, Gabriel Giroud who was later to relate just what a paradise Cempuis had been. There was a Cempuis former pupils' association that kept up links between pupils who had grown into adulthood.

A short time later, Robin was condemned for his writing about women's "health," and he quit France for New Zealand. He returned to France after he was granted an amnesty.

On September 1, 1912, at the age of 75, he took his own life by swallowing some chlorohydrate of morphine, keeping scientific notes on his demise right to the end. His well-stocked library and print shop were bequeathed to Sébastien Faure who carried on his work, after a fashion, in his Ruche colony.

Children belong neither to their parents, nor to society. They belong to themselves and their future freedom...Reason, truth, justice, human respect, consciousness of personal dignity which is all of a piece with and inseparable from other people's human dignity, love of freedom for its own sake and for everyone else's, the cult of labor as the foundation and condition of all entitlement: contempt for unreason, falsehood, injustice, cowardice, slavery and idleness. Those ought to be the underlying premises of public education.

Bakunin
Revolutionary Catechism (1869)

From 1904 on, there was a similar experiment conducted on a farm in Patis near Rambouillet. Sébastien Faure, that old stager of anarchy (1858–1942), leased twenty hectares of land on which to establish a school, La Ruche (Hive—The honey collected on the property would help to supplement its funds). He wisely set up a cooperative that bought up the farm's produce and marketed it. La Ruche was rather more than just an alternative school. It was an out and out anarchist enclave.

Faure also earned money as a lecturer, and from his books and the venture prospered. It represented a real model alternative for the proletariat. La Ruche was to survive right up until the end of the First World War when Faure was overwhelmed by financial difficulties.

The education doled out there was the "integral" education of Paul Robin, Faure's inspiration. In spite of its founder's tremendous prestige, La Ruche was a soviet, operating in accordance with the weekly general assembly of the staff, the older children, and Faure himself.

The teachers were fed and given lodgings but no pay. Their needs were met out of a common fund without any requirement that they be explained: in spite of this there was never to be any problem with the arrangement.

The fifty or so children aged from 5 to 16 had been selected from the cream of the applicants considered. The only difference Faure made in them was to favor the children of victims of political repression (such as Emile Henry's children, for instance).

They learned Esperanto and up until they were 10, the children did as they pleased. At 10, they were placed in a pre-apprenticeship (flitting from workshop to workshop two or three times each month). Apprenticeship to their chosen trade started at age 13. At that stage, they were given a wage and produced articles for the benefit of the school.

Faure was scrupulous about not imposing his own anarchist beliefs and left them complete autonomy. Freinet was to borrow heavily from this too. Sex education and mixed-sex classes were borrowed from Robin.

By the time the experiment came to an end, Faure was 59 years old. Aristide Lapeyre, a disciple of his, set up the Elan school in Villeneuve-sur-Lot during the 1930s, and that too would be brought to an end by the war.

Rather than enter into a lengthy description, the pictures below, based on actual postcards made and on sale at the time, offer a glimpse of this busy, alternative micro-society which was to survive for thirteen years.

3. RAMBOUILLET – "La Rûche", les Petits

5. RAMBOUILLET. "La Rûche". Départ pour les champs.

6. RAMBOUILLET. "La Rûche". L'atelier de Menuiserie.

4. RAMBOUILLET- "La Rûche", les Grands

7. RAMBOUILLET. La Rûche. L'Imprimerie

Mexico, 1910-1919
THE ZAPATISTAS

The land's going to break its chains
Poverty's heyday's over
The hills, the valleys and plains
Are going to blossom through work
Down with the liars and traitors
The tyrants and usurers
The peasants will be masters
In unison with the workers
Oh, hasten that great day!
Behold the thousands and hundreds of years
That Jean Guetre describes
As the Peasant Republic.

> Pierre Dupont
> *The Peasants' Song* (1850)

On the one hand, they fought. On the other, they built.

> Maurice Dommanget
> *The Commune and the Communards* (1947)

In 1909, in Anenecuilco, a little hamlet in the state of Morelos (Mexico), the recently elected village leader (its mayor and, in a sense, its spiritual leader) went by the name of Emiliano Zapata. His precise age would never be known. Some sources have it that he was born in 1873 or in 1877 or even 1879. He had a brother, Eufemio, who would often be found at his right hand. Zapata had been active since 1906 and his activity was the reason why he was elected.

The state of Morelos adjoins the state of Mexico where the capital city is situated. It is a southern state. Also in 1909, Zapata joined the Melchor Ocampo Club, a liberal and progressive political association. In turn-of-the-century Mexico, the great political agitator was Ricardo Flores Magón, founder of the review Regeneración which was to leave its mark on the times. But Magón was to be virtually continually in exile. Tremendous strikes in 1906 and 1907, though broken by the rurales, the army and the police, had prepared the ground.

The outlook was disastrous, chiefly on account of the despotic big landlords and the governor of Morelos state, Escandón. In 1911, following the revolution, he was to flee. Tracts of land were laying idle, the peasants denied the right to put them to work. Most of them were perishing of hunger.

Zapata, a farm laborer like so many others, armed eight hundred men and seized the land they needed. From then on every farmer had his plot and they worked the land in common. Such were the beginnings of Zapatismo in Morelos. It was to last for ten years, through ups and downs.

The owner of the hacienda upon which the entire village was dependent demanded that they pay him rent. They did nothing of the sort. They haggled. They were not supposed to pay except from the next year onward. The surrounding villages thereupon did likewise. Fences were torn down. Zapata, who was in the thick of the movement, was strategically well-placed: his village overlooked the entire state, or nearly so.

Things were on the move, politically, as well. Without going into the details, let us say that the dictator Diaz was overthrown by a man of the left, Francisco Madero. This was in 1910. In Morelos, Madero had his back to the wall: his supporters were being killed or arrested. Into his fight came two "gang leaders," two peasants, each of whom had been in revolt for several months in his particular locality: Pascual Orozco and Doroteo Arango, the latter better known by his nickname of Pancho Villa. He was indeed a one-time bandit. In fact he was one to the end. Zapata, of course, backed the movement. His own cousin, Antonio Salazar, had raised a troop of men in Yautepec. In Morelos state, Madero's coming victory was to be owed to Zapata who, along with his supporters, looked to the incoming president for the agrarian reform of their dreams.

Zapata captured Cuautla, then Jojutla, towns of some importance. He was now supreme leader of the Southern revolutionary movement. Authority came naturally to him. A rather good-looking, charismatic fellow of above average intelligence, he was respected, even loved. They did not follow him because of his beliefs but primarily because they loved and trusted him. Over the period of ten years, all of the peasants would be, if not his supporters, then at least his informants, his spies, his suppliers, and his accomplices.

Madero was quite the opposite. He was a bourgeois. None too intelligent, he had no conception of the peasant's lot and absolutely no interest in it. On the other hand, he was a decent if somewhat naive figure. In Morelos he had no interest whatsoever.

The revolutionaries joined Zapata, or stayed independent, but their campaigns ran in tandem. We might mention Genovevo de la O, an important leader in the Cuernavaca area, or Salazar, or Otilio Montano, an intellectual who threw in his lot with Zapata and became his secretary, before turning into a fighter. All of these people came to an accommodation: each was to remain master in his own area, but, whenever feasible, they would mount concerted attacks and keep in regular contact with one another.

The civil war ended in May 1911 when Diaz quit once and for all. Throughout this period, the Zapatistas had not laid a hand on the haciendas and they had stood guard over the harvesting work in progress. But, once in power, Madero diluted his promises and the agrarian reform was put on the back burner. The plantation owners (who owned the large haciendas) began to raise their heads again. Zapata bided his time for a while before seeking out Madero when the later was on a visit to the region a little while later. Madero came away with a bad impression, made worse by his entourage: the only things that he could see in all this were ruins and looting (for gangs of genuine bandits had been cashing in on the situation) and he reckoned that Zapata was behind it all. Zapata reluctantly agreed to disband his men.

Naturally, the planters lobbied Madero against the Zapatistas. And they also worked on public opinion, which was shaped by the newspapers in Mexico City, far removed from the hard realities.

In order to buy time, Zapata was appointed as chief of police for Morelos state. Whereupon he requested arms, which he was denied. He seized them off his own bat. The demobilization was to proceed but the peasants refused to return the land to the rich until such time as the agrarian reform might be carried through.

A single incident lit the fuse. The army inflicted fifty fatalities on the revolutionaries in Puebla and the dead included women and children. Zapata re-mobilized his men. The rebels' chief of staff, Abraham Martinez, was arrested. Simultaneously, the incoming Interior minister was very hostile toward Zapata, dismissing him as a bandit. The new governor of Morelos was one of the Figueroa brothers who led a revolutionary army, but they were only upstarts ready to turn traitor at the drop of a hat.

Wearying of it all, Zapata took time out to marry Josefa Espejo and to rest for a while. The army was to invade Morelos: at its head came General Victoriano Huerta, with the mission of "pacifying" the region. He wanted Zapata's guts for garters. Madero, on the other hand, was still making time for the peasant leader. They often met one another. At one point, Zapata's advisor was a well-known anarcho-syndicalist, Alfredo Quesnel. Not until October would elections be held (as part of the deal with Diaz under which he had agreed to leave). As yet, Madero was not formally president. There was an acting president, De La Barra, who was keen to see Zapata liquidated (it was De La Barra who had dispatched Huerta to Morelos). Madero failed to hold them in check and ended up letting things proceed.

The first of the manifestos to the people of Morelos penned by Zapata was a retort to the charges levelled against him and it took the government to task. Zapata just escaped capture by Huerta who recaptured Cuautla. He fled on a mule. For good measure, De La Barra announced an amnesty for everybody except "criminals," by which he meant the Zapatistas.

There was tough fighting but it went in Zapata's favor. In the end, he was able to pose a threat to Mexico City. The elections came along just in the nick of time. Madero was elected. The first request he made of Zapata was that he lay down his arms. But even as he was making it, his army attacked. Zapata fell back to Morelos. Battle had been joined.

Then, on November 25, 1911, the revolutionaries published the Plan of Ayala, drawn up by Montano and Zapata and spelling out their position. In it, Madero was referred to as a "traitor" and they promised to string him up. The Plan bore the signatures of Salazar and of Eufemio Zapata.

The situation moved slowly. Martinez was set free. Governor Figueroa tendered his resignation. Revolts erupted all over in January 1912. The new army commander in Morelos, Juvencio Robles, was very hard on the revolutionaries: he had all suspects shot and had Zapata's sister, mother-in-law, and two sisters-in-law arrested. He also tried his hand at a little "resettlement": peasants were corralled into ghettoes outside the towns and whenever he wanted a place emptied of people he simply burned it to the ground.

The Ayala Group, which embraced all the revolutionaries signatory to the Plan of Ayala, equipped itself with a chairman, the very popular Pacual Orozco, who controlled the state of Chihuahua, but entertained great personal ambitions. When Zapata was short of arms, Orozco refused to send him some.

Numerous arrests were made. Martinez was picked up again and the government captured important documents. However, the revolutionaries managed to pull off some great coups: De la O attacked a train and left one hundred of the enemy wounded; Salazar killed sixty-six of the enemy in one engagement; Zapata had help from the populace inside the town the day that he attacked the town of Yautepec.

In order to take some of the heat out of the situation, some of the more liberal elements were placed in positions of power locally. The new military commander, Felipe Angeles, took a more conciliatory line. The linkage, feared by Madero, between the Zapatistas and Flores Magón's supporters, never came about, and that was a real pity. The few remaining plantation owners well-disposed toward the revolutionaries had stopped supplying them.

Eugenio Morales, the speaker of the Legislative Assembly, a man tempted by anarchism, pressed for self-managed reforms. Zapata's family was released. Flores Magón joined a ministerial cabinet.

August 1912 saw agrarian and social reform at its peak. Never again would it be so far-reaching. Many revolutionaries availed of this lull to return to their homes. Slowly, however, the Assembly was to drift to the right and the projected reforms were increasingly to be drained of all content.

There was a re-organization of the fight: Zapata, Montano, Salazar, etc., levied taxes on all the haciendas in Morelos (in the event of a refusal to pay, they would burn them to the ground) in order to finance their struggle.

In February 1913, everything was turned upside down. Diaz's son and the sinister Huerta mounted a coup d'etat and overthrew Madero. This ushered in the Decena Trágica, ten days of bloodletting. Three days later, Huerta had president Madero murdered: this with the blessing of the United States (remember that shared frontier with Mexico). Every one of the old enemies of the revolution had a post in the new government: Robles was re-appointed military commander in Morelos and then was made state governor. Certain secondary leaders of the revolution opted for negotiation with Huerta, as did Orozco. Orozco thought of nothing but his own personal interests and jettisoned the Plan of Ayala.

Throughout the south, there was a state of siege. There was also an uprising by another, rather ambiguous individual, Carranza. More of him anon. Liberals were thrown into prison. Robles had the hacienda ranch-hands replaced by scabs imported at great cost.

Zapata had a new secretary, Manuel Palafox, a small, thin man of 26, with a face pock-marked by smallpox. From then on he was to pen the documents signed by Zapata. To curtail Zapata's successful offensive, conscripts were raised and compelled to fight. Draft-dodgers took to the forest or joined Zapata. Some of these rebels were very young indeed and they included some women: primarily widows and later girls attracted to the fighting such as La China, a sturdy woman who commanded a women's brigade which sowed terror wherever they passed in their ragged dresses, or, sometimes, in dresses stolen from the rich. With their guns, cartridge belts and great sombreros, they made a picturesque procession.

Zapata's charisma created havoc. From now on he was the leader of the Ayala Group which had been betrayed by Orozco. He established the Revolutionary Junta of the Centre and South of the Republic, of which he was both chairman and army commander. Palafox was its secretary: its chief leaders were Montano, De la O, Salazar, and Eufemio Zapata.

This time, Zapata moved up a notch in the re-organization drive. Self-management was in place. The big landlords were driven out and replaced by elected officials. The agrarian reform promised in the Plan of Ayala was at last implemented and each region was afforded a free hand to adopt whatever structures it deemed best.

There was requisitioning, which led to problems from time to time: looters capitalized upon the opportunity to burn, loot, and rape. All of this, although taking place far from the area under Zapatista self-management, was credited to the Zapatistas. In reprisal for raids close to Mexico City, Zapata's family was re-arrested. Entire villages were torched and their fields destroyed, and this included their harvests.

Zapata had settled in Huautla, in the mining valleys. In the end the city of Huautla was to fall, but not before the Zapatistas had evacuated it. The fascists found no one there other than corpses, including the body of the executed Orozco senior. This was in 1913. The general talk had it that Zapata was finished.

Meanwhile, Huerta was having trouble getting the United States to recognize him. Robles's actions had made an impression on President Wilson, Huerta sacked him.

Among the Zapatistas, a process of ideological toughening was underway. The fighting flared up again, but in the neighboring state of Puebla, the army was better organized, militarily. Circumstances required that this be so. Francisco "Pancho"

112

Villa, for his part, met with success and captured Torreon and was pretty much master of the states of Chihuahua and Coahuila. An attempt to assassinate him in February 1914 failed.

Thanks to a further coup, Huerta was propelled into the position of dictator, a position more lucrative than any presidential office. Whereupon the United States dropped him like a hot potato. This put paid to what was, in the minds of revolutionaries, the number one threat (U.S. intervention).

Zapata capitalized on this to draw all of the revolutionary movements into a federation. The result was only half a failure. In April, he captured Chilpacingo, inflicting a great defeat on Huerta: there were mass desertions and a great influx into Zapatista ranks. The territories under their control were vast now.

They recaptured the whole of Morelos, city by city. But they were short of munitions as the plantation owners were not paying up any more (it being impossible for them to pay the ransom sums as their fields had been burned, so further reprisals were not anticipated).

Mexico City itself was in jeopardy. Panic set in. In July, Huerta was obliged to step down and go into exile. Zapata would attack Mexico City if power was not surrendered to the revolutionaries and agrarian form not written into the constitution. He was also insisting on the liquidation of the Huertistas.

The government stalled for time. It came to an arrangement with Venustiano Carranza, leader of the Northern rebels, a man already greatly compromised. Zapata was left out in the cold. In the North, Villa was unhappy with the ascendancy enjoyed by Carranza.

Not that he was the only one whom the situation left with a sour taste in the mouth. Glittering intellectuals joined Zapata: Antonio Diaz Soto y Gama, for instance, a Kropotkinist who was to become Zapatismo's most important theoretician. There were also anarcho-syndicalists, quasi-Marxists, and even a veteran of the Paris Commune, the Frenchman Octavio Jahn. A Zapata-Villa alliance now became imperative against the turncoat Carranza.

Villa would witness an "agrarian reform" on his own patch. He did not know too much about it and it was not one of his political objectives. Carranza regarded such reform as plainly "absurd." Even so, Carranza and Villa met in Cuernavaca to thrash out some accommodation between them. Zapata refused to meet them, although he did send Palafox. But of course, there could be no *modus vivendi* between them.

This was perhaps the acme of Emiliano Zapata's achievement. His army numbered something in the region of fifteen thousand men. They were not really organized. Most were illiterate and they all wore the same peasant uniform of light sandals and white pajamas. So did Zapata.

He implemented his Plan of Ayala: the officers of his army took inventory and shared out the land which was allotted to the peasants and to the widows and children of fallen revolutionaries. The peasants elected agrarian commissioners from among themselves. In Morelos, the peasants had done that already, without prompting: Zapatismo was a frame of mind.

Felipe Angeles, the liberal who had been the military commander of Morelos, had become the Villista leader in Mexico City. He met with Zapata and formal negotiations were opened shortly after that. Zapata's chief negotiator was Paulino Martinez , a journalist, along with Diaz Soto y Gama and the Magana brothers. By the summer of 1914, the civil war had come to a halt. The Zapatistas managed to force through implementation of the Plan of Ayala. In return, Carranza was painted out of the picture.

In November, Zapata formally entered Mexico City. He shunned interviews and receptions and lived in a state of universal distrust in a tiny hotel. Villa then entered the capital also.

The two peasant leaders met for the first time on December 4, 1914, in Xochimilco, the in the presence of Eufemio Zapata and of Emiliano's son and his sister. There was a stark contrast between the two men. In a detailed comparison, the thoughtful peasant emerged as the better of the pair, being delicate and charismatic alongside the bulk and brutishness of Villa. Zapata was a heavy drinker, favoring cognac over everything else, whereas Villa gagged on it and could bear only water. There are stories galore about Villa's boorishness, machismo, and his morals, which were better suited to some factory charge hand than to a revolutionary leader.

The Xochimilco treaty was drawn up and they held a joint procession through Mexico City. However, Zapata got wind of a Huertista plan to drive a wedge between Villa and himself and this plot was to be a success, thanks to Felipe Angeles. Villa was in any case a mercurial sort, with a foot in every camp, changing his mind the way he changed his shorts and he was in any case swinging to the right.

A few days later, in confused circumstances, some Villistas murdered Paulino Martinez in Mexico. The Carranzistas, finding Zapata a much greater threat than Villa, attacked him. He retreated yet again into Morelos.

It was there that the Zapatista movement was to enter its most interesting period. A genuine Mexican-style self-managerial society was established there. They cleared the land and built, as if the civil war need not necessarily demolish all this: the peasants were reverting to an old Mexican communitarian tradition. Village leaders were of tremendous importance, more important even than the army officers. Moreover, the latter were answerable to them.

Municipal and judicial elections were held. Everything was taken in hand by the populace directly: including the railways. The acting governor was Genovevo de La O. Zapata was in Tlaltizapan. He arbitrated disputes better than Saint Louis under his spreading oak tree and acted as the peasants' champion in all circumstances. He was never to set up any police force; everything was decided by the village council. This showed remarkable political maturity for a comparatively uneducated peasant, albeit one possessed of an acute, almost animal-like feeling for democracy.

Every village selected its own way of re-allocating the land (dividing them up or holding them in common, or whatever).

Politically, events were taking a turn in their favor. A moderate agrarian reform was drawn up by the government. And Palafox, no less, became Secretary for Agriculture. On arriving in Mexico City, this little man had an agricultural loan bank set up, as well as agricultural training schools and tool-making plants and he pressed for agrarian reform and self-management.

Around a hundred agronomists set out to assist the peasants. The collectively-owned sugar cane mills were revived. For his part, Zapata had hospitals built and ambulance services arranged. 1915 was one of the freest years the people of Mexico had ever known.

But certain sinister interests were at work. For instance there was a swindle that came complete with an impostor. The Mormon, Hubert Hall, established a completely sham cooperative colony of the liberation army. His aim was to establish a modern agricultural complex near Cuernavaca. Diaz Soto y Gama was taken in by him. Palafox, though, had his misgivings and aborted the scheme just in time.

The government appointed Gildardo Magana (one of the Magana brothers) governor, and Salazar was made army commander in Mexico City. On the other hand, he dropped Palafox. Zapata kicked up a bit of a fuss and his friend Soto y Gama brought down the government and brought back Palafox. After this success came the successful harvest, the first successful harvest in a long time. A wide range of crops had been planted—a novelty in itself. Zapata, a close scrutinizer of local economics, urged his comrades to grow sugar cane, for which there was significant demand, rather than vegetables which would at best guarantee a degree of autarchy. He had even gone so far as to lend some of his own money to some of them.

While Mexico City was still in thrall to famine, Morelos was thriving. Tlaltizapan had become the de facto capital of the state. Zapata had set up his office in an old rice mill. He had some time on his hands to make babies.

Villa was taking a beating from the Carranzista forces of the one-armed General Obregón who had invaded Mexico City. There was a number of skirmishes between his supporters and the Zapatistas. The situation, politically, was confusing: in the north there was the president and the Villistas, and in the south the Zapatistas: they all professed to be the embodiments of the revolution. The United States recognized Carranza. Moreover, the landowners, most of them newcomers from the north, were also on his side.

After a few spectacular forays, especially into United States territory, Villa was beaten. As for Zapata, militarily, things were none too brilliant: his troops' homemade cartridges were of poor quality. He was under open attack again, on a larger scale this time. The agronomists fled to the cities. A number of leaders agreed to a government offer of amnesty. One of Zapata's lieutenants, Pacheco, betrayed him. Not really persuaded that he had been betrayed, Zapata saved Pacheco from execution. Luckily, De La O saw to it in his place.

To make matters worse, in April 1916, his cousin Amador Salazar was killed by a stray bullet in the neck near Yautepec while out horse riding. This was a huge loss to the revolutionaries. Villa, on the other hand, had resumed his raiding parties.

Zapata surrendered Cuernavaca and fled. He lost several cities in a row. Soon all that remained to him were Jojutla and Tlaltizapan which held out until June. His supporters were massacred out of hand. In Tlaltizapan, 286 men, women, and children were butchered. Zapata sought the safety of the mountains.

Carranza, driven by personal ambition rather than by political beliefs, followed the inevitable route where power leads: downhill into corruption. Having swung as far to the right as his former enemies had ever been, he enforced his dictatorship over the state. Elections were even cancelled whereas they had been held in "wise" states. The Zapatistas' harvests and achievements were literally pillaged shamelessly by the González government and its henchmen. Munitions were abandoned. What was recovered was sold on at a profit by the occupation forces. The resistance from the peasants was fierce. Taxes went unpaid. There would be skirmishing and many died. At the start of 1917, the Carranzistas eased up on the peasants and this brought some people over to their side.

In a devastated Morelos, Zapata dug himself in. He would have to start all over again. He set to the task, bravely. He set up a Consultation Centre for Propaganda and Revolutionary Unity, the members of which included Soto y Gama, Palafox, Montano, the Magana brothers... Its task was to re-organize everything: conferences, decrees, demonstrations, arbitration, and advice.

Every village saw its own Junta (Council) established: four officers and six elected peasants, rotated at four monthly intervals. Each junta connected to all the rest. One representative per village had responsibility for agrarian matters (the aim being a federal arrangement). Schools were re-established, not to mention adult night classes. Each village soviet was in contact with a district president who had responsibility for order. Alas, this was not always well-managed by the peasants.

Caught up in the squabbling between his lieutenants, Zapata was in no position to give this his attention. He was even to be forced to allow two of them— one of them his old friend Montano—to be executed. Others caved in from exhaustion: his own brother, Eufemio took to drink. Sorry to say, he was slain by a humiliated old man on the look-out for revenge. Salazar, Montano, Eufemio: Zapata had lost his oldest companions. He was overtaken by listlessness. 1915 and 1916 were a complete contrast.

1917 got off to an inauspicious beginning, too: in May, Carranza became president. He planned to negotiate. Magana was pressing for reconciliation or for a truce.

Zapata weakened. He wound up making references that were more and more far-removed from the Plan of Ayala. By March 1918, it was as if the Plan had never existed at all. His ranks continued to be eroded: Palafox caved in now, having lost all confidence in anyone except his leader. His homosexuality made him anathema to all these macho men. Zapata was forced to let him go. Palafox was to throw himself into the embrace of his adversaries. He died in 1959.

The winter of 1918 was a tough one. An outbreak of the Spanish flu decimated the population. All that Zapata had left now were his oldest surviving companions. De la O was still loyal. The weary who had departed for their home villages were to stay in touch and would supply him with provisions, intelligence, and hiding places.

The denouement came in April 1919. A dispatch from Zapata was intercepted by the Carranzistas: an ambush was laid. Zapata was intending to "turn" a Carranzista colonel who was at daggers drawn with his own side, Colonel Jesús Guajardo. With the leave of his superiors, the latter was to profess to be in a state of rebellion.

They were due to meet in Jonacatepec. Zapata showed up with thirty of his men. Guajardo showed up with six hundred and a machine-gun!

Their discussions made little headway. The following day, they met up on the Chinameca hacienda. The proceedings were interrupted by a report of troops in the area. Zapata made ready to resist and posted his escort around the hacienda before returning to the talks. At lunch time, he mounted his horse, with a ten-man escort. Guajardo's escort, drawn up in order, presented arms before him, then lowered their weapons and opened fire at point-blank range. Panicking, his escort fled in disarray. Zapata had been killed on the spot.

His body was taken back to Cuautla on a mule. The legend was born. Some Mexicans say that Zapata still roams the hills. And will return one day to free Mexico.

But the fighting was not quite over. Magana picked up the baton. He was 28 and lacked Emiliano's charisma. He entered into talks with Carranza and secured the yearned-for agrarian reform, on paper at least. The practical upshot was that the plantation owners returned in force. Magana sized up the situation, jumped ship and threw in his lot with Obregon. Soto y Gama and especially de la O also defected to Obregon who eventually overthrew Carranza in May 1920. Carranza was assassinated a short time after that.

Alvaro Obregón became president. Soto y Gama became Deputy Speaker of the Chamber of Deputies and went on to become the great leader of the agrarian party. Magana and Genovevo de la O were promoted generals.

Villa too made his peace. Not that it brought him any happiness for he was assassinated in 1923.

But Obregón showed a willingness to listen to Zapata's supporters. They were to control the whole of Morelos and agrarian reform was at last set in train. Magana

Eufemio et Emiliano ZAPATA . 1911

personally oversaw agriculture. Spectacular progress was made.

Magana died in 1939, de la O in 1952. In Zapata's village, his successor and curator of his archives, Francisco Franco (not to be confused with the European bastard of the same name) became village head. He was to ensure that the village's rights were established once and for all in 1935, before he, too, died by the assassin's hand in 1947. Those rights did not go untampered with for long.

Broadly speaking, while Obregon was president, Mexico enjoyed a period of contentment. Up until his sudden death in 1928. And how did he die? Well, pretty much as everybody else had: assassinated.

A footnote regarding the other towering figure in the Mexican revolution, Flores Magón. He led a restless life as an exile. Upon returning to Mexico, he was involved as charismatic leader in the Baja California venture. That Mexican-owned stretch of California, cut off from the rest of Mexico by an arm of the sea, rose in revolt on January 30, 1912. A Socialist Republic of Baja California was set up, but it was not to last, although it, too, was a model of libertarian communism.

The main slogan of Flores Magón's political group, Regeneracion (it was called after its newspaper) was Tierra y Libertad (Land and Liberty). That was the slogan that Zapata had opted to write on his banners.

Flores Magón, driven once again into exile in the United States, perished as his comrades had—but behind bars in 1922. Murdered.

Ukraine, 1917-1921
THE MAKHNOVSHCHINA

The only power possible for the proletariat is insurgent power, the power that sweeps all before it. Makhno's uneducated sod-busters, with their pitchforks, even though they be dead and buried, will always have the edge on Lenin, his lick-spittles and his cannons.

Alain Flieg
Phoney Struggle and Class Snare (1975)

The emancipation of the workers will be the workers' own doing.

Karl Marx and Friedrich Engels
Communist Manifesto (1848)

Much ink continues to flow regarding the 1917 Russian revolution, just as it caused the spilling of much blood. It is hard to come to grips with this taboo notion without running up against received ideas, ideas warped by upwards of a half-century of Stalinist misrepresentation. By way of summing up our starting point, which is the starting-point of any onlooker not blinded by ideology, let it be said that the revolution opened in 1917 and ended in 1918, when the Bolsheviks wrestled power from the people for their own exclusive advantage and wound up the soviets established by the workers, soldiers, and peasants who had made that revolution. It was to take twenty years of relentless massacres before the Leninist two percent would gain the upper hand in the country, under Stalin's mailed fist.

It was a daunting task, doing away with self-management and with the soviets. Outstanding proletarian leaders emerged to confront the bureaucratic leaders thrown up by the Russian bourgeoisie—Lenin and Trotsky—and were cut down after ferocious skirmishing.

The Kronstadt revolt, to quote only the most celebrated skirmish, was put down only by the strength of numbers of the a Red Army under the personal direction of Trotsky, Kamenev, and Zinoviev. They carried out a bloodbath against the workers and peasants before proceeding the very next day to celebrate the anniversary of the Paris Commune.

The most amazing episode in all this remains the civil war waged in the Ukraine from which one towering personality emerges—Nestor Makhno, real name Nestor Ivanovitch Mikhienko. Born in 1889 in Gulyai-Polye, a little hamlet in the Ukraine, to a family of poor peasants, Makhno became an activist at a very early age. Cowherd and farm-hand, in short, a working man, he was a member of the village's anarchist group. Along with his comrades he organized an attentat that went badly wrong and resulted in his being imprisoned. On account of his tender years, he escaped a death sentence but was not able to see the outside of prison until the revolution came to pass some nine years later.

It was in prison that his political consciousness was shaped, notably through an encounter with a remarkable militant Piotr Arshinov (1887–1936), one of the Moscow anarchist leaders, a locksmith by trade.

Makhno even then had the charisma that was to turn him into the "Batko" (Father) of the Ukrainian commune. The title "Batko" was not in regular use there but it was constantly bestowed upon him. (It hints more of the respect owed an object of admiration than at any fatherly authority). His face bore the traces of smallpox, but his prominent cheekbones endowed him with a rivetting gaze. His sense of humor and his legendary obstinacy and intelligence were to do the rest.

Released as a result of developments, he scurried back to Gulyai-Polye, to establish what was to prove a legendary soviet. Its first chairman was to be the village school teacher Chernoknizhny, who was blunt about the council's political outlook: "The notion of free toilers' soviets is generated by life itself. That transitional form of self-management leads on in practice to the non-authoritarian order to come, rooted in the precepts of absolute freedom and complete equality and fraternity." Rarely has so much been said in so few words.

Makhno threw himself headlong into the building of the soviet. Council members seized the land and livestock of the rich estate-owners and redistributed them to the poor peasants. Communes were set up in which participation was entirely voluntary (a far cry from the Stalinist kolkhozes that were to lead the Russian economy into disaster). They had around 100-300 members. What few factories the village had were taken into workers' control and management committees were put in charge of distribution and of the allocation of production. The most primitive forms of barter were established between the self-managing factory and the peasant commune.

The first of these free communes was to take the name "Rosa Luxemburg," in tribute to the revolutionary recently done to death in Berlin. These communes were self-generating and the poor peasants made up their initial membership. Everyone worked according to his abilities and egalitarianism was taken as far as practicable. Mutual aid became an obsession with them. All of the delegates and organizers were chosen by the entire membership. From time to time there were to be congresses linking the communes, three of them congresses covering the whole region. The revolutionaries took a hand in education and their system was inspired by Francisco Ferrer's theories.

But there was a war raging at the same time. There was the threat from the

Whites. Not to mention the Ukrainian nationalists led by a moderate upper bourgeois, Simon Petliura. As yet, the revolution had made few inroads into Ukraine, but the nationalists had already set up a Central Rada which had proclaimed the Ukraine an independent republic with its capital in Kiev.

The Bolsheviks responded by sending in the army. But the Treaty of Brest-Litovsk intervened. Lenin had no hesitation in sacrificing the Ukraine in its entirety and it was ceded to Austria-Hungary. The Austro-Hungarians appointed a governor, Skoropadsky, who replaced Petliura. Lenin pulled out of a Kiev which his troops had recently captured.

The Ukrainian soviets did not see eye to eye with this and from that point on they were to fight against the invaders. In Gulyai-Polye, Makhno had set up a farm laborers' union, and he was chairman of the peasant union, the metalworkers' and carpenters' union and chairman of the soviet. It only remained for him to conjure up his army. Which, after January 1918, was a fait accompli. It was quickly to come to be known throughout the country as the Makhnovshchina. It amounted to a column that would very quickly expand to fifty thousand people, complete with cannons, tanks, and armored trains captured from the enemy, and, above all with its celebrated tatchanki, highly mobile and light carts drawn by a couple of horses. These rode in the front of the column, with the infantry in the middle and the artillery bringing up the rear.

These carts were to be the essence of the "tatchanky republic," the Makhno column, which was to enjoy the support of the entire peasant and worker population over a two-year period. In military terms, this was a quality army; the peasants had fought from 1914 to 1918 and here they were, still in the thick of the action. They were all volunteers, discipline was freely embraced, and all post-holders and officers were elected by their troops. Makhno, however, had the final say in the selection of commanders.

All of the columns led by other revolutionaries, operating either independently or on behalf of the Red Army, were to throw in their lot with the Makhnovshchina. This was especially true of the column from Berdyansk led by an anarchist peasant, Vasil Kutilenko, of whom it was often said that he might fill Makhno's shoes, there was also the Dibrivka column led by the former sailor, Schuss, and Grishino's column led by Petrenko-Platonoff.

Obliged to fight nonstop and to move around, the peasants had a hell of a time trying to keep their communes afloat. The Makhnovshchina lacked intellectuals, the only ones to join it being Piotr Arshinov, from 1919 to 1920, when he left for Moscow to see to the disintegrating movement there; Voline, real name Vsevolod M. Eichenbaum 1882-1845, a member of the Nabat, the main anarchist organization of the day; Ossip and Aaron Baron (likewise Nabat members) who were to look after the cultural and educational side of things for a time. They would lay on conferences and draft leaflets and posters and see to the whole propaganda side. Voline was also to head the Insurgent Military Council for around six months. His essential testimony The Unknown Revolution is, along with Arshinov's History of the Makhnovist Movement, the chief source of all our knowledge about Makhno and his men.

The protracted nature of the fighting was another menace to the Makhnovists: Prolonged militarization rarely promotes self-managerial ideas and Makhno's supporters were often to fall prey to such contradictions. Especially as they were not without shortcomings: Makhno was a drinker, prone to become very violent and irascible when drunk, and was not always the perfect libertarian in his treatment of women, he kept bad company, even though his "clique" was often put in its place by the rank and file. To select one example out of the thousands: one of his commanders, the young, courageous, pugnacious giant Klein, who had been wounded time and again, was upbraided at one congress for having had too much to drink when the troops were forbidden to do likewise. He was to make a public confession, explaining that he had become bored, being far-removed from the fighting and that he was keen to be reassigned to the front line. He was forgiven and posted to the front.

The army's capacity for fight was not always helped by an enduring shortage in weapons and munitions. On the other hand, politically, the quality was high. The peasants adapted very quickly to self-management and between every defensive or offensive operation, they would turn their attention to practical achievements, urged on by a Makhno who was alive to the fact that construction and destruction are the two engines of change.

The black flag floated over the region. The magistrates and police were driven out or retained in a mere courier capacity.

But there was great danger. The civil war revolved around three forces (Makhno, the Bolsheviks and the nationalists), each at odds with the others, and in Moscow, fifty anarchists had been gunned down or jailed: the Makhnovshchina was starting to strike terror into the Ukrainian bourgeoisie…

Petliura had made a name for himself with his pogroms against Jews (he was to meet his end at the hand of a Jewish activist in exile), but he had also capitalized on a trip that Makhno made to Moscow (during which Makhno had an audience with Lenin who was, even then, incapable of the shifting situation, and met anarchists with whom he just could not see eye to eye, notably Kropotkin) to have Makhno's war-crippled brother murdered, raze his home to the ground and put a price on his head. The Petliurovski were to find the Batko's vengeance swooping down upon them: in every instance, the bullies, police, and officers were to be unrelentingly and often savagely executed.

It was the start of a struggle to the death. One that was to continue against the White armies of Skoropadsky, Denikin (who was to be defeated in short order), and then Wrangel. Simon Petliura stepped down in 1919. The clandestine Revolutionary Committee charged Makhno to orchestrate the fight against the Austro-Hungarian invaders.

His tatchanki worked miracles: in a single day they might strike in two different locations 100 kilometers apart. Their sorties brought in captured arms, provisions, money, and equipment. There was no battalion that could withstand him. The peasants, supplied him not just with billets and hiding-places, but also with fresh mounts, weapons, and priceless intelligence. Sometimes earning harsh retaliation for their pains.

The Bolsheviks, although they had the White armies at their rear, had no hesitation in attacking the libertarians with violence: arrests and murders proliferated. Trotsky, who never missed a chance to butcher the anarchist riff-raff, and Dzerzhinski, the dour boss of the Cheka, oversaw the repression. In September 1918, Makhno's wife and child were murdered. Non-Bolsheviks were being systematically disarmed everywhere. The fighters had either to enlist in the Red Army or make their way home. Meanwhile, Makhno launched an all-out attack on Skoropadsky, and then attacked Petliura in Ekaterinoslav, where he had support from the Bolsheviks, who were playing a double game. Makhno entered the city in a civilian disguise, travelling incognito on the train. Petliura's army was smashed and Makhno then abandoned the city to the Bolsheviks.

From November 1918 to June 1919, there was a breathing space during which Reds and Whites alike kept their distance and when the Makhnovshchina could develop, its army occupying the entire Gulyai-Polye district. For the first time there was time to reflect and even to indulge in a little theorizing regarding their experiences.

Petliura swept back for a time, capturing Kiev, whilst the Austro-Hungarians withdrew and the governor and great estate owners fled. In the end, the Red Army was to recover Kiev.

Throughout these developments, the area was blighted by gangs of looters. When the time came, this was to enable the united propaganda of the Bolsheviks and the Whites to depict the irksome Makhno as a highwayman (just as he would coldly be credited with Petliura's anti-Jewish pogroms. One "White" author was even to pen a defamatory novel called *Makhno and his Jewess*. That writer was one Joseph Kessel, whose admirers are careful not to reprint the novel in question).

1919 was marked by a four-cornered battle royal, as the Whites and the Ukrainian nationalists did not always see eye to eye. Makhno continued to waste time on Lenin. He played along and was reluctant to see the revolutionary forces split, even if he did not agree with the Reds. Having wrestled a hundred wagon-loads of wheat from Denikin, he sent them to Moscow and Petrograd to support the soviets there.

While the Denikinists enforced a horrific repression, the Bolsheviks made up their minds in March to attack them. Dybenko led their forces. An agreement was entered into with Makhno. They would come to some mutual understanding. The Makhnovshchina was to retain its independence, but Makhno would be afforded the status of a Red political commissar. The black flag would still fly over every tatchanka. We can just imagine what difficulty the Bolshevik leaders must have had in swallowing this—people like Trotsky, among others, or Dybenko who went on to be the military commander in the crackdown on Kronstadt.

Within weeks the Cheka had earned the hatred of the peasantry who detested the Chekists and their bureaucratic practices. In retaliation, there came a flood of complaints about the Makhnovshchina. Provisions were not always forthcoming, nor were munitions, and a number of arrests were made.

In January, February, and April, there was a congress of councils held in Gulyai-Polye. At the April congress, 72 delegates represented two million men. Dybenko declared it a counter-revolutionary assembly and a press campaign was launched against the self-managers who were written off as criminal types and kulaks (which took quite some cheek, since the peasants had stayed poor, and were, indeed, sometimes poorer than before). The ineffable Trotsky was to utter the historic pronouncement: "Better to surrender the Ukraine as a whole to Denikin than to allow any spread of the Makhnovist movement. Denikin's blatantly counter revolutionary movement, can easily be undermined later through class propaganda, whereas the Makhnovshchina spreads through the masses and indeed, sets the masses against us."

It was at this point that the first Bolshevik plot designed to have Makhno murdered was uncovered. It was foiled by Makhno himself. The plotters were executed out of hand. It was just then, as Denikin was launching his big push, that the Bolsheviks attacked Gulyai-Polye in June 1919. This spelled the end of the period of Makhno's complete power over the Ukraine.

Stabbed in the back, his communes destroyed, his supporters summarily executed, Makhno resigned his post with the Red Army. The Reds were once more under the command of Trotsky "a narrow-minded fellow of unwarranted arrogance and malice, a fine polemicist and orator who had—through the Revolution's having gone astray—wound up as the 'infallible' military dictator over a huge country," as Voline described him.

The Reds retreated in the face of Denikin's onslaught, so that the latter might outflank Makhno and dispose of him. Fresh Bolshevik forces under the command of Voroshilov arrived and it was suggested to Makhno that he fight alongside them. He declined. He was not wrong: Voroshilov carried in his pocket an order from Trotsky instructing him to seize Makhno and have him shot on the spot. Some of Makhno's men did take up commands in the Red Army, though.

On the day following Trotsky's announcement that Denikin no longer posed any really serious menace, Denikin recaptured Ekaterinoslav and threatened Kharkov. It too fell to him in July. The Red Army fled in panic, abandoning the Ukraine to its fate.

Now Makhno was the only remaining opposition to White terror. Those of Makhno's men who had stayed with the Red Army flocked back to him, with a

124

goodly number of Bolshevik deserters in tow. The local populace fled along with Makhno, terrified by the actions of the Whites who were shooting the men and raping the women (in the case of Jewish women, this was standard practice). The retreat lasted until September.

Surrounded, barely sleeping, forever on the move, Makhno had eight thousand wounded in tow. In Uman, which was in the hands of the last remaining Petliurist forces, he came to an accommodation with them in order to have his wounded men tended, but he was betrayed and utterly encircled by the Whites under General Slaschoff (who went on later to become an officer with the Bolsheviks!).

The turning-point came on September 26. Makhno switched direction and attacked the Whites in Peregonova. At the beginning of the battle he vanished from sight, only to turn up in their rear, covered in dust, just as his men were making a breakthrough. This sent the Whites fleeing. Makhno relentlessly pursued the fugitives who were butchered at saber point on the banks of the river.

Pressing home his advantage, Makhno broke through the front lines, taking the Whites by surprise (they had no defenses in their rear) and within days he had regained control of the whole of the Ukraine.

His progress brought panic. The Makhnovists razed prisons, executed officers and policemen and kulaks and priests and rich bourgeois. They swept aside any restrictions they came across. One poster put up everywhere stood out from the rest: it encapsulated what the Makhnovshchina was all about. "It is up to the peasants and workers to act for themselves, to organize and to come to some arrangement between them in every aspect of their lives, however they see them and however they would have them be. Let it be known to them from this moment forth, that the Makhnovist army will make no imposition upon them, nor dictate nor foist any order upon them. The Makhnovists can but assist them by making such and such information or advice available to them, affording them access to whatever intellectual, military, or other resources they might need. But they cannot and will not under any circumstances govern them or make any prescriptions whatever to them."

Denikin fled. He had been defeated once and for all. The Bolsheviks, no fools, scurried back and scored an easy victory near Orel—which would furnish the basis for the myth that it was the Red Army that had beaten Denikin. They sought to reinstall their bureaucracy wherever they went, but Makhno thwarted them in this.

There was an important congress in Alexandrovsk. It provided for everything to be organized along co-operative lines, pressed for self-management and commissioned Makhno to oversee military operations, with eighteen commanders at his disposal. A short time after that, there was a typhus outbreak that would not spare the Makhnovshchina and decimated its ranks. Makhno himself was to be sick for quite some time.

Yet again—not quite as ingenuous as some historians appear to believe, but having little choice in the matter—Makhno was to flirt with and, seemingly, to enter into an alliance with the Reds. There was fraternization between their armies. The Bolsheviks had no qualms about asking Makhno to mount an attack on the Polish front, far from his native province. He declined and withdrew to Gulyai-Polye once again.

Now declared an outlaw, Makhno was several times to give Trotsky's killers the slip. Bela Kun, who made his name during the Commune in Hungary, had allied himself with Makhno, only to vilify him once his back was turned.

The nonsensical propaganda directed against Makhno was, oddly enough, echoed around the world, the bourgeois press doubtless, and rightly, calculating that he posed a greater menace to capitalism than Lenin and Trotsky.

Wherever they could, the Bolsheviks destroyed what Makhno had built. A total of 200,000 peasants were to be shot down at this time. Gulyai-Polye changed hands a number of times and there were further executions each time, as Makhno was ruthless with the Red commissars and officers.

In the spring of 1920 came a fresh White offensive, in the Crimea this time, under the command of the former tsarist Baron Wrangel. Every time that Makhno, who had rearmed against the invader, mounted an attack, the Reds attacked him in his rear. For good measure, Red propaganda then made sure to accuse Makhno of treachery (allying himself with the Whites). They declined to respond to the appeal for anti-White unity launched by Makhno, who had been rejoined by Ossip and Voline.

As Wrangel made inroads and captured the villages of the Ukraine one after another (Gulyai-Polye included), an agreement was finally thrashed out between the Reds and the Makhnovists.

Voline was to be a beneficiary of this: a captive of the Bolsheviks, he would be freed on this occasion, as were some other anarchists. Together the anarchists and Communists sat alongside one another one last time in the soviets. Makhno was given a free hand to pursue his own strategy and the inhabitants of the Makhnovist-held territories had their right to self-organization recognized. This was a right which they had seized long before. The Bolsheviks publicly acknowledged that there had been no Makhno-Wrangel alliance.

Wrangel promptly suffered his first reverse, the prelude to complete liquidation in November 1920, which was a result of the concerted efforts of the two "allies."

In Gulyai-Polye they were starting all over again, beginning anew. The school was got up and running by followers of Ferrer. The Makhnovshchina made a splendid fresh start. On their side, Lenin and Trotsky ordered Makhno's murder and the extermination of his supporters. Now that the common enemy was no more, there was nothing to restrain them from an inevitable head-to-head confrontation.

The first plot had been cooked up prior to Wrangel's defeat. In a surprise move, the entire Makhnovist command in the Crimea had been rounded up. Its leaders, who included Simon Karetnik who was in command (often filling in for Nestor Makhno as supreme commander) and Piotr Gavrilenko, another anarchist peasant and one of the victors over Denikin, were executed out of hand. Only Martchenko, another peasant from Gulyai-Polye, the cavalry commander, managed to escape with 250 of his 1,500 men.

On their arrival, Martchenko and Taranovsky (another commander) presented themselves before an ailing Makhno. Martchenko reported to him: "I have the honor to announce the return of the army of Crimea." To which Makhno replied, "yes, brothers, only now do we know what these Communists are made of." Makhno had known this for some time, but events had left him with little option. Yet again he quit Gulyai-Polye, taking just 250 men, so as to make good speed. He was as sick as a dog and had a broken ankle. He needed time to recover from this blow.

Voline, who had been arrested at this time, reports that one of the Cheka chiefs, Samsonoff, who interrogated him, passed this remark: "We have now become real, shrewd statesmen (…) Now that we have no further use for his services—and indeed that he has turned into an irritation to us—we can rid ourselves of him once and for all." A better summation of the situation would be hard to frame.

But Makhno was not beaten yet. He put together an army of a thousand horsemen and fifteen hundred infantry. In a counter-attack, he recaptured Gulyai-Polye and took 6,000 Bolsheviks prisoner: 2,000 were promptly to desert to his side. It has to be said that it was beginning to become obvious to the Old Bolsheviks that their revolution had been hijacked by a cabal of upstarts and bureaucrats, most of whom had had no hand in the initial fighting or indeed had taken part only reluctantly: (Trotsky, Kamenev, Zinoviev, etc.).

The fighting was to persist until 1921. In the end, Makhno was forced into a retreat. The winter, the snow, the freezing conditions all conspired against him. A number of his faithful lieutenants (such as Martchenko or Grigory Vassilevsky, who often stood in for him as head of the army) had been killed. He himself had sustained several wounds, could mount his horse only painfully, and had a bullet in his thigh and another in his belly.

That summer saw the deaths of his last remaining comrades, like Schuss, Kurilenko, or Mikhaleff-Pavlenko. The peasants were forced to hide him as he could no longer walk or even stand. He overcame his debility and fled.

Outside of his regional base, he was a man alone. The Russian anarchists all disowned him, being misled about his true role and too susceptible to Leninist propaganda about him. At the Congress of Red Trades Unions, he was denounced by anarchist collaborators. Elsewhere in the world, he was looked upon as a bandit chief. When the Makhnovshchina had been thriving, it enjoyed the support of anarchists: once it went into decline, they all shamelessly deserted it. On the whole, the Russian anarchist movement was a Moscow-centered movement, most of it ignorant of matters Ukrainian or of peasant affairs. Such shortcomings and shortsightedness in the Russian libertarians who were also short of strong personalities, partly accounts for the ease with which Lenin and his henchmen were able to derail a movement as powerful as the Russian revolution and turn it into a bureaucratic, State capitalist system. In any case, Makhno had nothing but contempt for the Moscow anarchists.

In August, Budyenny defeated the Makhnovist forces once and for all. Nestor Makhno was wounded and Ivanuk and Petrenko killed (they being his last two faithful companions): he managed to escape with—so the sources say—250 or merely 77 surviving cavalry.

Later, concealing in a hay cart that was probed by bayonets at a checkpoint, he was smuggled into Rumania, where he could be tended and interned.

As the lingering remnants of the Makhnovshchina were being eradicated and as the sinister Frunze was butchering women and children, the whole of the Ukraine was subjected to such a dictatorship as none of the tsars had ever enforced. Scarcely had he recovered from his wounds than Makhno escaped from Romania into Poland where he was re-arrested. He then escaped again into Germany where he joined some of his supporters. He started to write.

He turned up later in Paris, a dour exile living in the poverty that attended the remainder of his life. He drove a taxi, was a factory hand with Renault, was deserted by his wife Galina Andreyevna (whose dream it had been to be the consort of the master of the Ukraine). His ankle never quite healed and his cheeks bore a huge scar. He wrote his memoirs (which were, alas, to remain unfinished and stop just where the revolution began). Increasingly he turned to drink. His heath was sapped by Tuberculosis.

He died in 1935 in an oxygen tent, with no one at his bedside. In Russia, the former fascist general, Slaschoff became an instructor at the Military Academy and peddled lies about Makhno. In France, the likes of Barbusse and Aragon distinguished themselves by their zeal in dragging his name through the mud. Stalin was in power by then, openly implementing the program which his predecessors had not been able to carry out with such cynicism.

In 1936, a few survivors from the Makhnovshchina joined the Durruti Column in Spain to meet a belated death. But in 1954, during a bitter strike in Norilsk, those who had never forgotten hoisted (for a time) Makhno's black standard with the device "Liberty or death" sewn across it. For it is easier to kill men than to kill off the myth.

Of Makhno's two best-known comrades, Arshinov was to meet the sadder fate: having survived the slaughter, he wound up in 1931 abjuring anarchism in favor of "the historic, ineluctable necessity of our age, the dictatorship of the proletariat." In 1935 he was even to write of the Makhnovshchina as a "tragic-comic farce." Having turned into a Stalinist, he was to receive the reward that was his due: Stalin had him executed in 1936.

Voline, who had been arrested along with the entire Nabat leadership in Kharkov, was to survive. As an exile in France he was to defend Makhno against his libelers (notably Joseph Kessel), before he died in Marseilles in 1945.

Germany, 1818-1919
SPARTAKUS

> Arise, proletarian! To battle! There is a whole world
> to be gained and a whole world to be fought against.
> In this, world history's class battle for the loftiest
> aims of mankind, there is nothing left to say to the
> enemy but 'Thumbs in eyes and Knees on chest!'
>
> Programme of the Spartakus League

> On safety and cost grounds, the State must countenance
> the deaths of revolutionaries, if not expedite them.
>
> Helmut Kohl, Minister-President
> *The Frankfurt Journal* (1974)

The German revolution started with the war in 1914. Or, to be more accurate, with the opposition to that war which was to prove one enormous massacre. An opposition group grew up around strong personalities like Karl Liebknecht, Rosa Luxemburg, Franz Mehring, or Clara Zetkin. Liebknecht was a parliamentary deputy, aged 43. They were all members of the Social Democratic Party, the S.D.P.

Aside from the Social Democrats, the left wing forces were the Communists of the K.P.D. , the anarcho-syndicalists (numbering around 200,000) opposed to any seizure of central authority and led by Rudolf Rocker (1873–1958), not to mention a few councilors, each beavering away in his own locality.

Agitation really got off the ground from 1916 onward. The first text of any significance appeared in January 1916 and was the famous "Pamphlet," signed Junius and penned by Rosa Luxemburg. Rosa was 46 years old, a matchless battler. Her legendary personality was familiar and attractive, even to those who are her adversaries these days. At the time, she was viewed primarily as a dangerous terrorist. However, her selflessness, gentleness, and strength of spirit struck all who had anything to do with her. There are strong similarities between her personality and that of Louise Michel, so much so that a cataloging of the one reads like a profile of the other.

The group launched a review *The International*, of which only one issue ever appeared. Its main editors were Rosa and Leo Jogiches, aged fifty, a figure of some standing in the socialist movement.

After that failed, they launched the *Spartakusbriefe* (Spartakus Letters), from which the name given to the hitherto nameless group would be taken. These were to appear up until 1918 when they switched to publication of leaflets only, due to pressures of time. In 1916, Liebknecht and Otto Ruhle, radical S.P.D. deputies, were expelled from the party on the grounds of leftism. This was a boon to the U.S.P.D., a socialist party tinged with leftism, something along the lines of the P.S.U. in France. The course of events was to present them with their chance.

In January 1918, there was a general strike right across Germany. Soviets popped up pretty well everywhere. The strike, which was outlawed, was forcibly broken in February. In March a number of Spartakists, not least Jogiches, were arrested. That spring there was a resumption of the strike in Berlin.

All of which carried the Social Democrats into government by that autumn. The rift with the extreme left was complete. The Spartakusbund (Spartakus Group) was calling for the formation of soviets and for revolution, whereas the Socialists were railing against adventurism. Liebknecht, who had by then been in prison for some months, was freed in October. Within ten days, the Baltic sailors had mutinied. In fact, on October 30, two warships had refused orders to put to sea. It took the dispatch of a submarine and some torpedo boats to force a surrender. Four hundred seamen were taken prisoner. The next day, in Kiel, all of the sailors there demonstrated to demand the release of the prisoners. A brawl ensued, with several lives lost. The government sent along a few Social Democrats to calm things down. Among them was one Gustav Noske (1868–1946), of whom more later.

The German military defected to the side of the mutineers and rebels in entire units. Numbering 20,000 by November 4, they set up a soldiers' council, chaired by an ordinary seaman, Artelt. They entered into negotiations with Admiral Souchon, who recognized their soviet, and agreed to their non-political demands, but not the others, the chief one of which was nothing less than that the Kaiser should abdicate. Among the civilian population, there was a general strike. Among the principal leaders of this ferment there was one Egelhofer who was to make his name a short time later in the Bavarian councils' republic. (See the following chapter.)

The rebels swept everything before them. The Konig was seized and red flags were flying everywhere. Noske's stroke of genius was quite simply to place himself at the head of the rebels and have himself proclaimed Kiel's governor. He was the worm in the bud.

Right across Germany—in Lubeck, Hamburg, Bremen, Cuxhaven, Cologne, Munich, etc.—the same scenario was played out. The government expelled the soviet ambassador, Yoffe. In Hamburg the lead was given by a very idiosyncratic far left known as the "Bremen tendency," who wished to remain as independent of the Spartakists as of the U.S.P.D. and whose theoretician was Johann Krief. Its leaders were Fritz Wolffheim and Laufenberg. A radical program drafted by Wolffheim was adopted, newspaper offices were taken over, and military garrisons drove out their officers. The movement was primarily led by workers. The prisons were thrown open. The very wishy-washy trade unions played no role. Revolutionaries had long since given them up as a bad job.

In Bavaria too, events had started to move. We shall skip them, since they are to be examined in the next chapter, but we need to be clear that, in their timing, they were closely matched by events elsewhere in Germany, even if the linkage between them never had time to crystallize.

Rosa Luxemburg was freed from prison on November 8. The very next day saw revolution in Berlin. Wilhelm II abdicated, the government broke up, and the military and police were at a loss to know what to do next. The Socialists immediately tried to lay claim to a revolution that was not of their making. They managed to foist a wholly sham workers' and soldiers' council upon Berlin. Thanks to which they ensured the establishment of a National Assembly and the appointment of one of their own — Ebert — as chancellor. Another Social Democrat, Scheidemann, proclaimed the republic in the Reichstag. Within two hours, from the balcony of the Kaiser's palace, from which a red flag now fluttered, Liebknecht was proclaiming his own republic, a Free Socialist Republic of Germany.

This sort of confusion and socialist chicanery were not to prevent an agreement between Social Democrats and Independent Social Democrats, which is to say, between the S.P.D. and the dissidents from the U.S.P.D.: six people's commissars were to be appointed. Ebert and Scheideman would be two of them.

Liebknecht alone spotted the trap and declined to accept the conditions attached.

In Brunswick, one crafty Spartakist, August Merges, a simple tailor, showed up the previous evening at the palace of the Grand Duke of Brunswick, brandishing a slip of paper signed by the Workers' and Soldiers' Council and insisting that The Grand Duke abdicate. In a panic, the Grand Duke agreed to pass his mandate on to the soviet, through Merges. But the Council was not in fact to be set up until the next day. Merges became Brunswick's representative on the Reich's States Council. He had earned it. There he moved that the land and the factories be transferred to the proletariat and that they proceed with this fait acompli.

In the Ruhr, the miners socialized (i.e., self-managed) the pits, in anticipation of the report from the official commission charged with deciding upon the matter: self-management ought not to wait upon officialdom. It cannot be legislated into existence.

The Spartakists published a newspaper that was to last for as long as their short-lived revolution would — *Rote Fahne*. At the same time, Wilhelm II fled to Holland. A new government was installed, indistinguishable from its predecessor, and an armistice was signed between France and Germany. It would be foolish to overlook the fact that they were still at war with each other.

While the laws were allowed to stand, a number of social measures were passed, particularly the introduction of the eight hour day and of a degree of co-management in firms.

The soviets, with lively backing from the Spartakists, in turn backed the government, somewhat naively. Unlike most of the other States' representatives, Merges was four-square behind dictatorship of the proletariat.

The right's analysis saw through the confusion. It had grasped the point. Henceforth, it set about openly supporting the Socialist, Ebert. Marshal Hindenburg popped up again and secured a hearing, openly criticizing the radicals. On December 6, a putsch was only just thwarted in Berlin.

The following day, for the first time, the Spartakusbund paraded through Berlin on its own. Liebknecht was even placed under arrest for a few hours. Among its leaders, in addition to those already named, we ought to mention Levi and Lange. Rosa was changing her address every evening as a precautionary measure.

The garrison commander, Wels, dispatched his troops to the Spartakusbund's premises. It was there that he earned his nickname of "Blutwels"(Bloody Wels).

The government then took a number of measures geared to moderation, not to say, sabotage, of the revolution: "socializations" there would be (they were inevitable), but they were to proceed with compensation for the capitalists; a national volunteer guard was set up, essentially to provide a pretext for dissolving the councils; and all weapons were required to be returned to the authorities.

On December 14, the Spartakusbund published its program, drafted yet again by Rosa. Naturally, it looked in a different direction. To quote at random:

—non-proletarian police and military would be disarmed: weapons and munitions would be placed under the control of the soviets.
—there would be armed proletarian militias drawn from the populace.
—there would be a freely agreed discipline and army officers would be elected and subject to recall.
—there were to be councils at every level of administration and at town-hall level.
—revolutionary tribunals would sit in judgment of great leaders and plotters.
—the republic would be one and indivisible.
—soviets would be elected by the populace, firm by firm; delegates would be liable to recall.
—there would be a central council of councils, all of the members of which would be re-elected every three months: matters executive, legislative, and administrative would fall under its remit.
—the working day would last six hours.
—all privileges and orders were abolished.

—all imperial and royal fortunes and assets were to be seized.
—expropriated estates would be given over to (centralized) agricultural co-operatives.
—factories, roads, banking, and transport were to be nationalized.
—Etc., etc. All of these are familiar demands. With minor exceptions, they have not varied for centuries past.

A little later, the First National Congress of Councils was held in the Landtag in Berlin: it was attended by 489 delegates, two out of every five of them Social Democrats. The real left was made up only of 11 United Revolutionaries (Laufenberg Tendency), and 90 U.S.P.D. members (only ten of them Spartakists). Although outflanked by the right, the Spartakists had the support of certain radical delegates who put their case to Ebert and his friends.

There was pressure from the streets and the Spartakist delegations jumped ship. They called for widespread self-management, called for dissolution of Ebert's Council of People's Commissars and the formation of a Red Guard, and above all, for organization of the fight against the reactionaries. Naturally, what emerged from the congress was the precise opposite.

We should not believe that the ideas and proposals of the Spartakists and other self-managers (including the anarchists) were confined to vague generalities. Alongside of all this, they were organizing society according to their lights. Ideas were fleshed out in practice, as they used to say prior to '68. For instance, on December 17, Liebknecht and the other members of the soviet, Berlin soldiers, passed a very radical motion to the effect that all ranks were to be abolished and a supreme soldiers' council established. This never got very far, for the revolution had only a few more days' life left in it. Sailors mutinied against Wels once again. They seized the government building and negotiated with Wels.

Even as this was happening, they came under gunfire. They then captured Wels and his cronies, releasing the latter in return for a withdrawal by troops deployed against them. That withdrawal never took place. The building came under bombardment and in the end they freed Wels in return for minor concessions.

The "Internationalist Communists" started to federate with one another. Their ranks embraced all sorts of tendencies, Moscow-aligned communists and Spartakists alike. The latter had seized control of Vorwaerts, which thereafter put out all their leaflets. In a number of towns, the soviets issued weapons to the workers.

Shortly before the end of the year, the U.S.P.D. walked out of the government, their disagreements with it being too great. Whereupon Noske, who was still governor up in Kiel, was recalled and put in charge of Defence. That very same day saw the opening of the Congress that was to mark the foundation of the Communist Party of Germany (K.P.D.) into which the Spartakusbund was absorbed. Lenin was represented at it by Radek who attended in an observer capacity only but who was to play a crucial part in the proceedings.

Rosa, Liebknecht, and Jogiches were in favor of contesting the elections, but the majority took a different line. Rosa delivered an important speech. The central committee was made up of Rosa, Liebknecht, Jogiches, Lange, and Levi, but it also included Meyer, Pieck, Thalheimer, and four "Internationalist Communists" (that movement having joined the K.P.D.), among them Frolich.

The Spartakists had a hard time getting the movement to budge for it was held back by the Stalinists (yes, I know—as yet they were only "Leninists" but I am using the word in its generic sense to describe a school of thought that predated Stalin by far, and of which he was the consummate expression), Radek and Yoffe (both of them Russians). Radek even dismissed Laufenberg and Wolffheim as "National-Bolsheviks." Their essential goal was to prevent an alliance between Germany and the Entente powers which could only rebound to the detriment of the Russians.

From Rosa Luxembourg's speech let us single out a couple of phrases that are plainly indicative of where she stood. Apropos of Ebert, she stated, "If we want a king, we do not need some upstart who cannot even conduct himself in a kingly fashion." And on the soviets, she said, "No matter the country where the revolution will erupt after Germany, its first act will be to create workers' and soldiers' councils." As we can see, she was anything but an orthodox communist.

The Socialists made a good start to 1919: they disarmed the 75th Bremen Infantry Regiment, the most revolutionary unit of them all. Berlin's prefect of police, U.S.P.D. member Eichorn, was stood down: and the revolutionary police force which he had made up of workers militia members was abolished. There were violent protests from the left (by which I mean the Spartakist revolutionaries).

In a handbill, socialists called upon the populace to turn against the "Spartakusbund bandits." Noske was to go down in legend with his celebrated exhortation: "If a bloodhound is what it takes, I am not afraid to take on the responsibility." He was secretly armed with the powers to deal with the Spartakist rabble. Everyone was out for their blood, especially the soft left, whose plans to take power they had upset. Ebert, Noske, Scheidemann, and Wels would shrink from nothing to have done with this nuisance.

The hatred they inspired was matched only by the degree of threat that they posed. Noske, nobody's fool, was to sum the situation up callously but correctly: "Had the mob had resolute leaders who knew what they wanted, instead of fine wordsmiths, they would have been the masters of Berlin by noon that day" (January 6).

The fighting raged in every city. In Bremen, a Councils Republic was proclaimed on January 10. In Essen, the coal mines were taken into self-management. Laufenberg, who chaired the Hamburg soviet, was arrested. The following day, Vorwaerts was under siege and the 300 persons on its premises surrendered to Noske. The other newspapers suffered the same fate. Meyer was arrested, as was Lebedour, the delegate negotiating a compromise with the government.

By January 14 the fighting in Berlin was over. The next day, near the Zoo, Karl

Liebknecht was murdered by Noske's troops. Rosa, captured the same day was beaten to death with a rifle butt by a man named Vogel. Her corpse, tossed into the river was not recovered until May 31 and her funeral was not held until June 13. The killers of the two Spartakist leaders were to be "tried," but Vogel was to escape with consummate ease.

Rote Fahne was banned, although it reappeared regardless in February. Elections to a Constituent Assembly were held. The councils, which were still around, were no longer able to nominate their delegates and so they ceased to be councils. The lingering skirmishing was fading out. Shattered by the failure, the elderly Franz Mehring died embittered and in despair. On February 4, the Central Council of Councils abdicated: it handed power to the Assembly. Only in Rhineland-Westphalia did the "socializations" endure.

What remained of the councils was taken in hand by the government which disarmed the workers and soldiers. Ebert was to be elected president of the Reich, with Scheidemann as chancellor (prime minister), Noske was minister of War and all of the leaders were Social Democrats or right wingers. In Bavaria, a parallel process drowned the debacle in a bloodbath.

On the eve of his death, in a pathetic note, Liebknecht analyzed the defeat: "Their strength was neutralized by indecisiveness and the weakness of the leaders they had chosen for themselves. And the tidal wave of counter revolution, emanating from the most backward strata of the people and from the backlash of the propertied classes, has swept them all away and drowned them."

There was a bit of an upset on February 22, when a Councils Republic was proclaimed in Mannheim. Within three days it had been mopped up, peaceably for once. Fighting and strikes were to linger through the spring of 1919.

On March 10, it was Leo Jogiches's turn to be murdered in his prison cell. The repression in the wake of the fighting was violent. The K.P.D. was outlawed. In April, it was the Ruhr's turn to lose out. Bavaria's turn came in May.

The German Revolution had had its day.

Rather more than is commonly believed. In August a nationwide clandestine conference of the K.P.D. saw the central committee's orthodoxy pitted against the representatives of leftism (Laufenberg, Wolffheim, Ruhle, Wendel, Schroder). By October, the leftist minority had been expelled. The dissidents went on to launch the KAP, which led a faltering existence. The Leninists had just dealt the death blow to the revolution's last survivors.

In April 1920, in a congress in Hanover, the supporters of self-management attempted to set up a federation of their own. The police had no difficulty in dispersing them. They went on to found the A.A.U.D., the most prominent leader of which was Hermann Gorter, celebrated as the author of *A Reply to Lenin*.

Bavaria, 1918-1919
THE COUNCILS REPUBLIC OF BAVARIA

ERNST TOLLER (1893-1939)

What was their meaning, real men down through the ages, when they spoke of giving their lives? One often reads it in books, and hears it told as in tales of wonder, and it commands admiration, filling the heart with joy and hope, conjuring up dreams of better men and better worlds. And then it happens that what one has been reading and hearing about turns into a reality, on a lesser scale. At which point one discovers just how hard it is to be a man...

Abdellatif Laabi Reports
The Citadel of Exile (1978)

Nothing so seduces a man as free will, but there is also nothing that is so painful!

Dostoyevsky

Although very closely bound up with the German Revolution as a whole and in particular with the Berlin "Commune," the Bavarian Revolution constitutes a separate entity, on two grounds: because it was slightly later in terms of time, the serious business starting only around two months after the crushing of the Spartakists, and also because liaison with the fighters in Berlin was not established with sufficient speed right from the outset, thus allowing their common foes to crush them one at a time, without their struggles ever managing to link up.

The main difference between the two uprisings relates to the pronounced working class factor within the Berlin Commune, whereas in Bavaria the peasant element predominated. These, it should be remarked, were rabidly anti-Prussian peasants and their anti-Prussianism was to be one factor in the option they chose.

It all started in November 1918. The mutiny in Kiel triggered a situation that was ripe for explosion. The example set by the Baltic sailors and soldiers acted as a stimulant. The following day, November 7, was also the first anniversary of the Bolshevik revolution in Russia.

The disintegrating monarchy failed to withstand the uprising. Bavaria's king,

Ludwig II, simply ran away. His regiments had refused to open fire on the crowds.

The demonstrations were led by a moderate, level-headed type, Kurt Eisner, a journalist and writer who was a member of the U.S.P.D., the Socialist Party's "independent" left which was just then at odds with the "softer" socialists.

The republic was proclaimed on November 8. Its president was Kurt Eisner and he also took charge of Foreign Affairs. A socialist called Erhard Auer took over at the Interior ministry. They set up headquarters in the Landtag.

Simultaneously, the first workers' councils were established, along with the first of the self-managing cooperatives. The Munich council running the city set up shop in a beer hall, as might have been expected.

Contacts with the rebels in Berlin were brief and by November 26 they had ceased altogether. It is worth noting that in early December (1918!) a soldiers' council was counseling caution with regard to Bolshevism. As we can see, the conflict between Leninists (or Stalinists, in the language we have adopted throughout this book) is no recent development. There are numerous texts testifying to that dating from during the Russian revolution, from after it, and, at any rate from long before Budapest, Prague or the nouveaux philosophes. Unseen by those who had every interest in not seeing them. The "disclosures" about Stalinism, the Gulags and everything that we have discovered in more recent times is—as far as they are concerned—merely the latest avatar of the rearguard action on behalf of their ideological authority. A repentant Stalinist is always worse than a Stalinist: not merely a hypocrite but a dissembler to boot.

Eisner pursued a policy that was rather moderate and it was opposed by the libertarians, as well as the Communists, and, naturally, the right wing.

The libertarians' leader, the man who incarnated the Bavarian republic, was forty year-old Erich Mühsam, a quite remarkable figure, who might have developed into a political figure of some significance. The Communist leaders fell into two categories, each of them typified by a Russian Social Revolutionary (S.R.) who had quit his homeland in the wake of 1905. And, to make things even more confusing, their names were almost identical.

The orthodox, Jacobin school—what was to develop into Stalinism—was represented by Eugen Leviné from Berlin. The more leftist trend, less inflexible toward the anarchists, was represented by Max Levien.

Anarchists and Communists alike were against the elections that the government wished to see organized. Eisner had his opponents rounded up, only to free them on the eve of the elections on January 10, 1919.

On January 16, Munich hosted a huge gathering on behalf of the Councils Republic.

The right was still very powerful in Bavaria, as the elections testified. Eisner emerged in the minority. It was he who turned to Gustav Landauer, an extraordinary figure in the German revolution.

Forty-eight year old Landauer had a tremendous record behind him. A writer and journalist, he had been a significant figure within the Social Democratic Party, and subsequently in the New Community, had been associated with the Localists and with the Freilanders (the latter being utopians who wanted to settle in Africa, there to establish an anarchist commune at the beginning of the century). Longtime director of the review *Der Sozialist*, he was the author of a number of authoritative books such as 30 Socialist Theses (1907).

A follower of La Boétie, Whitman, and Francisco Ferrer, Landauer was an independent thinker, not always well-regarded by the groups from which he had readily defected. A pacifist, he was probably one of the leading personalities in the history of anarchism, on a par with the likes of Bakunin or Durruti.

He was quickly disheartened by what he saw. And came into conflict with Eugen Levine.

The army, which was rather socialist in its leanings, did not take sides in the clash. Mühsam and Egelhofer, one of the leaders of the Kiel mutiny who had returned to Bavaria, led 400 of their supporters in an attack on the Munich presses and captured them. Eisner had them ejected. Whereupon they attacked the Interior ministry. Only to find themselves being scattered.

In addition to the government, a shadow authority had been established: the authority of the soviets. The revolutionary workers' councils, soviets, the trade unions, and the S.P.D. then set up a Central Revolutionary Council, the R.A.R., which was to oppose the authority of the lawfully constituted government, without managing to defeat it.

Eisner, at the end of his tether, decided to step down. On February 21 he travelled to the Landtag building to communicate his decision. But he was murdered en route by an aristocrat, Count Arco.

GUSTAV LANDAUER.

One month previously, let us not forget, the left had massacred the Spartakists. The Landtag was broken up. A state of siege was introduced.

Formal authority was then vested in the hands of the minister Hoffmann, a Social Democrat. He it was who would try to liquidate the councils. The government styled itself the Congress of Councils of Bavaria, but that existed only on paper. To be honest, by this time, there was no one who enjoyed uncontested authority. As we all know, it is at such times that the people's initiative is articulated best. From this point on, the essential struggle was the contest between Hoffman and the R.A.R. The far left was split. Some wanted to see a Councils Republic proclaimed at last. Others opposed this, especially the Communists of the Leviné tendency. The ones from the Levien faction, on the other hand, were all for it.

This takes us into phase two of the Bavarian revolution, the phase covering the period between April and May 1919. It all started in Augsburg with a strike led by Mühsam to press home the demand that a soviet republic should be proclaimed. It was eventually to be proclaimed in Munich on April 6.

Aside from Mühsam, its main leaders would be Landauer, who took charge of education, and Ernst Toller, a twenty-six year-old playwright of some quality. Egelhofer was to be in charge of the army. The cutting edge of the republic was the R.A.R. The Communists were against it, but the S.P.D.—ever the demagogues—reluctantly played along with it. As did the peasant league and the trade unions.

This was widespread self-management in all its splendor. Everything was reorganized at ground level, including food supply and defense. Other cities also switched to self-managerial arrangements. This was the case in Augsburg, Rosenheim, and across the region. There was naturally an effort made to orchestrate all their efforts, but there was not time enough for that. The Councils Republic in fact was fated to last no more than three weeks.

Within the R.A.R., Mühsam's influence was crucial, but we should remember that Levien had a foothold there too. He worked hand in glove with the anarchists, to whom he was indebted for his release back in February from the prison to which he had been consigned by the government.

The soviets then proclaimed the dictatorship of the proletariat, a nebulous idea whose ambiguity had yet to become plain to anyone. It would not be long before the confusion was cleared up in Russia.

The Landtag was dissolved. Bureaucracy was done away with, or at any rate a start was made on that. A red army was set up under Egelhofer and the press was taken under social control. It was loudly proclaimed that : "The Bavarian Councils Republic is following the example of the Russian and Hungarian peoples." (Hungary had risen in revolt at the same time, as can be seen from the next chapter of this book.)

One of the heavyweight arguments that the revolutionaries adversaries were to deploy against them relied upon the deep-seated anti-Semitism among the common people. For Landauer was a Jew, Mühsam was a Jew, Toller was a Jew, and Silvio Gesell (who looked after the financial side of things and was one of the theorists of the free school) was a Jew. The right did not spare its criticism of them. Hoffmann, who had fled to the safety of Bamberg, orchestrated the campaign against them. There was a putsch led by the socialists and reliant upon right wing troops on April 13. Mühsam was arrested.

It took Egelhofer's Red Army (one of its commanders was Toller) to stop the putsch in its tracks. Twenty people lost their lives. It was at this point that the K.P.D. (Communist Party of Germany) swung its support behind the councils. This was, of course, merely a ploy, but the libertarians had little option but to welcome it.

The Central Council had an executive made up as follows: Levien, Leviné, Toller, and Axelrod (another figure of Russian origins). There was a general strike enforced everywhere, weapons were commandeered as were food supplies and housing was re-allocated. Hostages were even taken. There was a shortage of foodstuffs and of coal. The peasants started to resist the requisitioning, which had never been popular. The absence of newspapers fed the rumor mills, especially rumors of an anti-Semitic character.

Internal frictions were added to the open fighting against Noske's troops.

In the end, the KPD withdrew. Egelhofer adopted a tougher line: he had ten hostages drawn from among far right wingers shot. Six of them had lined their own pockets by effecting requisitions on the strength of phony army bonds.

Whereas Landauer and Mühsam had been compelled on April 10 to step down after a week in power, the Communists who came after them clung on for just five days.

Betrayed by the Socialists, outmaneuvered by the Communists who were as yet weaker than them, the libertarians fought on. On April 21, Noske regained control of Augsburg. Having dealt with the Spartakists he was keen to be done with the Bavarians.

The attack on Munich was to last for three days in early May. By May 4 Noske had crushed the Councils Republic. It was the last bastion of the German revolution. The West warmly welcomed its demise. So too did Lenin, even if this was not plainly obvious at the time.

The reprisals were to be as harsh as they had been in Berlin. Six hundred lives would be lost. Landauer was murdered on May 2, his skull crushed by rifle butts. The soldiers who killed him were commanded by the Prussian, Major Baron Von Gagern, whom Noske as he congratulated him was to compliment upon "the discreet and highly effective manner in which he had conducted the Munich operation."

Egelhofer and Leviné were captured and shot without benefit of trial. Levien managed to escape—the only one of the Bavarian leaders to do so. He returned to Russia where, like everyone else, he was to be liquidated by Stalin in 1937. Toller and Mühsam who were somehow spared, were imprisoned. Toller was to serve five years in prison only to emerge after a worldwide campaign for his release and would go into exile in the U.S.A. He committed suicide in 1939.

Mühsam, too, was saved by his arrest, as this spared him the vengeance of the bloodthirsty soldiery whom Noske had unleashed against them. He was to get 15 years in prison but was released in 1924, in the same batch as a certain Adolf Hitler (Mühsam's inclusion was a cover, as the seemingly "liberal" amnesty from which left and right benefited, was primarily an excuse to set Hitler free). Attracted for a time by Leninism (we all have our weaknesses and many an anarchist was to suffer a similar infatuation), he was to reject it after the liquidation of Makhno and of Kronstadt. When the Nazis took power, they did not forget him (he had also written a Hommage to Landauer) and he was arrested in 1933. In 1934, the Nazis hanged him before making the announcement that he had "committed suicide."

Reckless or ingenuous, or worse, his widow agreed to donate all of Mühsam's papers and archives to Stalin, who naturally disposed of such dangerous evidence of a self-managerial revolution which had almost been brought off in Germany.

> The soviets, but not the Bolsheviks. Freedom and not dictatorship. Socialism, and not state capitalism! Everything for the councils and no power above the councils! Such is our watchword, which will be the Revolution's watchword too.
>
> Rudolf Rocker
> *The Bankruptcy of Russian State Communism* (1921)

> The State is the sum of the denials of the individual liberties of all its members.
>
> Bakunin

Between 1917 and 1921, the entire world came within an ace of being turned upside down. In the wake of the upheavals in Russia and then the twin upheavals in Germany, it was Hungary's turn to stir. On close examination, in fact, it emerges that there were stirrings in many lands around the globe, almost as if the echoes of aborted revolutions were bouncing back from different cliffs. There is much that could be said about the striving toward worldwide revolution discernible over those few years, a striving discernible also in the titanic changes which took place pretty well universally in cultural and philosophical affairs, inspiring phenomena as divergent as Dada, Sexpol, expressionism, or councillism. Although these were but scattered fragments that never knit into a single phenomenon. We shall be returning to this phenomenon when we come to examine the next phase in this worldwide awakening in our chapter on May '68.

In 1919, what we today call Hungary was an Austrian possession. The Russian revolution had raised a morsel of hope which was quickly to take effect. In the Hungary of 1919, a land of aristocracy, the reprisals visited upon such incomplete revolts were severe. We ought to take note of the significant influence wielded by the Galilee Circle, a real Philosophical and political melting pot in which anarchists, revolutionary syndicalists, and far-left socialists (what are commonly called these days the SRs, Social Revolutionaries,

142

reminiscent of the PSU in today's France) rubbed shoulders.

But the uprising proper started in Budapest in October, 1918. The huge central barracks and telephone exchange were seized. In the course of these events, the aristocratic prime minister, Count Tisza, was executed.

A new government was installed under another count, Mihaly Karolyi, leader of the nationalist opposition, a man of the center-left who embodied the "decent left."

The first councils started to emerge from October 16 on. The symbol of this revolution was to be the chrysanthemu flower that in Hungary does not carry the association with death that it has in France. It was something of the equivalent of the carnations in the Portuguese revolution.

At the time, the German revolution was in full flood. Which was to have a horrific

influence upon events in Hungary. In November, the land was seized, the factories occupied, prisoners released, and communal councils set up. A start was made upon an agrarian reform that was a lot more ambitious than the one the government intended. There were councils directing the police, the students, the workers, the engineers, the clergy(!), the teachers, and the housewives. Budapest city council was under their control. The leader of the soldiers' soviet was Joszef Pogany, of whom more later.

At the same time, the republic was proclaimed. But all power was in the hands of soviets. This was on November 16. On November 17, two figures of importance arrived in Budapest. The first, Bela Kun, was returning from Russia. He was a Bolshevik. The second, Tibor Szamuelly, was an anarchist. They were the Hungarian revolution's first leaders. Hitherto, it looked as if the insurgents were coping quite well without any.

Meanwhile, of course, everything had fallen apart. A republic had been proclaimed in Vienna in Austria as well. There was a race between the King of Hungary and the Emperor of Austria to see which would be the first to abdicate. French troops in alliance with Romania launched an attack. To what end? Well, Romania had had ambitions to annex Hungary for quite some time and this had been an ongoing source of frictions between them.

Bela Kun had returned with one, very definite aim in mind: to set up a

Communist Party in Hungary, where there was not a single Communist to be found. He gathered together 11 individuals and launched a party, complete with its review, *Voros Ujsag*. He would have to wait until March 1919 before his party amounted to anything.

In Szeged, a workers' council also seized power and supervised food distribution. Throughout the revolution and at the instigation of Andorka Kovacs, it was to be the most radical presence.

Kun was an orthodox Stalinist, even if Stalin had not yet properly "arrived" by that time. He had but one idea in his head: to make the Hungarian revolution the closest possible imitation of the Russian revolution.

Szamuelly, also returned from Russia, had been closely involved in the soviet revolution. He was an admirer of Kropotkin and had met him in person. He and Kun were acquaintances and were to work hand in glove. In those days, it was still possible to find a Communist Party with anarchist members! And Kun had no option if he was to build a Communist Party on just 12 people—anarchists included. Anyway, Kun tried to make reassuring noises: declaring among other things, "The dictatorship of the proletariat means (…) the straightforward seizure by the people of the tools of production." Out of craftiness or naivete, he gave every encouragement to soviets. These soviets, who had not been waiting for his permission before starting their operations, were spreading like wildfire. Joszef Pogany was quickly admitted to the Karolyi government as commissar for war. And a queer sort of commissar for war who had no compunction about declaring: "The soldiers' council can have but one program; to see the army disbanded once and for all." Instead, the people were to be armed directly.

Karolyi's agrarian reform was a fiasco. Karolyi may well have been a moderate with an interest in the Russian model, but he was still a Jacobin at heart. Instead of urging the peasants to get themselves organized, he imposed technocratic reforms which promptly failed. For instance, rationing of sugar was to be introduced, when Hungary was a bulk producer. Karolyi launched the much needed land survey, but the lawyers in charge of carrying out the work contrived to ensure that it resulted in as much litigation as possible, which lined their pockets but made the survey useless.

The peasant soviets, on the other hand, seized the lands of the estate-owners, setting up cooperatives instead of stupidly parceling out the land, and they launched cooperatives handling purchases, sales, and production.

Karolyi alienated the upper bourgeoisie by introducing one good measure—taxation of large fortunes. As for the Hungarian Communist Party, it launched a rent strike. The councils kept the factories, weapons plants, gasworks, and construction industry in operation. Self-managed hotels and newspapers operated as normal.

Politically the situation was moving along. The Hungarian Social Democratic Party, the H.S.D.P. (which owed its foundation to the former Communard, Frankel) expelled its left wing. The Third International was launched. Kun was arrested and beaten up in March 1919. All of this culminated on March 20, after a huge demonstration calling for socialization, in the downfall of the Karolyi government.

Then the H.S.D.P. and the H.C.P. amalgamated. Fear was the spur: each was afraid of the other and saw this as a way of controlling the threat.

Kun was released from prison. Everybody thought that now Lenin's Russia would help them and send troops to fend off the Romanians who were making dangerous progress. On March 21, 1919, the Hungarian Councils Republic was born. Its life span was to be exactly 133 days.

There was a final falling-out between the Bolsheviks and the anarchists. The party that emerged from the amalgamation of the two great left-wing parties took the name of the Unified Socialist Party of Hungary (U.S.P.H.); within three months it had become the Party of the Socialist and Communist Workers of Hungary. Self-management was proliferating but the authoritarians were ready for it.

Kun, the Communists and the Socialists (trade unionists included)—being already very hierarchy-conscious and bureaucratized—flirted with the soviets. At the time, power in Hungary lay with the Council of People's Commissars. Its chairman was a Social Democrat, Sandor Garbaï. Kun was in charge of foreign affairs, Pogany of war (with Szamuelly as his adjutant) and, note this, the man in charge of public education was 34-year-old Gyorgy Lukacs, not yet the brilliant philosopher into which he turned, but well on his way to becoming such. Even then he was very popular in Hungary and this experience was to prove crucial to the subsequent flavor of his works.

The anarchist movement was in the throes of crisis and split into two. At the same time, the Council of People's Commissars adopted its first measures: generally speaking, it endorsed everything that the soviets had done over the past six months. The left had no option, not being in a position to defy the will of the people. The soviets were granted recognition and formalized, the land was taken under social ownership and trial judges were henceforth to be elected and subject to recall. And so on.

Tipped off in advance. Lenin asked Kun for assurances against the Social Democrats and asked for the date of the first congress of the soviets (it was possible at congresses to try some chicanery and seize the advantage). He also wanted to know the precise meaning of all the talk about dictatorship of the proletariat.

There were other bad omens: many of those who had rallied to the new government were suspect. For instance, support for it had been expressed by Count Karolyi and indeed by the Archduke Franz Joseph. A National Assembly of Councils was also set up. The soviets were to retain control over the security forces, the civil service, the banks, food supplies, production, and the seizure of castles and works of art.

By April, all urgent measures were in place: an inventory had been made of consumer goods, price controls had been introduced, buildings had been nationalized, certain civil servants and police officers dismissed (and replaced by hand-picked volunteer militias). Supporters of self-management forced Kun to accept self-managing farming. Panicking, the Social Democrats obstructed all these steps. So did Kun, primarily because whatever was beyond his control frightened him.

Liaison with the revolutions in Berlin and Bavaria proved elusive (they had been crushed too quickly and the Hungarian revolutionaries had been a bit lackadaisical). There were a few executions carried out, but only a very few.

There were certain results produced by the farming sector. But the Social Democrats, Communists, and libertarians were continually sniping at one another. Kun could not see beyond bringing everything in the world under state control. Sometimes, he found some middle-of-the-road stratagem, as he did with the railways: they were taken into state ownership but handed over to the soviets who were to keep them running as normal.

The cooperative stores were reserved for unionized workers: so the bourgeoisie flooded into the civil service en masse, where it found it easy to lie low. Fortunes were frozen, the banks socialized, and store managers elected by the soviets. A black market emerged. Little prepared for such problems as these, the revolutionaries were floundering. Strict rationing was introduced.

Accommodation was taken into communal ownership and everyone assigned his space. This proved a success: district councils re-housed 300,000 people. Rents were cancelled for the duration of the commune.

The sexes were proclaimed equal and free unions were legalized (a world first!). While there was not a single woman on the Council of People's Commissars, a women's liberation charter was promulgated, dealing with basic issues like education, rape, pregnancy, marriage and, prostitution. Churches, playgrounds, and holiday camps were set up. In the schools, rudimentary sex education replaced catechism classes. There was a recruitment drive aimed at getting education back on the rails.

Entertainment outlets at rock bottom prices were to operate throughout the commune's life. For the most part, these had been transformed by Max Rheinhart, whose stage decor became a byword. Art and culture were to develop as never before witnessed in Hungary and the government commissioned huge numbers of posters from the most modern artists. Within four months, 31 films would be made! Confiscated objects of art were placed on exhibition, masterpieces of Hungarian and international art that

Hungarians had never been able to view before.

The great names of Hungarian culture banded together in the artist and writers' associations: on the musical side, there was Bartok, and on the literary side there was Tibor Dery, Bela Balasz, and Lajos Kassak, not to mention Lukacs. Kun was personally hostile to any modern art form, an imitator in this of his mentor, Lenin, whose conventionality in cultural matters was legendary.

Pharmaceutical treatment was free of charge and basic social insurance was introduced and all minority languages were rehabilitated. Quite some accomplishment for just 133 days!

Three quotations by way of illustration. The first is from Lukacs: "Politics is only the means, the end is culture." The second is from Lajos Kassak: "With us, art is not wanton play. With us, the beautiful is tantamount to the good. With us, the aim of life is not the class struggle, the class struggle being merely one means of reaching the rounded man whose only way of life is revolutionary action." The third comes from Bela Balasz: "The Commissariat being perfectly well aware that art needs complete freedom in order to survive, it does everything it can to prevent literature's turning into official literature and, for its own part, places literary freedom beyond reach of harassment, beyond even its own influence." It could not be clearer: the Hungarian intellectuals, spokesmen for a popular revolution, knew where they were bound for. So too did their adversaries.

For the political squabbling was still going on. Following Kun's reckless chicanery, the libertarians had split: Pogawny and Szamuelly, who was in charge of National Defence, resigned on April 2, 1919. Another resignation followed, that of Cserny, an anarchist who had set up an assault commando called "The Lenin lads!" (As yet the manner in which Lenin was treating the Russian anarchists was not fully known, that would not remain the case for long.). These resignations came under pressure from the revolutionaries, who had long since grasped that Bela Kun was a very wily, slavish, and hypocritical petty chieftain. It was Kun (acting in concert with one Boëhm) who would take over the Defence portfolio.

It has to be said that, in terms of the war, things were not going well: as the government had shown itself to be incompetent, the workers centuries (self-managed units) gave a lead in the fighting. The Romanians launched a large-scale offensive. Kun had wasted too much time and the Entente forces were behind the Romanians. The cry went up: "The fatherland is in danger."

In the end, Hungary's Red Army went

on to the offensive. It made incursions into Slovakia (for Czechoslovakia too was aiming to carve off a slice of Rumanian territory). The Entente forces were primarily concerned to break the back of the revolution which might prove contagious and afford too great an advantage to Lenin (according to them).

At the start of June, Karolyi threw in his hand and fled to Vienna. From there he would head the right opposition after that. In Szeged, a shadow counter revolutionary government was set up. It was a hollow sham, funded by Marshal Franchet d'Esperey, and it was headed by a certain Horthy, who would later re-emerge as a leading agent of the Nazis. In Vienna, there was also an Anti-Bolshevik Committee under British direction. Clemenceau, then in power in France, a one-time socialist turned shooter of striking workers, issued an ultimatum to the Hungarians: they must evacuate Slovakia. That very day, Kun offered to negotiate with (a defeated!) Czechoslovakia. There was utter confusion.

The Romanian offensive, however, forced the Hungarians to retreat. It was a rout. Once again, the soviets rescued the situation. The peasants themselves laid on an effective guerrilla campaign. Szamuelly persuaded Kun to leave the conduct of the fighting to the soldiers' councils. The Social Democrats strenuously opposed this: they were the ones who had been in charge from the outset and who had brought the country to the brink of disaster, but they were not about to give it up.

Lenin, for his part, stayed well out of it. His troops were waiting for something before they would intervene. What, no one knows. The crushing of the soviets, no doubt. Also, one of Lenin's zealot supporters, the economist Jenö Varga, who went on to become a celebrated Stalinist and to lead Hungarian agriculture to catastrophe, was a rabid opponent of anything reminiscent of self-management.

It was only in May that Szamuelly forced a decision. There was a massive mobilization and a well conducted counterattack brought a succession of spectacular victories. Councils sprang up everywhere in the wake of the victorious forces.

Meanwhile, in Budapest a Congress of Councils met on June 14, 1919. The matter of affiliation to the International arose. Kun was keen to espouse the description "Communist Party": in fact he was afraid that the anarchists might beat him to the draw and we ought to remember that many anarchists would long describe themselves as "communists" in the original sense of the word, in that they had devised a communist theory long before Marx and his successors (this may seem a bizarre point today, such has been the Leninist and Marxist, generally efforts to take out a patent on the term communism.)

Varga drew up an assessment of the economic position: a million hectares had been taken into social ownership, as had 800 banks. He proposed that the bureaucracy be expanded in order to run it all. It was primarily its interest that he was looking out for.

On June 16, the offensive proved so successful that a Councils Republic was proclaimed in Slovakia. But the Communists turned traitor the very next day. The push was halted by Bela Kun, who, being frightened by the possibility of a probable victory for the soviets, opted instead to enter into negotiations with a Clemenceau who was less demanding! The soldiers of the Hungarian Red Army then withdrew from Slovakia, which they had so recently conquered.

The anarchists were outraged. The Slovak Social Democrats, abandoned to their fate, were butchered by the Czechs.

All of a sudden these Czechs seized the tiger by the tail, attacking and defeating the Hungarians at Kisuszallas. It was a rout.

Kun's downfall came on July 31. He fled to Vienna. He was replaced by a Social Democrat and trade unionist government. Szamuelly attempted to organize resistance and tried to enter Austria to that end. He was recognized at the border and was murdered by the frontier guards who were to peddle a story about his having "committed suicide." Some peasants disinterred his body to mutilate it. The other anarchist leader, Corvin, was hanged.

On August 6, the Social Democrat paper government was swept aside as the reactionary Friedrich took power. Private property was re-introduced. By the very next day, the Rumanian army was in Budapest.

Mihaly Horthy became army chief. In the countryside, the fighting lingered until August 15. As ever, the reprisals were horrific. In this the fascists were abetted, belatedly, by Stalin, who was to kill off the survivors who had escaped to the U.S.S.R. Some 30,000 members of the Hungarian soviets were dispatched to Stalin's concentration camps, with 9,000 lives lost.

There may be surprise expressed at the lame response from the revolutionaries. It has to be said that Kun had cut the legs from under them and broken their morale. Many, disheartened, simply gave up. The peasants were no longer sustaining them. And, to cap it all, Kun had had 5,000 Polish Jews deported. The Red Army was to be crushed with ease. Kun's treachery had done him little good: the Entente was to honor not a single one of the commitments it had given.

He was to flee to Russia where he would fight against Makhno and become a Zinovievist (birds of a feather flock together, after all). In 1918, before events in Budapest he had made a name for himself by cracking down on revolutionary socialists. Kun was a high-ranking member of the Comintern when he was arrested in 1937. According to a contemporary dyed-in-the-wool Stalinist, Gyorgy Bersany (in the anthology *Budapest* 1919 published by Editeurs Français Réunis) "the circumstances of his death are not known. What we do know is that, like so many others, he was a victim of breaches of law generated by the personality cult." What Bersany means is that his political friends did him to death in the depths of some prison on the grounds that he was becoming too important. But Bersany's is such a pretty phrase that it deserves to be reproduced here.

In Szeged, Franchet d'Esperey personally dispatched 600 revolutionaries (including Kovacs) to hard labor. The Rumanian occupation was to end in

November 1919. Horthy assumed power when, after allowing restoration of the monarchy (in February 1920), he mounted a coup d'état and proclaimed himself regent (March 1920).

He was to line his pockets with the property of the revolutionaries. Looting and summary executions were to be the normal fare in post-revolutionary periods which have not lasted.

Hungary was literally dismembered by her conquerors—Yugoslavia, Rumania, Austria, Czechoslovakia, everybody snatched a piece. A third of the population overall wound up living outside of Hungary's borders after that.

THE RIO GALLEGOS WORKERS' ASSOCIATION

EL TOSCANO

There are defeats which are really victories and victories that are more shameful than defeats.

Karl Liebknecht's final article, written on January 14, 1919, on the eve of his murder.

Our defeats today prove nothing except that those of us engaged in the battle against infamy are not sufficiently numerous.

Bertolt Brecht
Against the Objectors

In 1920, Argentina—and especially Patagonia—was in ferment. It can be argued without any exaggeration that at the time it was one of the world's main hotbeds of revolution. Many immigrants had settled there for economic reasons—the availability of work, as well as for political reasons—in that the exiles found there an international community ready to welcome them with open arms.

Hence the blend of experiences, theories, and the unsolicited spirit of brotherhood that was to leave its mark on these few years.

The great ranchers seemed untouchable. Yet the overly exploited Farm laborers launched a determined strike. The contest was a violent one and the police were very harsh. At first, in February 1921, the government looked as if it was about to cave in to the peasants' and workers' demands; it awarded certain wage increases and acknowledged that wages should be paid for the days spent on strike. In return, the strike should be ended.

Among the extremists who had for several months now been waging a veritable armed struggle, there followed the inevitable disintegration: around 350 of them laid down their arms and gave it up, returning to work. That left 200 diehards. It was they who were to write the name of Rio Gallegos into the history books.

While the Argentinean and world press railed against them, workers' communities grew and managed their own affairs just about everywhere, in Puerto Deseado, Santa Cruz, San Julian, and above all in Rio Gallegos where the workers' association was to become a real force to be reckoned with. It ought to be said that in its ranks it numbered some extraordinary figures:

—Alfredo Fonte, born in 1888 (and thus aged 33 years), who was known by the nickname of El Toscano. An Italian émigré, he was—in spite of some dissent—to be their unchallenged leader, as he was the most determined of them all.

—Jose Aicardi, who was known simply as "68"—the number he had had when a convict in Ushuaia prison. He had travelled widely. At the outset at any rate, he was to provide the military leadership.

—Antonio Soto, born in 1898 and thus only 23 at this point) was secretary of the Rio Gallegos Workers' Association. He had arrived in Rio Gallegos with a travelling theatre group. A Spaniard, he was one of several personalities influential after May 1920 and frequently clashed with El Toscano in that he was firmly in favor of action within the law and opposed to direct action.

After the carrot came the stick. The government harried the workers. In fact it had a lot of them arrested, especially the trade unionists. There was a proliferation of strikes: in retaliation, the country was rocked by some attacks and hostages were even taken on occasion.

This mini-guerrilla war was fuelled by extremists of every hue. The international context was to be a significant factor in the whole affair. Business was booming for the American and British corporations and their governments were anxious about the safety of their nationals (the same old refrain). The press and these governments spare nothing in their efforts to vilify and bring down the "bandits." The final straw was to come with the sentencing to death in the USA of Sacco and Vanzetti, two innocent anarchists who were to be executed six years later in spite of world opinion. The verdict in their case unleashed fury among revolutionaries in whose ranks libertarians (and consequently, internationalism) were in the ascendancy. The extremists won the argument and an all-out armed struggle was launched.

Along with 200 men, El Toscano took to the brush and controlled a whole region which was run along self-managerial lines. Elsewhere, they commandeered weapons, horses, and the foodstuffs which fed both the guerrillas and the strikers who had stayed behind. The red and black flag fluttered at the head of their columns.

There was wholesale direct democracy. It so happened that El Toscano, a member of the Rio Gallegos association, was side-lined by his colleagues who were afraid of his unduly overpowering personality. They recalled him on a regular basis.

It has to be said that things were proceeding apace on the other side. The government sent in the troops under the command of the formidable Colonel Varela. The struggle took a violent turn.

Rio Gallegos appointed a new military commander in the shape of Ramón Outerelo, an erstwhile Spanish sailor, known as "El Coronel." There were two columns, led by Antonio Soto and by José Font, alias "Facon Grande" (Big Knife), respectively. They would oversee the later fighting.

The ranchers took off the gloves: confident that victory would be theirs, the great estate owners succumbed to a blood-lust: one of them who had lost 27 horses to raiders, had 27 farm laborers executed in retaliation.

The revolutionaries were short of weapons and above all of communications resources and little by little they found themselves being encircled. El Toscano and his band were captured and he was executed. Outerelo, too, perished in an ambush.

Facon Grande, on the other hand, successfully defeated Varela in battle and saved face. The government was alive to the danger. So was Varela. Facon Grande was promised an amnesty for himself and for his men. Well aware that to go on fighting was hopeless, as they were now badly weakened, he agreed to surrender.

Varela thereupon had his entire band murdered. Facon Grande he had shot where he stood, without benefit of trial. His officers seized the body, tied it to a stake, and roasted it over a fire lit for that express purpose. Relishing their success and blood-crazed now, they danced around the corpse and fired shots as it roasted on a spit to their cries of delight.

As a finishing touch, the workers' pay was cut by 50 percent. One thousand and five hundred workers were butchered. For the succeeding quarter of a century, Argentina was to see no strikes or rebellions of any description.

By the way, it has to be said that, having stalked Colonel Varela for some time, a young, nonviolent German, by the name of Kurt Wilckens, fair-haired and an underpaid proletarian, threw a bomb at him. Wilckens used his own body to shield a young girl who happened to be passing at the time. Both he and Varela were injured. Varela drew his saber but Wilckens finished him off with five bullets from his Colt. "His killing days are over now. I have avenged my brothers," Wilckens told the policemen who dragged him away. Sentenced to life imprisonment, he was murdered, beaten to death by a rifle butt in his prison cell a few months later by Jorge Ernesto Pérez Millán Temperley, a 24-year-old fascist and member of the Patriotic League. The murderer was to receive a light sentence and would be sent to a mental hospital, pending his release.

It was there that Guerman Boris Wladimirovitch, an inmate of Russian extraction, a crippled bank-robber and violent anarchist, successfully killed him in 1925. The circle was complete: Wladimirovitch was sentenced to 25 years imprisonment and died in Ushuaia penitentiary.

Spain, 1936
THE SPANISH REVOLUTION AND THE DURRUTI COLUMN

> The enthusiasm for destruction is also an enthusiasm for creativity.
>
> Bakunin

> Better the fascists than the anarchists.
> Ilya Ehrenburg
> *Novy Mir* (1962)

> Under the dictatorship of the proletariat, two, three, or four parties may exist, on just one condition: that one party be in power and the others in prison. Anybody who fails to understand this just has not got the slightest idea about the dictatorship of the proletariat, about the Bolshevik party.
> Tomsky (trade unionist liquidated by Stalin) *Pravda* (1927)

In 1933, the Left, ranging from moderate social democrats through to anarchists, became the majority in Spain for the first time since the beginning of the 1930s. However, it had just missed its chance for power in the elections. The National Confederation of Labor (C.N.T.) established in 1911, and its sister organization, the Iberian Anarchist Federation (F.A.I.), which embraced libertarians from Spain and from Portugal and had been in existence since 1927, had declined to be associated with the wishy-washy socialists.

Their boycott tactics had proved very effective. In May 1936, by contrast, they determined to conclude an alliance with the Left which was offering concessions. There was a landslide vote for the Left. Catalonia returned Lluis Jover Companys as the president of its Generalitat (home rule government). This signaled the start of what has come to be called the Spanish Revolution, which is amazing, for it was merely a lawful assumption of power by a Popular Front, made in the image of the one so recently formed in neighboring France.

The C.N.T. was a mighty trade union confederation. It had for a time been affiliated to the Third International (back in 1919), before quitting with quite a to-do after the massacres carried out on workers (notably in Kronstadt) in 1922. This was a union without bureaucracy, having no apparatus and no paid staff (it had only one paid officer!). Yet in 1936 it represented a membership of one million—out of a total population of 24 million! For the record, the P.O.U.M., the C.N.T.'s nearest rival organization, had barely 10,000 members at this point. All of the C.N.T.'s cares worked in factories or offices. Its daily newspaper was *Solidaridad Obrera* and the F.A.I. had its own *Tierra y Libertad*.

At this point, the Communist Party of Spain (PCE) was virtually nonexistent. To counter the libertarian organizations, Stalin was to import a ready-made party, making use of and turning around right-wing workers—all of the other sort were affiliated either to the C.N.T. or to the social democratic trade union, the UGT. In pursuit of his aim, he made full use of the International Brigades. Communists—sometimes foreigners—infiltrated the police, the army, the civil service, and whenever possible, captured the positions of importance.

And they did not forget to fight against the legitimate social democratic government of Largo Caballero. At the outset of the civil war, they frustrated its plans to strike in Extremadura, where it could well have won.

The process of liberalization was underway in Spain. Spain still had a colonialist foothold in Morocco. Moroccan revolutionaries were keen to rise in revolt in July 1936 with C.N.T. support. They even had the backing of Companys. However, Companys needed the green light from the French Socialists—they being the only ones in a position to furnish the requisite weaponry. Léon Blum refused all assistance. So the uprising never took place.

This is a crucial point. The civil war might well have been averted if it had. It was in fact in Spanish Morocco that the fascists were to hatch their putsch and it was there that it started. A fascist uprising took the place of the one that ought to have taken place there. It was led by the quickly rising star of Francisco Franco, who had made a name for himself with the savagery of his repression of a revolt in Asturias in 1934. The fascist revolt occurred on July 7, 1936.

On July 18, a putsch was mounted on the territory of Spain proper. On July 19, Andalusia was captured. By July 21, a third of the country had fallen to the rebels. The C.N.T. retaliated immediately with a general strike. In Catalonia, the fascist attack was beaten off. President Companys proposed to the C.N.T. that it assume power. Scarcely prepared for that task, the libertarians declined. However, they exercised a de facto authority. In Aragon, for example, where the republican mayors and leaders had turned tail and run, the communes held out on their own, managing their own affairs for as long as the fighting lasted.

In some places held by the C.N.T., those in charge organized distribution of consumer vouchers, introducing a family wage, overhauling local finances, printing their own currency and a point-based consumer voucher system (money having been abolished), and set up cooperatives and municipal storehouses where they marshalled whatever businessmen had not fled. They defeated the July revolt (remember that the men were all on the fronts), commandeering farm machinery and livestock, setting everyone to work, especially the womenfolk.

There was collectivization on a greater or smaller scale, depending on the locality. They had no one to rely upon except themselves. No help would be forthcoming from the social democratic nations abroad. The danger poised by the revolution outweighed the fascist threat. The French Popular Front, headed by Blum, refused again to lift a finger to help.

From autumn 1936 on, there was Stalin's promise of regular supplies of weapons. In return, the legitimate government was to use all of its resources to apply a brake to the revolutionary process (which would set a very poor example for the remaining positionists still alive in the U.S.S.R.). In the U.S.S.R. too, a non-Leninist revolution was regarded as a greater danger than fascism. Anyway, the Russian Communists were on the verge of concluding an agreement with Hitler and they would shortly be supplying arms to Mussolini for the invasion of Abyssinia.

Only in exceptional cases did any of the Russian arms make it through to front-line fighters. The front was manned by anarchists and members of the P.O.U.M., whereas the Communists in the towns in their rear had weapons galore (and would soon be finding this very useful). Stalin was the sole arms-supplier available. It was arms from him, or no arms at all.

In a recruitment drive, the Stalinists easily stirred up the rich farmers and moderate bourgeoisie hostile to self-management and collectivization. The Right, having donned camouflage, bounced back with a vengeance, discreetly operating through the administrative posts held by the P.C.E.

In November 1936, at the insistence of the C.N.T.'s general secretary, Horacio Martinez Prieto, libertarians agreed to join the Largo Caballero government. Juan Garcia Oliver became minister of Justice, Juan Peiró took charge of Industry, Juan López Sánchez took over at Commerce and Federica Montseny at Health. There they were, in the cabinet, powerless and in positions of insignificance, furnishing the respectable left with its alibi. They represented the soft leadership of a C.N.T. that was hard-line but which had been eaten away by incipient bureaucracy. The mediocrity of its leaders, who fell for every promise made to them, was to prove a considerable factor in the defeating of the revolution.

In December, Stalin gave his answer: he would offer formal support to the government, in exchange for decision-making posts—but not for him meaningless posts. For instance, he wanted the Supreme Security Council, the secret police body. Two days later, *Pravda* was brazenly announcing: "In Catalonia, the mopping up of Trotskyists and anarcho-syndicalists has already begun. It will be carried out with the same vigor as in the U.S.S.R.."

Earlier, after the proclamation of the Republic, The Communist paper *Batalla* had carried the headline: "F.A.I.—ism = Fascism."

Little by little the Caballero government was to slide into slavish obedience to Stalin. And abandon the accoutrements of its powers to the Stalinists, local and international. On December 24, 1936, for instance, it banned the carrying of weapons. So, while the Communists were betraying their "allies," the people were denied the means to defend themselves. From December 27 on, a campaign of vilification was mounted against the P.O.U.M., the Workers' Party for Marxist Unification, which, although Trotskyite, was close to the revolutionaries (in spite of his hatred for anything redolent of self-management, the exiled Trotsky was to urge the P.O.U.M. to ally itself with the C.N.T.—but his missive was intercepted) and it advocated a united front which anarchists stupidly rejected "so as not to get involved in politics."

It was the beginning of the shambles on the left, especially within the International Brigades made up of activists from all over the world who had rushed to the aid of the Republic and who were to be adroitly manipulated by Stalin. The Comintern (Third International) had in any case long since infiltrated the ranks of all its adversaries. Those who proved of service in paving the way for the grand treachery of May 1937 were to be richly rewarded after the war: take Enrico Berlinguer or Jacques Duclos, for instance—they reached the top of the Italian and French Communist parties, respectively.

A soft-handed start was made to the butchery. Curious killing passed unnoticed. In January 1937, a right-wing moderate, Joan Comorera, minister for supply, abolished the Supply Committees and Bread Committees. Plainly this was indicative of a deliberately contrived food shortage that had a particular impact upon the fighters on the front lines.

After April, it was weapons that were being withheld (completely) from Catalonia. This overall boycott of the revolution was mounted by the Stalinists and also by right-wing social democrats and by the moderate right-wingers (a term indicating the non-Francoist right, the right-wingers who abided by the voters' decisions).

And what was the C.N.T. doing all the while? When I say the C.N.T. I mean those close to its activities as well. Not all members of the union were anarchists— far from it—but they were all keen to defend autonomy, self-management, and direct democracy.

In mid-February, the collectives in Aragon formed a federation in Caspe: 275 villages, banded together into 25 federations, speaking for 40,000 active members. And this latter figure just grew and grew.

Borders between villages were ignored and volunteers travelled from one township to another, the forests were tended, livestock herds increased, and seed sowed. Experimental farms and nurseries were established and small holders were allowed to stay outside of the collectives, although, on the other hand, they were not entitled to enjoy the benefits accruing from membership. In contrast, the assets of fascists were impounded and the peasants assumed power on their farms. Technical schooling was arranged, leisure and cultural activities organized, and unemployment evaporated as if by magic. Wages were paid on a weekly basis and the townships catered for refugees. The police chief was replaced by a defense committee. For the minutiae of this activity, the reader ought to consult the accounts of collectivization in Graus and Binéfar in Gaston Leval's remarkable study.

Come harvest time, people were mobilized street by street, especially the young girls. The crops harvested were used primarily to feed the men at the front. In many places, marriage was done away with, but every new couple was entitled to accommodation and furnishings. The electricity was the power they themselves produced and use was made of water courses. A dam was built at Villajoyosa to bring water to a million almond trees. This out-and-out economic miracle (taking into consideration the circumstances and the time involved) was the achievement of solid organization and imaginative planning. Collective teams would tackle a particular problem and work on several villages at a time.

In Levante, the peasants even devised a brand-new dessert, "orange honey"! Elsewhere, they came up with a new poultry feed. To counter illiteracy, a secretarial school was set up under the Moncada Agricultural University (with its 300 students). Wealthy villages helped their poorer counterparts. In a socialized restaurant, a meal was only a quarter of the price charged in a normal restaurant.

Production was sharply stepped up everywhere. In pursuit of this increase, libertarians had no hesitation in diverting streams, clearing the land, erecting mills, setting up farms, and refectories.

Inside the unions, collectivization was also on the agenda. Collectivized factories and transport services were emblazoned with the notice "Incautado" (impounded) to indicate that the workers were now in control. They even assumed responsibility for the debts incurred by the previous capitalist owners. For the first time ever, the tram service operated properly in Spain: they were painted red and black, the twin colors of the revolution.

And all of this was the work of just a few months! During this short span of real power, libertarians organized and overhauled the water, gas, and power services; overhauling the railways, medical services, educational services (in conjunction with all the other republican factions), maternity services, and the provision of mills. In Elda, they even devised 900 new shoe styles. In Barcelona, they launched a brand new funicular railway service.

On the front lines, the columns wrought miracles daily in spite of the embargo placed upon supplies of arms and ammunition to them by the Communists in their rear. The Durruti Column (see below) was the most remarkable and most respected of these columns. We might also mention the Iron Column, made up of ex-convicts, old lags, and others, freed by the revolution. Fed by the peasants, they captured their weaponry from the enemy or simply stole them. Looked at askance by the republicans (who dismissed them as "bandits" or, worse still, as "uncontrollables"), they were nevertheless among the most dependable revolutionaries, whether in battle or in day-to-day life. Property-owners were terrorized and the Communists simply itched to have done with the Iron Column. For months, the column's very egalitarian members drew not a penny of their pay: their delegates had no special status and no special privileges over the ordinary column member. In March 1937, they were to be incorporated into the regular army.

In March 1937 came the first friction, which was promptly snuffed out by the C.N.T.'s ministers. But in May, the Communists and the right mounted their definitive attack on the libertarians and on the P.O.U.M.. A week of bloodshed in Barcelona began on May 3. Although conflict had been on the cards for quite some time, the treachery of the Communists left most of the combatants stunned.

The chief of police, Rodriguez Sala, had taken it upon himself to issue orders without reference to the government. After ferocious fighting, he drove the C.N.T. out of the Telephone Exchange which had been held by it and been managed by the workforce. A general strike erupted and everybody seized their weapons and took to the streets.

But Rodriguez Sala had spent the previous few months building up an 11,000 strong armed police force (who might have proved very useful on the battle front). When the alarm was raised, the anarchists fought with rifle, pistol, and grenade but they were facing Communist artillery, Communist machine guns and Communist tanks—the sort of equipment that the Durruti Column had been asking for for months, only to be fobbed off with the excuse that it was elsewhere on the front!

This time, the anarchist ministers halted nothing. As blind as ever, they even tried to preach calm to the armed workers and merely provoked their wrath. The workers felt that there was treachery all around them. For some months, the Communist workers had been sabotaging the self-managed firms, while the authorities had been "commandeering" the equipment needed to keep them in operation. Allegedly so that it might be dispatched to the front lines, which had of course been pressing for the equipment…but never ever got it. There were whole depots filled with machinery and equipment stockpiled to no purpose.

The fighting only lasted until May 6, at which point the anarchist ministers intervened. The Stalinists had captured Barcelona city center while the C.N.T. controlled the suburbs. The order to fall back came before the fight was finished. Solidaridad Obrera was even to denounce the erection of barricades.

As calm returned, the government sent in 6,000 men to disarm the workers. Officially, everybody was to surrender his weapons, but the Communists were to be allowed to hold on to theirs! The incident had cost 500 lives and left 1,000 wounded. The central government had moved to Valencia. The C.N.T. was beaten and the F.A.I. outlawed.

At the same time, the P.O.U.M. too was targeted. Its headquarters in the Hotel Falcón in the Plaza del Teatro in Barcelona was turned into a fortress with barricades and sandbags, its terraces bristling with militias. They too were to observe the cease-fire. To tell the truth, the tragic retreat by the C.N.T. leadership was taken very ill. The Friends of Durruti group, the most determined group of all perhaps, even in the absence of its hero who had been killed in November 1936, ordered that the fighting should be carried on. But no one followed the lead they gave.

As anticipated, there was a crisis in the government. On paper, the right-wing republicans assumed power. In fact, real power lay with the Communists. From then on, the Communists alone were the sole organized force. Stalinist ministers held the key positions. Take Uribe, the minister of Agriculture: his first move was to insist that the P.O.U.M. be outlawed. The new prime minister was Juan Negrin.

There was to be a horrifying crackdown on the P.O.U.M.. A number of its leaders were former associates of the Third International. Most were done to death in the secret prisons which the PCE had scattered around the city. Andrés Nin and Kurt Landau were the best known of the victims. Nin had been Trotsky's secretary before going on to defy him by launching the P.O.U.M.. The crackdown was spearheaded by, among others, Orlov, the head of the NKVD in Spain, one of whose lieutenants, Carlos Contreras (alias Vittorio Vidali) had Nin murdered while his killers acted out the farce of posing as Nazis pretending to release him only to murder him.

Pillage, murder, illegal abductions (the government was never to be briefed on the whole thing), private NKVD prisons (with 15,000 inmates!), such was to be the lot of revolutionaries.

In August, a ban was placed on criticism of Stalin or of the U.S.S.R.. The last remaining bastion of the revolution—the Aragon Defence Council—was wound up and its chairman, Joaquin Ascaso, was arrested. Uribe, the Agriculture minister, was systematically with rare venom to dismantle everything that had been achieved. Divisions pulled out of the front lines for the purpose of being dispatched against the communes. Their chief commander was the sinister Lister who was to display somewhat less enthusiasm when confronting Franco a few months later (when he simply took to his heels). It was Lister who deployed the International Brigades to break up the collectives.

From 1938 onward, the great estate-owners were invited to recover their estates. The factories found their self-managerial structures being dismantled.

Uribe used a simple ruse to carry out his tasks discreetly. He would send in his supporters "to assist" the peasants. Then he would send in the police (who were also Communist-controlled) "to requisition" their harvests for "the front," which, naturally, never set eyes on them. Such "assistance" would subsequently provide the basis for hints that the Communists had organized the communes.

Order was soon restored. When the fascists came, there was nothing left for them to do. It had all been done for them. This treachery, licensed by the lawful government, is reminiscent of the betrayal of the Paris Commune when Thiers reached an accommodation with the German occupation forces over the crushing of the Commune, which he viewed as the greater danger.

Inside the army, ranks, saluting, hierarchy—all abolished by the revolutionaries—were restored. Once again, soldiers were in receipt of lower pay than their officers.

And calumny ran riot. The press abroad blithely echoed tales of an "anarcho-Trotskyite" plot, glossing over the nuances: it was either totally pro-Nazi or utterly pro-Stalinist. No matter, it told the same story in either case. The Spanish socialist press was to pull off the feat of allowing the events in Barcelona to pass unreported at all!

Forty years on, Santiago Carrillo himself was to concede: "The collectivization forced upon the peasants, and the small-holders who found themselves stripped of their livestock, their hams, and their produce, in return for worthless vouchers turned a segment of those social strata off the fight for the Republic." If only that had been the only culprit...

Once the revolution had been finished off, Stalin was to send no more arms, as if succeeding operations were only a trifling matter. His supporters were to be all the more easily swept aside as a result. As for the arms which he had sent, he received payment for those in gold.

Apart from Orlov, his chief henchman was an old acquaintance, Antonov-Ovseyenko, whom we met earlier grappling with Makhno. Within a short time, Stalin was to get rid of him, for he was decidedly looking out for interests of his own. Lister was to outlast him. He went to become the leader of the orthodox Communist Party in exile in Moscow (as opposed to Carrillo's "Euro-communist" party). These were the men who spearheaded the repression and ordered the killings of the Spanish revolution's leaders—Nin, Landau, Wolf, Mouiln, Camillo Berneri (one of the two Italian leaders of the Ascaso Column and an anarchist militant of some stature), and Barbieri. There never has been a shortage of red Gallifets.

The C.N.T., or at any rate its leaders. failed to respond to this menace. Back in May 1937, three British warships had arrived to "protect British interests" and were ready to intervene. This was a factor in inhibiting them.

George Orwell, one of the best witnesses to this reversing of the revolution, and himself a socialist enlisted in the P.O.U.M.'s ranks, tells of the awful impact that Stalinist propaganda had upon the fighters who were not all conversant with the subtleties of the struggle for power: "This then, is what we were according to the Communists: Trotskyists, fascists, traitors, murderers, cowards, spies, etc. Just imagine how odious it must be to see a young 15-year old Spaniard brought back from the front lines on a stretcher, to see, poking out from under the blanket an anemic, bewildered face and to think that in London and in Paris there are gentlemen dressed to the nines, blithely engaged in writing pamphlets to show that this little lad is a covert fascist. One of the most despicable things about war is that all the war propaganda, the shrieking and the lies and the hate, are invariably the handiwork of the folk who do not fight. The PSUC militants whom I have known at the front, the Communists from the International Brigades whom I have happened to meet, have never, not one of them, ever called me a Trotskyist or a traitor: that they leave to the journalists in the rearguard."

France and England were full of just such jackals far from the firing line. In May '37 *L'Humanité* displayed the headline: "Hitlerite Putsch." But its targets were not those who had paved the way for Franco; its targets were the revolutionaries. Cachin and Vaillant-Couturier went to it with customary venom.

There is no doubt but that the PSUC rank and file steered clear of this, as Orwell suggests. Many front-line fighters, International Brigade members, were to be liquidated themselves upon returning to the U.S.S.R..

It is almost pointless to relate what followed. Franco had not expected such an easy time of it. He had no difficulty in routing the Communist armies which no longer had much stomach for a fight (and questions were to be raised there, in spite of the propaganda). Negrin was beaten. Companys was to flee to France. The idea was not such an awful one but Pétain was to hand him over to Franco and he was to be shot in 1940.

We can only regret that Durruti had not been more influential inside the C.N.T.. And, above all else, that he was not spared longer.

(1896–1936)
THE SOUVENIR ALBUM OF BUENAVENTURA DURRUTI

text by
YVES FREMION
and ILLUSTRATIONS by
GUILLAUME KEYNIA and VOLNY

a CARTOON STRIP

1 1917: The railwaymen's union hits out. The union is frightened by its own sabotage.

1919–1924: The time of the pistoleros. Along with many of his comrades, Durruti participates in many attentats at this time. He founds the Solidarios group along with Gregorio Jover, Francisco Ascaso, Juan Garcia Oliver, Garcia Vivancos, Antonio Ortiz, **2** Ricardo Sanz. etc.

3 1923: Ascaso and others slay Cardinal Soldevila in Zaragoza. Soldevila was the money behind the yellow unions. The money came from brothels and gambling dens.

He invents bank robberies for political purposes. Uses the loot to finance a school in La Coruña.

4

1923: They buy 1,000 repeating rifles and 20,000 cartridges and, with the aid of smelter Eusebio Brau, make their own grenades and bombs.

5

6

Argentina: exile, hold-ups and fugitive status. Passes himself off as a vulgar sportsman: travels first class and is ignorant of refined manners.

With 500,000 francs stolen from banks, finances the International Bookshop in Paris. An attempt to relocate to Barcelona falls through on the border at Port Bou. The Civil Guard burn all the books.

7

8

1924: Meets the exiled Makhno in Paris. Greatly admires him. Also meets Mühsam and Rocker in 1928.

9

1926: Plan to assassinate Alfonso XIII aborted in Paris. Denounced by a taxi driver. Jailed with Ascaso, he spent a year in Marie-Antoinette's lodge in the Conciergerie prison.

10 1932: Revolt in Llobregat. Five days of self-management as the troops fight the rebels. Arrested along with Ascaso. They are deported to Africa.

11 The 170 prisoners are stifling below decks on the prison hulk. Ascaso revolts. The mutiny is halted but they complete **12** the trip in the open air.

"Go ahead then you coward. If you don't shoot me right now, I'll bump into you on some street corner and cut you down like a dog!"

"Go on then. We are not armed. But just you wait and see the reaction in Spain if you gun us down."

Solidaridad Obrera is impounded. Its equipment is auctioned off. Ascaso buys up the lot at a bargain price.

13

1000 Pesetas!...EUH, NON...Rien...

20 Pesetas!

14 Lays on a caravan of trucks to carry away the children of strikers arrested in Zaragoza. The children will be taken in by workers all over Spain.

166

1936: out of work. Since 1927 he has been living with Emilienne Morin. They have one daughter.

In prison with Ascaso. The warders bring their young girlfriends along to stare at the strange beasts.

July 18, 1936: Resistance to the Francoist putsch. On the balcony of the Government Palace while the military arms the workers.

July 19, 1936: Foundation of the Antifascist Militias Committee, an umbrella group. It includes Ascaso, Jover, Garcia Oliver, Sanz, and Ortiz. The Committee includes socialists, communists, the POUM, etc.

167

19 July 20, 1936: The fascists are repulsed in Barcelona. Durruti wounded while trying to take a machine-gun nest. Ascaso killed. He was 35 years old.

20 July 24, 1936: Launching of the Durruti Column. It sets off for the Aragon front. Initially it has 3,000 men. This will grow to 8,000.

The people's wrath is terrible. Durruti has difficulty restraining the pillaging of church **21** properties. On occasion, he manages to save a few likeable individuals' skins.

Take off those trousers. They are the property of the people!

22 Relentless but fair, intolerant of his men's shortcomings. These two had abandoned their post to go off for a drink. He sends them packing.

168

23 Interviewed by the Toronto Daily Star in October 1936: *"We are the ones who built all these palaces, these cities in Spain and in the Americas and right around the world. We workers can replace them with newer, more beautiful buildings. Ruins do not frighten us. The earth will be our inheritance, no doubt about that. Let the bourgeoisie blow its world to smithereens before it leaves the stage of History. We carry a new world in our hearts and that world will go on growing. It is growing even as I speak…"*

24 Arms were not reaching the front lines. Durruti traveled up to Barcelona to make his protest heard. Everyone there was over-armed. He was furious. He was forced to seize what had been promised to him.

25 He set up a farming commune in Los Moegros when he could find the time.

The Durruti Column—no officers, but elected delegates on the same rates of pay as the soldiers under them. Courts martial made up of the troops. Soviets. Foreign anarchist brigades. No saluting, **26** no hierarchy.

169

November 1936: In Madrid, Largo Caballero offers Durruti a ministry. He declines. The Column is relocated to an under-strength Madrid (which had in fact simply been abandoned by the Stalinists).

Over Madrid radio he announces that the Government has fled Madrid and that he will see to the city's defenses.

November 19, 1936: Durruti is mortally wounded while inspecting the front lines. Was it a fascist bullet? Or a Communist one? Or an anarchist one? The provenance of the bullet has never been established as fascists and revolutionaries were occupying the building opposite at the time. There is just a chance of an accident with his own gun.

He dies on November 20 without regaining consciousness. Brought back to Barcelona the next day. Buried on November 22. A quarter of Barcelona's population pass by his grave. The revolutionary ethos is laid to rest with him.

HIJOS DEL PUEBLO...

On November 21 a vast crowd walks behind Durruti's coffin in Barcelona.

Budapest, 1956
THE PEOPLE'S UPRISING IN HUNGARY

The workers ought to place themselves, not under the authority of the State, but under that of whatever revolutionary community councils the workers may establish. On no pretext must weapons and munitions be surrendered.

Karl Marx and Friedrich Engels
*Address to the Central Committee
of the Communist League* (1850)

A people can never have too much freedom.
John Warr
The Privileges of the People (1649)

Hungary is a charming country. Twice in the one century it has come within an ace of turning into the pace-setter for world freedom and just failed to introduce a self-managerial society. The first time was, as we have seen, in 1919, in the wake of the tremors in Russia.

In the interim, the Communists took power in Hungary and within a few years they installed a tyrannical regime at the behest of Stalin's agents. The all-powerful Comintern dictated its will to half of Europe. But Stalin died in 1953. Less than three years later, Hungary was in the throes of insurrection again. To understand this, we need to know one thing: when the Russians overran Hungary in 1944, they installed a government headed by Bela Dálnoki-Miklos, who had been Horthy's personal representative to Hitler and who had been decorated by the latter. His lieutenant in the ministry of Defense was János Vörös. And this was the government in which Imre Nagy cut his teeth as minister of Agriculture.

In Hungary, before the eruption, the A.V.O. (the secret police) gathered together—to borrow Andy Anderson's description—"the old dregs from the Horthy regime and the new dregs connected with the Communist Party." Its members, who enjoyed enormous privileges, were greatly despised. In the socialist economies, nationalization served primarily to bring everything under their supervision (being State-controlled thereafter). The master changed over some holiday, with notification to none. Inside the factories, police terror reigned and everything was closely monitored. There was massive absenteeism. Old activists quit the Party, having lost all faith in it. Every day, the reading of the Party newspaper for a quarter of an hour was compulsory—it was the only way it could get readers.

In 1949, the Rajk affair was staged by Rákosi. Following the death of Stalin, the ripples were felt in the G.D.R. and in Poland. Mátyás Rákosi (1892–1963), friend of Lenin and erstwhile collaborator of Bela Kun, hero in the struggle against the tyrannical Horthy, Comintern agent, Russian citizen and friend of Stalin as well, became prime minister. Then in 1953 he was forced to hand over to Imre Nagy as part of a liberalizing trend, which necessitated that hand-over, in order to preempt disorder. Nagy had to be released from prison for the purpose.

But Nagy got a little carried away with the liberalization. After the lurch to the left came another, to the right as Rákosi resumed the helm.

The opposition rallied around the Petöfi Circle, frequented by the Young Communists, most of them students of working class extraction. Established in 1956, the Circle became the locus of intellectual ferment, in short, the spokesman for the people's aspirations. The review *Irodalmi Ujsag* (Literary Gazette) was also to play a crucial part in the molding of a collective consciousness. Its issues sold like hot-cakes and there was a black market in them: it ought to be said that the review was highly critical of the regime. Among its editors was Gyula Hay who was calling for unrestricted freedom.

It was partly due to these critical intellectuals that Rákosi was toppled a second time in July 1956. His enemies—like János Kadar (born in 1910), a former worker, ex-cop, ex-Interior minister, who had twice been expelled by the Hungarian CP and jailed and tortured—were rehabilitated. Rajk too had been rehabilitated, and in October was given an official funeral. The very people who had ensured his conviction officiated at the ceremony and this outraged the populace which had not been taken in.

While the events in Poznan in Poland date from 1953, the charges brought against the perpetrators were not heard until 1956, at which point Gomulka was elected Party secretary. All of this helped to create a climate of agitation in the socialist countries.

There was a first demonstration in favor of self-management. The trade unions did what they could to keep things in check. The heartland of Hungarian radicalism was, precisely as it had been in 1919, the island of Csepel in the Danube between Buda and Pest.

The Petöfi Circle clamored for Rákosi to be expelled from the Party, for (the despised) General Farkas to be brought to trial, for dealings with the U.S.S.R. to be on an equal footing, for Nagy to be brought back, etc. Prior to the actual uprising, no one had it in mind to go for revolution. Nagy was to be brought back.

It all got underway for real on October 23, 1956. The Petöfi Circle orchestrated a huge demonstration. Ernö Gerö, who had been appointed as the new secretary of the C.P., had been an exile after 1919, a Russian citizen of course and had stamped down on the Spanish Revolution, like most of Stalin's agents. At the time of the demonstration, he was in Yugoslavia. At a loss of what to do, the

173

membership of the C.P. banned the "demo," while Gerö scurried back as fast as he was able.

But the demonstration proceeded. The Stalinists, now resigned to it, then gave the go-ahead, which was evidence of the weakness of their position, if any were still needed. The placards read: "Freedom!", "Let every nation have its own army and territory!" and "Down with Stalinism and the bourgeoisie!" Peter Veres, the president of the Writers' Union and leader of the Petöfi Circle, read out a statement by the Union to the same effect. The Writers' Union did not play the role it did in more recent times, as a faithful mouthpiece for the bureaucrats. In 1956, it was very forward-looking. Gyula Hay, Tibor Dery, and Lajos Kassak were still members. There was also a demand that the workers should be in charge of their factories and that the peasants should have freedom of choice. But all of this was, as yet, very vague.

The procession arrived in the Kossuth Square where 100,000 silent people halted outside Parliament. It was evening. Parliament turned off all its lights in order to hurry them along. But they all set alight to newspapers to improve visibility.

The crowd decided to insist that the radio station broadcast a list of their demands. The 100,000 made their way to the studios. In the Stalin Square, 3,000 people gathered in front of the 8 meter-high statue of the late dictator and, in a state of euphoria, lassoed it around the neck with a rope and pulled. It toppled to the sound of cheering. The entire exercise was followed by a tide of laughter that shook the square. The only thing left in position now was…Stalin's boots (the aficionados of symbolism had a field day with this). The toppled portion of the statue was taken to outside the National Theatre and broken up.

The A.V.O., brandishing machine guns, stood guard over the approaches to Radio Kossuth. The recently returned Gerö had just delivered a diatribe against the demonstrators. Only a delegation was allowed to go inside. They failed to re-emerge. The temperature started to rise with cries of: "Give us back our delegates!" The tension grew. The machine guns opened fire and two people died. The crowd pressed forward. Whereupon Radio Kossuth announced that it was under attack from a "fascist gang."

The rebels fetched weapons from the factories. The crowd's numbers were swelling and swelling. A few police were fraternizing with them and were even content to let them have their guns. Some military did likewise. Barricades were thrown up everywhere and A.V.O. vehicles were commandeered. The entire city was occupied.

The following day, Imre Nagy (born in 1896), one of the founding fathers of the regime, and himself a Russian citizen, who passed—wrongly, no doubt—as a "liberal," which made him popular, became prime minister. Jänos Kádar was the secretary of the Hungarian C.P. Martial law was introduced to counter "looters" (a useful stratagem).

After the carrot came the stick: on October 24, the Russians were called in, 24 hours into the uprising. The formal announcement stated: "Soviet troops, in keeping with the government's request, are assisting in the restoration of order." This of course was done prior to Gerö's being formally dismissed. We ought to note that Gyorgy Lukacs was brought back as minister of Culture.

This did nothing to add to Nagy's popularity. He, who was regarded as the man who was independent of the Russians, had been installed by them. As much of a Stalinist as Gerö, Nagy's reputation was a figment of circumstances. From start to finish, he was to be a mere puppet in the hands of History. He was primarily highly regarded by those intellectuals most remote from the working class.

A Revolutionary Workers' and Students' Council which was in permanent session issued some tracts. The radio station continued to thunder against them: it was one place they were never to capture.

Gerö had been dismissed by Mikoyan and Suslov no less, and they had replaced him with the "Titoist" Kádar, whose reputation was, to say the least, overblown. When the time came, Kádar would know just how to conduct himself like a good Stalinist.

Nagy appealed for an end to the fighting and promised democratization. To no avail. He had lost all credibility. The country was brought to a standstill by a general strike. The first of the Russian tanks rolled into Budapest. They were immediately attacked. On occasions when they did not open fire, arguments broke out and these gravely troubled the young Russian soldiers who had come intent on fighting "fascists" but who found themselves confronting Communist workers.

In the working class districts in particular, the fighting was tough. In the Széna Square, barrels and diverted (but not looted) railway carriages were used to erect

barricades. The tanks were often ablaze before they could crash through these: thirty-one tanks were burned in one week, thanks to Molotov cocktails alone. Whenever one caught fire, cries of "hurray!" resounded everywhere. The overall atmosphere was not grave but rather light-hearted and there was plenty of humor in evidence on the streets. At the Kilián Barracks, Colonel Pál Maléter, a one-time Horthy officer turned by the Russians, a veteran of the International Brigades had assumed command of the rebels. In the street in front of a cinema, their sole artillery piece was firing, manned by a simple tram driver. Most of the insurgent military had also been in the International Brigades. In the lulls between the fighting, there were heated discussions. The fighting dragged on for three days without a break.

On October 25, in front of the A.V.O. headquarters, demonstrators insisted that the Russian star be removed from the facade. After negotiation, they were allowed to draw nearer before they were mowed down by dumdum bullets. A hundred were to lose their lives and these included many children and women. The insurgents were beside themselves with fury. The A.V.O. headquarters were stormed and its occupants lynched.

They raced on to the Parliament building where Russian tanks fraternized with them; they had come to an accommodation, worker to worker. One officer even ordered his men to fire on the AVO sniping from the rooftops and trying to pass themselves off as rebels, such provocation being the only way of preventing such fraternization.

Soviets had seized power everywhere. The strike spread to every sector throughout the country. Their basic demands were: that the Russians should withdraw; that the A.V.O. be disbanded; and that social freedoms, self-management, a general amnesty, and political pluralism be introduced. There was huge variation from place to place.

Every town had its Central Revolutionary Council to orchestrate all this. The peasants supplied them with food. There were even soviets among the peasants (the largest was in Bábolna). On the State-owned collective farms, the land was redistributed. The rebels held all the radio stations, except for Radio Kossuth, the main one. The bureaucrats were ousted from all of their positions. There was a council republic again, almost completely autonomous. Just like in 1919.

In Budapest the Central Revolutionary Council was chaired by Sándor Ráez, born in 1932, an electrician and former member of the Hungarian Communist Party, and its secretary was Sándor Bali, another electrician. They oversaw the distribution of foodstuffs, medicines, and fuel. Everything was up and running again but on behalf of councils this time: the miners sent coal to the power stations and hospitals and there were convoys of trucks, and sometimes of trains, on the move. There was one oddity who made a name for himself. With his revolver on his hip, wearing leggings and a Tyrolean hat, Jozsef Dudas (born in 1912) was scarcely one to pass unnoticed. A mechanical engineer, he had been a Communist before defecting to the Small-holders' Party. Having been a deputy at the end of the war and having been a prisoner in a camp up until 1954, he had had an eventful life. Politically ambitious, he was a forceful personality. He headed a "National Revolutionary Council." He had his own newspaper, with its headquarters on the premises of the former *Szabad Nep*. A very dubious character, he was to be placed under arrest by Maléter when he attempted to seize the Foreign Affairs Ministry along with a 50-man commando who were ready for anything. It is hard to get to the truth where he is concerned, for reports about him are very contradictory. He was most likely one of these adventurers who pop up in every revolution, who capitalize upon the occasion to accomplish what they hold to be their destiny.

In the outside world, as ever, nobody went into the details of the soviets. The talk was all of a nationalist uprising and that suited the Stalinists fine. Stalinist slanders would be all the more credible once repeated in the west. However, inside, say, the French Communist Party, there were stirrings: Vaillant, C. Roy, and Sartre came out in favor of the soviets. The spokesman for the hard-line Stalinists was Roger Garaudy.

On October 26, a National Council of Free Trade Unions issued an important document wherein it demanded that Nagy be made premier, that an amnesty be declared, that a National Worker Guard be established, that the Russians pull out, that workers' councils be formed in the factories, that workers should oversee planning and the economy, that wages be increased, that productivity targets be abolished, that they construction of housing be stepped up, and that Hungarians enjoy parity with the Russians.

The army, the press, and health services were overhauled. The newspaper *Szabad Nep* became the *Népzabadság*, thereby supplanting the Hungarian C.P.'s mouthpiece. Twenty-five brand new dailies appeared. The prisons were emptied. A.V.O. personnel were systematically gunned down or hanged and the mob spat on their corpses. Theie be^te noire, General Mihaly Farkas, a dyed-in-the-wool Stalinist, whom the Russians had ended up arresting but who had never been brought to trial, was executed.

On October 27, Nagy declared that the A.V.O. was to be abolished and that a cabinet reshuffle was imminent. But on October 29, delegates from the councils handed him an ultimatum for nothing had been done. On October 30, it was announced that the Russian pull-out had begun. It started immediately, but they pulled out only to surround the city. Nagy claimed that the Russians had been called in by Gerö and not by himself.

On November 1, Russian troops crossed the border and headed for Budapest. Nagy refused to respond to appeals from the councils. A reshuffle had resulted in the installation of Pál Maléter as Defense minister and General Istvan Kovacs became chief of staff. It was they who would be negotiating the Russian withdrawal. Nagy, who was trying to calm everybody down, was dumbfounded by the arrival of Warsaw Pact forces. He proclaimed Hungary a neutral nation. Too late. on November 2, the Russians themselves made the announcement that they would not be withdrawing. The Stalinists received every encouragement from everywhere, in particular from the United States, in the shape of Foster Dulles' words. The whole of the socialist bloc cheered them on: Mao, Tito, and Gomulka. (The latter was to say a year later that "the councils and all such thinking is an anarchist utopia. I reckon that it is a waste of time to spend any longer talking about it.")

The make-or-break action came on November 3. Maléter and Kovacs, dispatched as delegates to the Red Army Headquarters for negotiating purposes, were arrested by the very Russians with whom they had meant to negotiate. Kádar at first fled to the Russian Embassy and then on to Russia itself and thence to Szolnok. We shall see why anon.

By November 4, Budapest was under artillery assault, as were the other big towns. Barricades were thrown up everywhere. Fires were raging out of control as the Russians were using phosphorous shells.

Nagy also fled to the Yugoslav Embassy, along with 15 of his supporters, including Lukacs. There was ferocious fighting in the Széna Square and at the Kilián Barracks. Revolutionaries took on the tanks with Molotov cocktails and grenades. These had to be placed directly inside the tanks after the hatch had been lifted.

At the suggestion of Tito (and one would have to be a right twat to describe him as an advocate of self-management after this) Kádar established in Szolnok a "workers' and peasants' government" which yet again appealed to the Russians for help. The object of this was primarily to set down his own marker, for the Russians were already on the scene. The only reform his government seems to have introduced was to change the name of the A.V.O., to the A.V.H., without, of course, altering either its structures or its personnel.

Imagination was scarcely his forte. It was the Russians', though, and it was rampant on the streets, notably in the sometimes poignant posters that covered the walls.

Those captured were immediately hanged with a placard around their neck reading "This is how we treat counter-revolutionaries" scrawled by the very people who were engaged in the crushing of this proletarian revolution.

By November 10 the major fighting was over. "Kádar taxis" (Russian talks) were rumbling about all over the place. Ruin was heaped upon ruin. Mikoyan had correctly seen that artillery bombardment offered the only way out. It could be delivered at some distance, thereby averting fraternization between the Russian troops and the rebels...

The last remaining pockets were mopped up by November 14. But skirmishing continued into January 1957. And there were still strikes erupting in 1959.

Kádar had the officials from the soviets placed under arrest, as he slowly dismantled them. Support for the councils was still running high. For good measure, he expelled the 12 most despised Stalinists, of whom Gerö was one. For a time, the soviets were still spreading even as the situation was being resolved. Nagy became a symbol (which was more honor than he deserved, but at that time not everyone was au fait with his chicanery).

By November 16 Kádar was in negotiations with the soviets. He agreed to recognize some and to permit the creation of factory militias. At the same time, he contrived to sever their connections with the peasants who had been supplying their food. Then he grew angry and turned on them, dismissing them as "fascists." The Russians had problems restraining their own malnourished and shaken army. The other socialist nations were also asking questions.

Arrests were made among the Russians as mutinies multiplied. Abroad, the tanks were beginning to inspire indignation. The National Council of Trade Unions revamped itself and called for a laying-down of arms. Its idea was to urge the formation of "soviets" but issued "directives" (!) to this end and declared that these "soviets" were to be "answerable to the State" (!!) and that they would have a duty to guarantee "order and discipline." Straight up. The man in charge, Sándor Gáspár, was one of Kádar's henchmen.

On November 23, Nagy refused to accept Kádar's conditions: that he speak out against the rebels, resign, offer a self-criticism, and go into exile in a socialist country. All this in return for his freedom. Nagy was well aware that none of these promises would be honored.

Kádar pretended to "give way." He agreed to let Nagy go free. He would not stop him. There was no need. He had not promised that the Russians would not impede his going. Nagy left with his supporters and was picked up by Mikoyan's people who had set the whole thing up. Yugoslavia did protest. In 1958, in Rumania, Nagy and Maléter were discreetly executed. Kádar, who could not deny for long that he had been in on things, was to announce that they had been "murdered" by "counter-revolutionaries"—and in a way, he was telling the truth.

Meanwhile, Kádar broke off negotiations with the soviets. The negotiators— and this really was getting to be a habit—were arrested. They were Raez and Bali, leaders of the Budapest soviet. There was an immediate downing of tools at their factory and it took the police three days to get on top of things again.

The rest was more symbolic than anything else. The Communist Party newspaper was burned in the streets and 30,000 women paraded past the tomb of the unknown soldier. Calling for Nagy and for the Russians to clear out. Cardinal Mindszenty fled to the U.S. Embassy, which drew some crocodile tears from the West.

On December 9, all councils were disbanded, except for those in the factories and mines. Martial law was re-imposed. The death penalty was revived for strikers.

This signaled the start of summary executions and arrests, not to mention executions after due "legal" process.

In Poland, there was a demonstration in sympathy outside the Russian consulate in Sczeczin. Intellectuals like Gyula Hay and Tibor Déry were arrested. The councils were replaced (and some persisted up until November 1957) by company councils under the jackboot of the Stalinists.

The Social Democrat minister Marosán even announced that if he had to liquidate 10,000 people, so be it. In all, there were to be between 20,000 and 50,000 killed or murdered as against the 4,000 Russian soldiers who lost their lives. Certain members of the nationalist right had taken part in the uprising, although they had not had any input into its ideology. These were to be used as a pretext for denunciation of "fascists" during and after the rising.

The reorganization went swimmingly. Hungary was brought back into line. The Writers' Union was purged and the factories held in check by the trade unions. In spite of it all, the lesson was learned by the Stalinists. There was to be an enormous change in Budapest: the toppled statue of Stalin was replaced...by one of Lenin.

China, 1967-1968
THE RED GUARDS OF THE SHENGWULIAN

Tremble, ye new bourgeois bureaucrats, before the true socialist revolution that is going to shake the world! The proletarians have nothing to lose but their chains. And a world to conquer.

Shengwulian
Whither goes China? (January 12, 1968)

Tremble ye bureaucrats—STOP—The worldwide power of the workers' councils will soon sweep you aside—STOP—(...) Long live the proletarians of Canton and elsewhere who have taken up arms against the so-called People's Army—STOP—Long live the Chinese students and workers who have attacked the so-called Cultural Revolution and the Maoist bureaucratic order— STOP—(...).

The Sorbonne sit-in committee
telegram to the Politburo of the Chinese C.P. (May 17, 1968)

It is not easy to get a handle on the Cultural Revolution in China. And it has to be said that the "China-watchers" are of no assistance here. The confusion could not be greater. In the midst of all the misrepresentation, we are obliged to go by the evidence.

Mao Ze Dong had lost central authority prior to 1965. Since 1959 at least (he was paying the price for his mismanagement, for which the CP had not yet forgiven him). And he was ready to resort to just about anything in order to regain that authority. The struggle had been waged against Marshal Peng Dehuai, who had been sidelined, but, in the rough and tumble, Mao too found himself sidelined by the third thief, the orthodox Stalinist Liu Shaoqi, who was well aware that Mao still posed a threat to his personal authority. Feudal squabbling, the sort of thing commonly encountered in the apparatuses of single parties.

By this point, Mao's sole support came from Lin Biao, the minister of Defense, who was banking on his victory, and the old fox Zhou Enlai, who was still playing one faction against another.

What is incorrectly termed the "Cultural Revolution" (or, to those of us who are in a hurry and who are not Leninists, the "Cult. Rev.") opened in November 1965 with a nondescript article in Shanghai's *Wenhui Bao*, a four-year-old review of a historical play, *The Deposition of Hai Rui*. But no one was taken in by this: the play was an anti-Mao and pro-Peng Dehuai allegory, and the playwright, Wu Han, was the No. 2 in charge of Beijing, no less.

The author of the review, one Yao Wenyuan, who was in his thirties, had done his homework. In January, Mao had published his *Twenty-Three Articles*, wherein all of the elements which were to come together in the Cultural Revolution were spelled out. The wisest heads realized that Mao, his back to the wall in Beijing, had created a personal fiefdom for himself in Shanghai. Moreover, Lin Biao published his very pro-*Mao Long Live the Victory of the People's War*.

Beijing mayor, Peng Zhen, who was being targeted through his No. 2, retaliated by setting up a "Group of Five," Central Committee members placed in charge of purging the CP and wringing out the "Maoists." By "Maoists" we mean of course Mao's supporters proper, since in the China of the time, everybody was claiming to be a "Maoist," the better to advance themselves. But the Maoists were making headway. Lin Biao eliminated Luo Ruiqing, the chief of the general staff, on charges of conspiring against the State. In response to these charges, Luo Ruiqing attempted suicide. He threw himself out of a window but suffered only broken legs.

This left Lin a free hand in Beijing as he assumed control of the army himself. What followed was tantamount to a coup d'état. The police switched to the Maoist camp, as did the secret services through Kang Sheng, the 62-year-old member of the Group of Five who had jumped ship just in time and through Xie Fuzhi, a 68-year old model bureaucrat.

The Group of Five was disowned and in June 1966, Peng Zhen was brought down, followed by propaganda chief Lu Dingyi. Mao had won. It was at this point that in order to make a propaganda point he swam the Yangtse river in front of cameramen. From this point on, his purge was to affect the entire party hierarchy and spare no one. The "Cult Rev." was underway.

The Red Guards at that time were a shapeless mass: young people full of illusions, who would have their eyes opened later, as the struggle proceeded. For the time being, though, like good little lap-dogs, they swallowed everything that Mao told them. Mao's supporters were victorious in Shanghai as well as in Beijing. This led to the creation of the Central Cultural Revolution Group (C.C.R.G.) which was to operate as a sort of Maoist general headquarters in matters of ideology. Its chairman was Chen Boda (61), Mao's secretary. Jiang Qing (Mrs. Mao) was its first vice-chair. Kang Sheng was an advisor and the membership of the group included Yao Wenyuan.

The first of the dazibaos, or wall newspapers, was put up on May 25, 1966 in

Beijing University. From then on, they popped up everywhere. They were a pointer to the fact that there were as many ideas abroad as there were Red Guards: every viewpoint, every ideology was represented and they were, naturally, all "Maoist."

Among the radical leaders, the equivalent (making allowances) of the West's leftists, we ought to mention Qi Benyu, a member of the C.C.R.G., and another C.C.R.G. member, the 47-year-old Wang Li, one of the directors of *Red Flag*. Whereas by August the palace revolution was at an end, it took three years for it to be followed through in all of the provinces. This was to be their assignment.

Mao had been clever, successfully redirecting discontent (a product of his own initiatives and his bureaucratic rule) against those persons who had taken over from him in the running of the bureaucracy. The Red Guards, lacking experience, cadres, and political maturity, blithely allowed themselves to be manipulated by Mao and the C.C.R.G.: a 16 point charter of the Cultural Revolution was published. It was often to serve as a reference point.

Thanks to his Red Guards, Mao had all local leaders who failed to declare allegiance to him denounced. The most quick-witted of them realized what was afoot: and set up Red Guards of their own to counter the first set. The confusion became complete (everybody abroad was championing the faction of his choice, which was doubtless a significant factor in the still extant misrepresentation of what was going on). In September, Zhou Enlai made a brave effort to bring all of these Red Guards together in order to control them and to single out future victims to them. But it was an impossible task.

The struggle was particularly bitter in Shanghai: the Maoists there had set up the Headquarters of the Revolutionary Rebel Workers of Shanghai in December 1966 under the leadership of Zhang Chunqiao, a 52-year-old member of the C.C.R.G.. One of its founders was Wang Hongwen, whose name was never mentioned in the outside world at the time, which only made his spectacular promotion in 1975 a bolt from the blue to all observers. As we can see, along with Jiang Qing and Yao Wenyuan, what went on to become the "Gang of Four" was active in the city.

To counter that organization, its opponents set up the Headquarters of the Red Labor Defense Units for the Defense of Mao Ze Dong Thought. (Now don't be getting confused. Remember, it was the other guys who were the Maoists!)

At this point the so-called "Black December Wind" incident occurred. In point of fact, certain Red Guards had begun to ask questions about things and about the various cliques of bureaucrats. Light was beginning to break through. On December 1, 1966, a dazibao signed by one Li Hongshan, a Red Guard from Beijing, asserted: "Screw the C.C.R.G.. Let's make the revolution ourselves!" This school of thought which was to spread to many very libertarian and like-minded radical organizations, was to take a firm stand. More details anon of their activities.

For the moment, they organized a 30,000-strong demonstration, which was broken up. Li Hongshan and the organizations' leaders were arrested and vehemently denounced by Zhou, by Chen Boda and Jiang Qing from the C.C.R.G.. These bureaucrats were alive to the danger. The Red Guards, especially the ones from Liangdong, often singled out the Public Security offices as targets.

In January there came a turning of the tide in the contest. This was the so-called "January storm." The Headquarters of the Revolutionary Rebels, etc.—in short, the Maoists—took over the leading daily newspapers and put them to good use. There was vicious fighting with their adversaries, especially as this was all taking place against a backdrop of riots and leftist workers' strikes and peasant uprisings against the bureaucrats and that the extremists were regrouping, notably into "Workers' Struggle" which attacked Zhang Chungqiao.

The dockworkers especially were immersed in a complete shutdown directed equally against the Maoists and their competitors. Student "scabs" were sent in to do their work, but this ended in a resounding failure. For the very first time since the crushing of the revolutionaries in Canton back in 1927, the proletariat was making its own voice heard in China. And it had plenty to say. The ghastliness of the regime stood exposed in all its starkness. The countless testimonials collected by the Red Guards (and published in France in the anthology *Cultural Revolution in People's China*) spare no one's sensibilities.

The Maoists from the C.C.R.G. tried to calm the workers' and peasants' revolt, which they had not anticipated. The unrest was getting out of hand and the brakes had to be applied. This was sometimes difficult and confusing. In February, with support from the army, the C.C.R.G. seized power within the Shanghai Party Committee and amid the furor proclaimed the "Shanghai Commune," in commemoration of its Parisian predecessor. That imagery which proved difficult to control was quickly erased: within two days, there was merely a less suggestive "Revolutionary Committee." The restoration of order was underway.

But this was not the doing of the Red Guards: they carried on bursting into barracks, looting arms depots, and provoking the military who were already made uneasy by the dismissal of their officers. The Maoists had to veer to the right before it would be too late. This was the "February Counter-current." Numerous leftists and libertarians were rounded up. Wang Li, representing the left wing of the Maoists, was obliged to call upon them to show respect for the army. Zhou Enlai capitalized upon a gathering of Beijing Red Guards to urge them to stay in their universities and stop wandering all over the place. He spearheaded the entire campaign, even though his own situation was a difficult one, with some of his close associates being attacked and others, like Zhu De, brought low.

Elsewhere, though, the Red Guards were stymied by the regional magnates, the new feudalists. The latter passed themselves off as "Mao supporters" and had themselves appointed as Cultural Revolution bosses in their regions and in that capacity went on to crush and butcher the Red Guards. Wang Enmao up in

Xinjiang was the prototype of this.

In July 1976 came the Wuhan Mutiny, the most serious episode of the entire Cult. Rev. Wuhan is a strategically situated city where the army held power but where 54 different factions were competing to wrest power from army hands. The army commander, Chen Zaidao, threw his support behind the "Million Heroes" faction which comprised the anti-Mao peasants and workers.

Mao dispatched two envoys—Wang Li (one of the big wheels in the Cult. Rev. and the propaganda boss) and Xie Fuzhi (one of the main Beijing leaders and vice-premier).

Fighting erupted as the city rose in revolt. Wang was arrested, beaten up, and thrown in prison. Zhou Enlai was forced to travel up in person on July 22, to open negotiations for Wang's release. But on July 24, marines and paratroops, led by no less a person than Lin Biao, flooded Wuhan, disarming the Million Heroes faction and arresting Chen Zaidao, who got off with a token punishment. In the context of the times, this fact was significant. It was obvious that Zhou had left him in the lurch in the negotiations with the army.

The army was at loggerheads with the Maoists, while remaining very loyal to Mao personally. On the other hand, it was distrustful of Lin Biao who had eliminated some highly popular officers from its ranks. Mao had got the point: he would have to switch allies, or, rather, turn his famous Mao coat.

Gradually he came to depend upon the military and dropped his "supporters," deserting the Red Guards. It was his only chance to consolidate his authority once and for all.

The Red Guards started to find themselves being disarmed in September. One after another, their leaders were to fall into the snares of the lickspittles. The first to fall was Wang Li who had been too critical of the army earlier on (that is, a few months previously). His close cohorts, Lin Jie, Mu Xin, and Yang Dengshan, followed close behind. All were accused of connivance with the extremists from what came to be called the May 16 Corps, of which more later. In fact, certain Maoists had supported the corps for a time before turning against it, somewhat belatedly in the view of their adversaries who seized upon this pretext to bring them down. After the "August Storm" came the "September Turnaround," and a U-turn it was.

Doubtless a western mind used to the rather lame writings of the handful of China-watchers who carry a lot of weight in our native lands will have problems unraveling all these interests. By way of a summing up, let us review the main groups at work. As in every other country, there was a formal left and a formal right, the practices and thinking of which differed little from each other: their essential object was to achieve power and to hold on to it.

The right was made up of the bureaucrats, the privileged, the ruling class, the bourgeois, the leadership cadres, which ran China like a private business. Liu Shaoqi was their representative, but behind the scenes, the notorious Deng Xiaoping was making ready to seize power, which he would do, on two or three occasions. To these right wingers we should add a more moderate, more flexible, and craftier right—the centrists, if one will—whose unchallenged leader was Zhou Enlai.

As for the left, it ranged from outright adventurists (like Lin Biao) who had simply backed what looked to be a rising star, to the softest of "leftists" who supported Mao and restrained the extremists. The latter sort were represented by the line-up of the C.C.R.G., Wang Li, Qi Benyu, and the like. Caught in the middle between these two groups were the C.C.R.G.'s moderates, Yao Wnyuan, Jiang Qing, Chen Boda, Zhang Chungqiao, (who would become the Gang of Four) and their supporters.

In opposition to all these power-crazy fetishists of bureaucracy, left and right alike, stood the revolutionaries. They too came in all sorts of varieties: Leninists on the brink of ideological breakdown, anarchists, "trotskyists," advocates of self-management, and others. Every one of them still invoked Mao, either honestly (out of naiveté), or as a ruse (it provided a very effective cover). These diehards, these anti-bureaucrats, these ultras wished above all right then to carry on with the Cult. Rev. in society and that included inside the army.

Mao's about-turn was to oblige them to go underground. Even as Mao was calling off the Cultural Revolution, he and Lin Biao were announcing that it had just triumphed! In spite of everything, they could do nothing to prevent the downfall of Xiao Hua, Lin's No. 2 who had committed the error of attacking Jiang Qing, Mao's wife. In November, it was the turn of Guan Feng, the sole survivor of the Wang Li group. Every grouping changed tack and lost important supporters. But the alliance between Lin Biao's left-wing military and Zhou Enlai's moderate bureaucrats brought things to an end. From the end of that year, the first victims of purge to be rehabilitated were emerging once again. At their head was the former marshal, Chen Yi.

It was also at around this point that Lin Biao was appointed as Mao's official heir apparent. Bureaucrats in Mao's pocket were appointed to positions throughout the country, with compliant "revolutionary committees" at their command. All in the name of the revolution, of course. The rebels were at a loss but their resistance persisted. In March 1968, Chen Yi was restored to his former duties. It was the best possible symbol of how things had been turned around.

Those who had made their U-turn in time with Mao were to hold up longer. Not until 1971 would Xie Fuzhi and Chen Boda be brought down, and the Gang of Four was not brought down until after Mao's death. Lin, whom his adversaries forgave nothing, watched his No. 2 brought low for a second time (in the ultra-left's dying gasp), followed by two of his chief supporters. By May 1968, only 26 out of 190 members of the Chinese Communist Party's Central Committee were still in place!

In the provinces, old scores were being settled as the Red Guards were hunted down and massacred. In July, the death throes came to an end as bureaucratic loyalists recaptured the universities. Mao's victory was complete as his adversaries were eliminated in a pincer movement. The four chief personalities by whom he was surrounded—Zhou Enlai, Lin Biao, Kang Sheng, and Chen Boda—were powerful…but had no supporters. Chen Boda, who had been all but eliminated in 1970, was brought down in 1971. Lin was to embark upon a dangerous conspiracy in 1971—one that was to cost him his life, as well as the lives of a few accomplices, in a plane crash in Mongolia. (Lin had been executed in a secret prison: yet the story was put out that he had been on board the plane.)

From 1973 on, Mao was growing weaker and Deng returned to power along with the right-wing bureaucrats. What followed is a separate story.

We now have to turn to our subject matter proper: the revolutionaries. We referred earlier to the May 16 Army Corps. Rarely can any group have been so misrepresented by its enemies, during and after its period of activity. In spite of the florid labels hung upon it, it was an "ultra-left" group that had been launched on July 1, 1967. Its supporters appear not to have left any printed declarations behind and that does nothing to assist us in our examination of the group. They were very active and very libertarian in their outlook. Their activities were underway prior to the establishment of the group, an act that set the seal upon their retreat into clandestinity following the arrests of their leading lights.

They were to be very active indeed at the time of the "Black December Wind" which occurred, let us remember, in December 1966, six months ahead of those arrests.

The Black Wind was rooted in Beijing, in the Forestry Institute, the Institute of Siderurgy, the Aeronautics Institute and the Foreign Languages Institute. The leader of its core group was one Li Hongshan (author of the "Screw the C.C.R.G." dazibao) and that group amalgamated with the Academy of Sciences group to form the May 16 Corps. For a time, they were, as we have seen, beneficiaries of the support of the most left-wing members of the C.C.R.G.—Wang Li, Qi Benyu, Lin Jie, Guan Feng, Mu Xin, and perhaps Xiao Hua. Politically speaking, they were against the "capitalist roaders" (right-wingers such as Liu Shaoqi or moderates like Zhou Enlai) but they also opposed the "new capitalists" (such as the army, Lin Biao, etc.)

Once they got themselves properly—if somewhat belatedly—organized, they set up eight front-line armies. But that is as much as we know about their goals and whatever other ideas they may have had, at the present moment.

They were, however, also powerful in Canton, through the May 16 Committee for Tao Criticism, the leader of which was Wu Chuanqi, head of the Beijing Philosophy Department. The membership of the group included Mu Xin and Pan Zinian, both of them prominent officials. Canton itself was teeming with little groups which were all affiliated to this current. Examples are the Canton Combat Group, the Municipal Alliance for Tao Criticism. These groups had seized the offices of the Central Committee of the local Communist Party, and the like. They eliminated the city's military commanders.

In August 1967, they attempted to seize power at the Foreign Affairs Ministry (which was headed by Chen Yi), under the leadership of Yao Dengshan, former ambassador to Indonesia, one of the most radical figures. Wang Li, Lin Jie, Mu Xin, and Guan Feng afforded them keen support on this occasion—something that was shortly to prove their downfall.

Six weeks after the group had been launched, its leaders were rounded up and in this they were soon followed by the extremists from the C.C.R.G.. The crack-down was to prove so ferocious that there is still talk of public executions of "May 16 personnel" in Beijing in December 1969! Perhaps correctly, they were to be credited with the death of Xie Fuzhi, whom they detested as he was in charge of the repression (having been minister of security).

This group was not alone. It had ties to other groups, especially to the Shengwulian which had the good idea of leaving texts behind. The Shengwulian, launched somewhat later, on October 11, 1969, which is to say toward the end of the upheavals, was an abbreviated name for the Unity Committee of the Proletarian Revolutionaries of Hunan. In fact it was a federation of some 20 groups active since that summer at least. Certain of their members were also members of the May 16 Corps.

In their province—Hunan is situated in southern China—these Red Guards were zealots. The Maoists did not fail to grasp this fact and made them their No. 1 enemies, desperately misrepresenting them in an effort to dismiss them as fascists. Their chief writings offer us an insight into their theories and the practices they implemented during the short time they were allowed by the bureaucracy.

Their *Programme* was written in November 1967 by Yang Xiguang, an 18-year old high school student who was a member of the "Let's seize military power" group. Couched in Maoist terminology, his was a violent attack upon all who wanted to apply the rein in the Rev. Cult. Another text, doubtless also by Yang, leaps to the defense of the peasants and workers.

Yang was scathing about Zhou or the opportunists, having grasped the crux of the struggle for power in China and even talked about "dynastic change": he could not have been more explicit. The finest analysis of the phenomenon appears in their text Where is China Going?, probably drafted by Yang and amounting in fact to a platform for debate offered to all Red Guards in January 1968.

Yang, or his colleagues, set out in plain language their angle on their struggle, on the revolution which had been effected (despite the efforts of the bigwigs of "Cultural Revolution" to disguise the fact), "at the hands of a people which, driven by boundless enthusiasm, had organized itself and assumed control of political, administrative, financial, and cultural authority in the townships, in industry, in commerce, in communications, etc. The editorial which had urged the masses of the populace to get themselves organized in order to take in hand the destiny of the socialist State and to run city affairs, industry, communications, and the economy themselves had thus been implemented to some effect. (...) Society suddenly discovered that not only could it survive without the bureaucrats but it could operate better, that it could develop more quickly and more freely."

He then went on to offer numerous specific instances, invoking the Paris Commune and drawing analogies between the two situations, before exclaiming, "The spectacle of workers running the factories themselves following the January revolution was truly moving. For the first time, the workers had a feeling that it is not the State that leads us but we who lead the State. For the first time, they had the impression of working for themselves. Their zeal had never been so great nor their sense of responsibility run so deep." He is talking here about the "January Storm" in 1967.

It was at this point that in Hunan some 90 percent of the corrupt local cadres were eliminated. One of the most important of these, the governor, was called Hua Guofeng, who later achieved supreme authority: prior to his accession to power he was known in China solely by his nickname "Executioner of the Shengwulian"—in radical circles at any rate. He returned to his office in February, only to be dismissed again that August. It was he who was to spearhead the crackdown on the Red Guards a short time after that. In the west, being unfamiliar to the China-watchers, he was depicted solely as Mao's heir apparent and for a long time our China experts were puzzled about which camp he belonged in.

The members of the Shengwulian were scathing in their criticism of the conversion of "communes" into "revolutionary committees." They had understood that this signified the elimination of "soviets." Yet again. George Santayana's famous dictum to the effect that "Those who do not remember the past are doomed to repeat it," was never so true. Still ignorant of how Lenin and his henchmen had conducted themselves in Russia, the Red Guards were to let Mao adopt the same tack. The power of the soviets was to turn into the "dictatorship of the proletariat," which is to say, "the dictatorship of the self-proclaimed leaders of the party of the bureaucracy ruling over the proletariat."

They could not attack Mao directly, but they resorted to roundabout stratagems to get their viewpoint across. They were still too much in thrall to Maoist ideology, too tainted by the Leninism and Stalinism which constituted their entire political and historical culture. The authors of *Cultural Revolution in People's China* were quick to spot this shortcoming: "Lenin, that red lantern, and Leninism, that white affliction, are still regarded there as the mightiest beacons of revolution."

The self-managerial potential of their revolution still escaped their notice: some of them honestly thought that they were being loyal to Mao Zedong. They were to let themselves be manipulated by the ruling class and the bureaucrats and this was to cost most of them their lives.

Their final spasm came at the beginning of 1968. In August 1967, they had briefly snatched back power and high school students were to be seen occupying security and communications premises, directing traffic in the cities and successfully overseeing finance and the economy. They refused to give up their weapons to the bureaucrats. Stolen arms were hidden away.

The peasants, profoundly intimidated by the might of the army, failed to follow their example. Bewildered by Mao's U-turn, the rebels were still making excuses for him as well as for Jiang Qing and the people from the C.C.R.G. The more radical among them became embittered, none of their goals having been achieved for any length of time: "All that effort and not a thing changed." The Shengwulian now had but a few more months to live, before it disintegrated under the weight of the repression.

The Shengwulian which thought of itself as "a fresh growth on a par with the soviets," and without doubt the most radical development ever seen in China, suffered the same fate as all the rest: all because it dallied with the bureaucrats for a time in spite of all their failings, in search of endorsement by them.

The Chinese ruling class had allowed it to operate over a two year period for one reason only—and the Situationists at the time hit the nail squarely on the head when they concluded that the class was about to split in two. In time, one faction would eliminate the other and the license afforded the revolutionaries would be withdrawn. Order was restored in China and the most spectacular demonstration of this was the announcement that Liu Shaoqi was being formally rehabilitated even as we write.

California, 1960-1969
THE SAN FRANCISCO DIGGERS

Of all social models, the anarchist society is assuredly the one most demanding of its members. Liberal society, where everything is law-bound and compartmentalized, is, in the end, the easier life: tolerance boils down to ignoring one's neighbor. As for the structured, hierarchical, Stalinist society, where one leader decides for everybody, plainly, few people would wish for that.

Henrik
Christiania (1979)

But in order to be achievable, communism requires tremendous moral progress on the part of the members of society, and also a high-minded, thoroughgoing sense of solidarity that revolutionary vigor may well not be enough to conjure into existence.

Malatesta
Programma (1884)

The end of the 1960s saw the emergence of a phenomenon that is both universally familiar and, in its essence, profoundly misunderstood. Much has been written about the Hippie movement, and rarely has ink flowed to such stultifying effect. It has to be said that the movement began in 1966 and fell apart in the autumn of 1967. Whereupon the press started to talk about it, literally conjuring the movement into existence as a media phenomenon, complete with its Flower Power ideology, the flower in the rifle barrel and the turning of the other cheek.

The reality was very different. The broad dropout movement of the time embraced a wide variety of things. Amid all the whining pacifists (most of them mystics), the apostles of liberation through drugs and the imbecile gurus, there were a number of quite radical acts which have been shrouded in deliberate silence. It is into one such action which we will be looking here.

It started with a theater troupe that was very well-known in its day, the San Francisco Mime Troupe, led by R. G. Davies. It was based in the celebrated Haight-Ashbury district which gave its name to the Hippie movement (Haight-Ashbury Independent Property—H.I.P.—laid back—in the swim—lots of other

191

meanings). Within the troupe there were a number of personalities, the most outstanding being Kenny Wisdom (1944-1978), better known by his nom de plume of Emmett Grogan.

Grogan even then had a checkered history: brawler, former addict (having come off the heroin he had been taking since the age of 13), thief and all-round rebel (for a time he had flirted with the IRA in Ireland). Grogan had been around and done a bit of thinking. He was shrewd and he was bored. He was none too excited by what was going on in San Francisco but it was fertile ground. As a result of a break-in, he and his pals found themselves with access to a certain sum of money. He eventually came up with a way of putting it to good use—"Chow!" he shouted, in a flash of inspiration.

He broke into the produce market on the city outskirts and loaded up his Ford pick-up with crates of fruit and vegetables, hens, and rabbits. He and his pals stole two huge 90-liter milk churns in which they cooked the whole lot up. At 4:00 p.m., they showed up at Golden Gate Park where they were expected by city residents who had been alerted by a following handbill: "FREE CHOW—HOT STEW—FRESH FRUIT—BRING A BOWL AND A SPOON—ASHBURY STREET OPPOSITE THE PARK, 4:00 P.M.—FREE CHOW—EVERY DAY—FREE CHOW—FREE BECAUSE IT BELONGS TO YOU!…THE DIGGERS"

That signature was a puzzle only to the ignoramuses, for it was assuredly a reference to the old Diggers, the English yeomen who made up the left wing of the Cromwellian army. Grogan had been an avid reader, too. He had signed the handbill almost without thinking. But he had just launched one of the most splendid self-managerial experiments in U.S. history.

Around 50 folk turned up, some of them with a bowl dangling from their belts. This was quickly to become the standing signal of recognition among Digger loyalists. Not that the original 50 were to be on their own for long. That day, their number swelled to 200. All week long, Grogan and his cronies carried on feeding the hungry, the marginalized, the bums, the junkies, the hoboes, the runaways, the passers-by, the hippies, and the rubberneckers.

At no time were they willing to say who they were, nor whence they had come. The many underground newspapers of the day were to add fuel to the mystery. Everyone was intrigued and wondered about their motives. What could be in it for them? Donors flooded in from all over, some of them disinterested givers, but above all, givers for a purpose. The only answer they got from Grogan and his friends was the sight of their dollars and their checks being accepted and promptly burned.

Grogan's friends, the core Diggers, were Billy Landout, Slim Minaux, and Butcher Brooks (the latter a photographer who owned a yellow Volkswagen beetle—known as the "yellow sub-marine"—daubed with the graffito "The path of excess is the route to the palace of wisdom.") This was the beetle that ferried the

192

chow along with the girls who prepared it. Some commune-dweller girls were helpers in the preparation of the meals; Suzanne Natural, Fyllis, Cindy, Bobsie, and Nana-Nina were the names given by Grogan in his astonishing autobiography *Ringolevio*.

As it happens, Butcher Brooks was wont to tour round and round the district, under the very noses of the volunteer charity workers, just to show them that this was no part of their doing. Grogan saw to it that food was found, collecting it or stealing it that morning for afternoon use (the Diggers had no refrigeration facility). They ended up renting a garage on Page Street where his friends Simoleon Gary, John-John, and Richie-the-Biker set up the first free store, the Free Exchange Market, as the huge billboard overhead announced.

The Diggers also laid on entertainment, also free of charge, with the San Francisco Mime Troupe. Ken Kesey and Neil Cassady could be seen there. Kesey lent his multicolored school bus for the runs (its windscreen bore the legend "Onwards").

Grogan's friends, the ones known as The Hun and Coyote, ran the shows. Five live marionettes were ordered by the police to move along. Whereupon The Hun, Grogan, and Slim Minaux—the marionettes—danced around the cops and improvised. They wound up down at the precinct with Butcher Brooks.

Emmett Grogan then played a crucial part in the framing of hippie imagery, somewhat in spite of himself. He had bugger all to do with the hippies but it was he who devised the famous V-sign finger gesture, which the press took to be a reference to Churchill, when in fact it was his V-sign reversed, a gesture employed by the IRA to say: Fuck you!

After these adventures, Grogan wrote two books, songs, became an anti-nuclear activist, and made some movies before he died of a heart attack in the subway in April 1978.

Alongside the Diggers' activities, a few people carried on with the theater shows that Grogan and Landout had allowed to fade away. In particular, with Hell's Angels assistance, they mounted "*The Death of Money.*" Grogan was to play a part in this, and just as soon as it was finished, he was hauled off to the precinct to face charges of meat theft. At his trial, Grogan's lawyer had a grand old time demonstrating that Grogan "does not steal for himself nor in order to sell the meat on, but merely to share it with the poor and the hungry invading the Haight-Ashbury district." He was given a six months' suspended sentence.

In return, the Hell's Angels laid on a thank-you party on New Year's Day (1967). They paid for the beer, the sound system, the stage truck, and invited along the Grateful Dead and the Holding Company (with which Janis Joplin was playing at the time). It was the first free rock festival in history. The police kept a low profile. "The park belongs to everyone," said those attending.

The role of the women in all of this was crucial. Grogan was to say: "They represented the real strength of the Haight-Ashbury community. They were the real Diggers. Cooking up two or three hundred-liter churns of stew for two hundred people may well be amusing if done once a year, but just try and stick at it two or three days in a row, for two or three weeks or two or three months. Without payment, without receiving a cent. It's a killer!"

A system was worked out and seemed to work well. Landout dropped out for a time. There was too much noise involved for his taste. The city health services impounded the Free Exchange Market. So they set up shop again in Frederick Street, where they had a kitchen, a bathroom, and a basement. There they provided shelter on an ongoing basis for heaps of folk on mattresses set out on the floor. There was a plate-glass window on which Grogan painted their insignia. Their buses had broken down. Richard Brautigan, who has since gained fame as a leading novelist, then made them the offer, through the rich daughter of one of his girlfriends, Flame (a name given to her by Grogan on account of her long mane of red hair), of a Chevrolet '58 truck. The truck was used as a free bus and ferried passengers all over the city, when not being used to ferry food.

Inside the Free Exchange Market, there was a cost-free store filled with "liberated produce," that is, liberated from the world of money and "commodity" (to borrow the Situationist terminology). Passing dropouts, whom the media unashamedly called the "Love Generation," could "crash" in the hall.

The Quakers then approached Emmett Grogan with an offer of $10,000 a year to do the very same thing but in the name of their church. Other, competing churches pestered him with equally dishonest offers. On every occasion, the Diggers suggested that they lead by example and distribute their (considerable) wealth among the poor.

Also on the point of rackets, one big-time LSD dealer offered the Diggers 10,000 acid tabs. The Diggers promptly handed these out, free of charge, along with the accompanying offer of 75 turkeys, in order to outflank the dealer.

The big underground stars—the Ginsbergs, the Learys, and the Alperts—the likeable and the weaklings, showed up in order to be seen. They found themselves turned away as if they were unclean.

The house next door was occupied by a Swami who had set up a Krishna store on the premises. Relations between them were very hostile. One day the Swami, who preached nonviolence, simply called in the cops because of the noise next door. Seizing on this pretext, the police rushed to the scene. So as to be sure that some might be found there, a brigade commander brought along some syringes and they were planted there. Grogan floored one cop before he himself was clubbed to the floor. The Free Exchange Market was smashed up by the police who trampled the food, showered it with water, and spattered all of the clothing with paint.

At a further trial, the Diggers were laid-back, for the judge was afraid of being made to look ridiculous in the press.

They then organized the big Human Happening (Be-In), complete with all the stars of the psychedelic scene and the leftists of the day—Jerry Rubin, Leary, Gary Snyder, the HIP traders and, pop groups (Quicksilver Messenger Service, Jefferson Airplane, Grateful Dead). Stewarding was left in the hands of the Hell's Angels, the only people who carried any authority at such gatherings. The menu offered turkey sandwiches with a dash of a sauce that was nothing less than LSD. Grogan was against all this, being, correctly, of the opinion that this was serving the interests of the dealers and feeding the illusions of the dropouts who thought that in Haight-Ashbury they were living a life of happy poverty when, in fact, all this was a sticking-plaster approach to poverty relief.

A poetry evening "to benefit the Diggers" was laid on and Snyder, Ginsberg, and Brautigan took part. There was no entrance charge, but the poets passed the hat. Grogan announced: "What benefits the Diggers is what benefits everybody," and promptly spent the money raised by standing everyone a round at the bar. Then there was the memorable party in Glide Methodist Church. Reporters present could not find anyone to answer their questions and were so shocked by what met their gaze that they breathed not one word about the event.

The Diggers' minds were not filled just with partying and enjoyment but also had time to spare for matters of benefit to everyone. Places for teenagers were set up across the city and everyone was welcomed, provided that they showed up without weapons or needles.

But little by little they were undone by myth. Thousands of youngsters at war with society, their circumstances dramatic or critical, turned out in the belief that the Diggers were offering a solution for all of their problems. They were encouraged by the thought that there was a different way of living and it was impossible to make them see sense. The police started to mount raids to pick up runaway minors. Whenever they came upon one of these poor endangered teenagers, they always began by reassuring him with their billyclubs, doubtless to protect him from evil thoughts.

The health center at the Free Exchange Market was exemplary: care was free of charge and certain doctors would even offer home treatments, particularly for Blacks and Chicanos. These were young neighborhood doctors in sympathy with this alternative society gnawing away at the city from within. Nurses or attendants would filch medicines to issue free of charge to those in need. The Grogan system was bearing fruit. Alienated products had to be "liberated" from the consumer society and put to their proper use, rescued, by confiscation, from a world of corruption and given a real life, just the way that birds should be freed from their cages. In spite of the good service the director of San Francisco's health services took a very dim view of the practice. He dispatched inspector after inspector to scrutinize hygiene conditions and he encouraged the local bourgeois and landlords to seize upon this as a pretext for evicting their tenants. A few of them did not let this chance go a-begging: there was money to be made from turning out hippie dropouts and moving in wealthy bourgeois looking to slum it for a bit.

It has to be said that the film industry started to muscle in on things and arrived to film sensational scenes on location. Big business also muscled in on this newly profitable district and there was a rash of nightclubs and "hippie" boutiques opening in the area, amid the joints touting "love-burgers."

The Diggers and the HIP businessmen just could not get along with one another. The city shut down the Free Exchange Market. So they moved to Cole Street, to a glass-fronted store with an upper story and inner balcony. But things just were not the same. Everyone was out to exploit them and use them—often the very people they were trying to help. One day Grogan caught two women scooping up everything they could from the free store for resale elsewhere. He gave them a piece of his mind about this. They merely replied: "You give the stuff away, so what the fuck has it to do with you what becomes of it?"

At the same time, certain frictions were coming to the surface in the Digger ranks. The media was cashing in on them in spite of their wishes. And that created jealousy. Grogan took six weeks off to unwind a little.

By common accord—albeit without discussing it among themselves—they all seized upon the chance to lead the media to believe that Emmett Grogan did not exist, that he was a myth, a collective name used by them all, that each and every one of them was Grogan. Even though he had gone, things carried on without him. On his return, he picked up where he had left off.

A further free rock concert was laid on in a park, with two flat-bed trucks back to back and two enormous screens. The Grateful Dead, Country Joe & the Fish, Janis Joplin and Big Brother & the Holding Company showed up to perform under multicolored lights. It was a resounding success.

Grogan received some strange threats and left once again. At this point, what has come to be known as the Summer of Love was in progress and the media were revelling in it all. Concerts organized by the Diggers (who never ever claimed any credit for anything) were credited to other people, who took pride in a celebrity that had cost them nothing.

Grogan was in London, where he met Alexander Trocchi, an ex-Situationist whom he admired. He took part in a debate on the "dialectics of liberation." He was surrounded by intellectuals with great notions about their own brainpower. He then delivered a thrilling address which he had simply lifted from a very demagogic speech of Adolf Hitler's about revolution, socialism, community life, etc. He was acclaimed. It only remained for him now to reveal the deception. The rage of the participants and audience could not have been greater and he was shown the door.

He travelled on, to see the Dutch Provos first hand, visiting Kommune 1 and Kommune 2 in Berlin, drifting through May '68 and dropping over to Prague before hanging out with Black Panther Party personnel.

On his return to Haight-Ashbury, he got involved in the home distribution of free meals, with the much-touted slogan "It's free because it belongs to you." By the end of a week, he had a hundred names on his list and was left to cope by himself. Some people shunned him, while others staked their claim to the credit for activity in which he had been careful to remain anonymous. The atmosphere was becoming strained and he had had his fill, so he quit.

Such disillusionment produced the inevitable results. He turned back to hard drugs. And was no longer up to taking on his "work." His most loyal friends took up the baton but things were still not going terribly well. Grogan entered a detox program again.

With Black Panther support, he revived the old idea and laid on breakfasts for the black kids of Oakland (the Black Panther capital). He supplied milk and groceries which were distributed by the city's Panthers. Exhausted by it all, he left California in January 1970.

With him went the Digger movement from the scene, after more than two years in operation. Which political party can brag of comparable success?

Those who speak of revolution without explicitly referring
to daily life, without understanding the subversive content
in love and the positive content in the refusal of
constraints, such people have a corpse in their mouths.

Raoul Vaneigem
Treatise on Living for the Use of the
Younger Generation (1968)

At this point France experienced the most extensive, most
prolonged general strike ever to have brought the
economy of an advanced country to a standstill (...) and,
at the same time, history's first ever "spontaneous" general
strike; all of the power of the State, the political parties
and the trade unions themselves were quite simply erased
for several weeks, while factories and public buildings were
occupied in every city (...) The events of May were
profoundly revolutionary and potentially a lot more
dangerous for the world than the Russian Revolution...

Gianfranco Sanguinetti
True Report on the Last Chances to
Save Capitalism in Italy (1975)

Much literature has appeared on the May '68 events in France and yet no book
offers an all-embracing and fundamental handle on the most formidable upheaval
History has to offer. At best, they offer a more or less adequate summary of the
"happenings." That, moreover, is where we should begin.

The agitation started in the autumn of 1967, but the disturbances are traced
back to January, when minister Missoffe arrived to inaugurate a swimming pool on
the restless Nanterre camps. He was taken to one side by a group of students
including Daniel Cohn-Bendit (a 23-year-old of German Jewish ancestry, as all his
adversaries never wearied of reminding people) who asked him why his report on
young people had made no mention of their sexuality. Missoffe made do with
advising Cohn-Bendit to take a dip in the pool to cool off.

The agitation was to linger for two months. Even then there was talk of the
Nanterre Enragés, that is, of folk like Cohn-Bendit, as well as like René Riesel,
Patrick Cheval, Gérard Bigorgne, and others. Bigorgne was expelled from the
university. Later, there was a further expulsion, this time of Xavier Langlade and

this was to trigger the occupation of a lecture theater (promptly renamed the "Che Guevara") on the Nanterre campus. One hundred and forty-two students then seized the council rooms and launched the Movement of the 142, which was to change almost immediately into the 22 March Movement, so there you have it.

Apart from Cohn-Bendit, the other Enragés wanted nothing to do with it because of its refusal to expel the Stalinists from its ranks. As a result, it embraced anarchists, Trotskyists, and soon, Maoists too.

The Enragés took a very radical line which had earlier emerged at the instigation of the Situationist International, a radical group from the years 1957–1971 and without question the most prolific nursery of ideas and personalities in a long time. In 1966–67, some students advised by the S.I. (especially Mustapha Khayati) had taken over the students' union in Strasbourg and caused a scandal by publishing the legendary (and sensational) pamphlet *On the Poverty of Student Life* (re-reading it today, there is not much that needs rewriting), written by Khayati; they had then dissolved that association, and suggested that the UNEF (French National Union of Students) follow suit; and finally, they had abolished the University Psychiatric Assistance Bureau which stood accused of referring deviants to the mental hospitals (it has to be said that their opponents were forever labelling them as "madmen"). One lecturer, Abraham Moles, then much in fashion, was even driven out of his chair and this heralded many similar actions.

The S.I.'s two most heavyweight theorists at the time published two highly important books in 1967 and 1968, books that were to have a tremendous impact on the few thousand minds which had read them by then. The books in question were Guy Debord's *Society of the Spectacle* and Raoul Vaneigem's *Treatise on Living for the Use of the Younger Generation*. Both books are worthy of perusal by today's "younger generation" for they are the only books from that time to have withstood the ravages of time.

On March 22, as they were leaving the Che Guevara lecture theater, the Enragés started to daub slogans on the walls to plant ideas in people's minds. For instance, there was one that read: "Never work" or "Treat your desires as realities."

While Riesel was the leading light among the Enragés, Daniel Cohn-Bendit, a sociology student and member of the Noir & Rouge anarchist organization, a fellow with a certain charisma and an infectious sense of humor, was undeniably the pacesetter of this pre-history of the upheavals.

The man who would become familiar as "Danny the Red," the "German Jew" or "Con-Bandit," or called by a heap of other names and labels in accordance with the horror he struck into the media, was to campaign unsuccessfully against his own "star" status for a few weeks. This was a stardom for which he was indebted to the press, although his own personality was a large factor.

The other leftist groups (not to go into detail here, suffice to say that there were anarchists, Trotskyists, and Maoists who—ALL OF THEM—at one point or another, were to do their damndest to apply the brakes to the movement, because none of them could control it) were very jealous of one another and this hatred lingers yet. More heavyweight historians (Ragache and Delale, say, who bear the marks of Leninism) try to play down their real influence. The fact of the matter is that Cohn-Bendit was May in all its splendor, what with his sense of humor, his naiveté maybe, his ambiguity and his imagination. Which does not mean that he was its leader. He was merely one of the more gifted of the people on the streets.

In view of the tension between the far left and the far right, the dean, Pierre Grappin, ordered the closure of the Nanterre campus on May 2. On May 3, a meeting between the UNEF (the main student union, which carried some weight at the time) and the 22 March Movement in the Sorbonne dragged on and on. The police cordoned off the university. Brawling erupted. For the first time the chant went up "CRS=SS" as the first tear-gas grenades exploded. There would be 72 police officers injured. The like of it had never been seen before. Six hundred arrests resulted in four sentences to close custody. An unlimited nationwide students' strike erupted.

On May 6, there was a demonstration in Paris, timed to coincide with the appearance of Riesel, Cohn-Bendit and six other Enragés before a disciplinary panel. It was to last for 16 hours. For the first time, young workers joined forces with the students and tilted the violence into the realms of the revolutionary and the radical. Cars were overturned and this left the bourgeoisie, press reporters, and other onlookers and property-owners stupefied. Barricades were even erected.

On May 9, Grappin backtracked and announced that Nanterre was to reopen. This was after negotiation with the trade unions, the UNEF (led by its vice-president, Jacques Sauvageot, who was close to the PSU) and the SNESUP (led by Maoist Alain Geismar). But the Education Minster, the ineffable Peyrefitte, vetoed the reopening. It was Peyrefitte who lighted the fuse of a powder keg that, within days, would strike such terror into him.

It should be made clear that the prime minister, Pompidou, was away on a visit to Afghanistan and that De Gaulle was asleep that evening. And that everything depended upon a handful of inept ministers and bumbling underlings. The Night of the Barricades arrived on May 10, 1968. Hundreds would be wounded. Outlying radio stations (less tightly controlled by the authorities than today) monitored developments second by second. In a single night the government lost the battle so ill-advisedly joined by Peyrefitte. An awful shudder was to travel through the country.

At a single stroke, everyone was made conversant with students' problems, but everyone also let loose his own desires and frustrations. At a stroke, France swung behind the barricades.

There was a rash of sit-ins the following day. Pompidou, terror-stricken by the situation, scurried home from Afghanistan. De Gaulle learned of the situation into which his ministers had plunged him. Initially, they backed off: the police pulled out of the Latin Quarter. Paris was in student hands.

From the outset, the political parties were hostile to the students, as were the trade unions (with the exception of the CFDT which held dialogue with them: Sauvageot was a CFDT member, too). The hatred from the French Communist Party and from the CGT was to reach unprecedented levels. It was at this point that a little squirt none too well known to the French public—one Georges Marchais by name—was to come to prominence. He was only the deputy of Waldeck-Rochet, the party's leader at the time, but Waldeck-Rochet was more of a softy.

The CGT was already under the control of Séguy, a dyed-in-the-wool Stalinist, some of whose utterances deserve a place in any anthology of silliness. While these events were in progress, this pair were to be De Gaulle's staunchest supports. He could scarcely count upon his own foot soldiers who were unlikely to be found in the factories.

On May 13, though, in spite of Marchais' racist slanders (while Marchais talked of "the German, Cohn-Bendit," some of his supporters used the term "carrot-top" and a few even referred to "Cohn-Bendit the German Jew"), the trade unions joined in the demonstrations, or at least went through the motions of doing so. Some 500,000 people demonstrated. There was a sit-in at the Sorbonne. The general strike was observed everywhere.

On his way into the Sorbonne, the Situationist René Viénet (whose book on *The Enragés and Situationists* in May, written in July 1968, remains one of the best analyses of what was radical about that upheaval) scrawled on a famous picture: "Mankind will only be happy on the day when the last bureaucrat has been hanged with the entrails of the last capitalist." The press kicked up about the defacing of a work of art, yet Viénet had just created a remarkable one of his own by putting into practical effect the S.I.'s theories about détournement.

Moreover, the Enragés and Situationists were to devise the best of the slogans that turned up on the walls of the Sorbonne and elsewhere, the ones that were to be reproduced the world over. Riesel and Christian Sébastiani, future S.I. members (whose star was to fade inexorably after May), were often the authors of these.

Riesel was also one of 15 people elected on to the Sit-in Committee, all of the members of which were liable to recall daily in an election. This was a student soviet in the grand tradition. They were to argue for direct democracy and for the Councillist tendency. An Enragé-Situationist International Committee also emerged to steer the Sit-in Committee over a three-day period, from May 15 to 17. It was they who issued the appeal to all the workers to sit in the factories and to establish workers' councils everywhere. They also dispatched stinging telegrams in every direction, notably insulting ones to Beijing and Moscow.

By May 15, the red flag was flying over the Renault plant. Red and black flags were visible on the streets. The wildcat strike became general from May 18 on. Now there was nowhere in the country unaffected by it. From the outset, women were to play an outstanding part in the insurrection.

The Odéon was occupied as well. This was the start of de facto self-management. Workers reopened the canteens and telephone switchboards for the insurgents' use. They even reopened a walkie-talkie factory because its products would be of service. The bakers supplied the strikers with bread and the farmers supplied vegetables and the fishermen, fish. A system of parallel intercourse in goods was introduced. Goods were given or sold at cost price. Trucks were bought or borrowed for transportation of foodstuffs.

Open-air centers were established. In every town a Central Strike Committee took power. These soviets ran whole cities whose municipal authorities had sometimes abdicated their responsibilities. Elsewhere, they merely helped. They were in charge of supplies of provisions. The strikers doled out food and fuel.

Rubbish collections were organized and free dispensaries opened. Special "strikers'" price charges were drawn up. Money was collected and subsidies wheedled out of sympathetic municipalities. Food vouchers were issued. An alternative society was in the making. In some places money was even replaced by bonds.

The notion of self-management as a flesh and blood political arrangement took hold in people's minds. The fact was that a proletariat that had for 2,000 years been unwittingly groping for self-management started to grapple with it consciously now and even to theorize about it. There was panic among the bourgeois but there was even greater panic among the professional leftists, the trade unionists, and party leaders. Hitherto, the notion of self-management had been the preserve of the PSU or of the anarchists.

Some sectors, such as the hospitals, were operational: and there were train services for the transportation of certain goods: penury had to be avoided. In the factories, there were debates and film shows and discussions about politics, society and sexuality, etc. In every regard the organization by the workers was remarkable. Hence the headway being made by the notion of self-management: everything was going so much better without the bosses. And yet, there was no one so surprised as the workers themselves.

Other committees were set up at the Sorbonne. Tiny groups started to wheel and deal, gutting one another over derisory morsels of power. A certain Krivine— at that time an obscure figure—panicked at the very idea that the students could have issued a call for the formation of soviets everywhere. Understandable. That had given his master nightmares in Kronstadt back in 1921. Little by little, the apprentice bureaucrats wormed their way back in everywhere. Disgusted, the Enragé-Situationist International Committee packed things in. Once it was gone, there was no more talk of re-electing the members of the Sit-in Committee.

The Mandarins were suffering badly. They were publicly insulted, if not driven out of their tenured posts. No one was spared and anyway, no one had grasped the potential behind the revolt: Touraine, Chatelet, Moles, Lefebvre, Morin, Axelos, Godard, Lapassade, and Aragon—they were all in the same boat.

Then the Enragés and Situationists set up the Committee for the Maintenance of Sit-ins (in French, the CMDO) which set up shop on the premises of the Educational Institute. It was to issue important texts and even a list of radical slogans for daubing everywhere. The list included the famous "Down with the spectacular commodity society" which still sends a shiver down the spine of récupérateurs of every hue. In fact, the CMDO realized that it was time to move beyond the student strike. The workers had realized this too after a fashion as their actions showed. From then on, the fight was carried by the workers. The student upheaval merely retreated from this point on.

On May 22, Daniel Cohn-Bendit set off on a European publicity "tour." He was banned from staying in France. He was to return, but, what with the recession of the student revolt, his role was going to be negligible. De Gaulle spoke for the first time on May 24, to no effect. The regime had disintegrated in a fortnight.

In Parliament, there was tough talking but it was greeted with general indifference. The opposition had been overwhelmed at the same time as the authorities. Society hovered on the edge.

In Nantes, the prefecture was taken over for a time. This was the Nantes Commune—the description may be a bit excessive, but it conveys the point that in that city, where the workers were more hard-line, where the FO was under the sway of anarchists, where the UNEF was headed by Enragés, there were more radical goings-on than elsewhere. Moreover the CMDO was still in touch with the personnel of the Enragé-influenced UNEF, notably with Yves Chotard and Juvénal Quillet.

Every town had its "barricades night" on May 24 or over the succeeding days. In Lyon, a police inspector was killed by a truck whose brakes had been released by demonstrators. One Parisian demonstrator was killed by a grenade. Five hundred people were injured. There was tremendous violence all over. Police excesses were countless. On De Gaulle's own recommendation, the police were doped with alcohol.

May 25 saw the opening of the Grenelle negotiations, which were to save the face of the Communist Party and of De Gaulle. Pompidou, his Employment secretary (Chirac), and his Social Affairs minister (Jeanneney) negotiated with the unions of the employers (the CNPF) and of the workers (André Jeanson and Descamps for the CFDT; Séguy, Frachon, and Krasucki for the CGT). Séguy uttered the historic words: "This is not the time for chatter about thoroughgoing changes in society."

Agreement was quickly reached. The government conceded some minor social advances (a lot more could have been negotiated in that sphere). The working class was tremendously disappointed and there was a universal and wholesale rejection of these shabby accords. Séguy got a heckling in Billancourt, the like of which he had never met with before.

In Nantes, the soviet—the Central Strike Committee—exercised all de facto authority: the prefect was virtually a prisoner, the police had pulled back, the municipal authorities had resigned, and the CGT was virtually nonexistent, for the local unions were very left-wing. This was to last until early June.

On every side, all sorts of Action Committees sprang up in schools, universities, factories... before developing into inter-professional ones (Worker-Student Committees). There was a flood of resignations from the CGT and the Communist Party. Even the less decrepit student organizations were being left behind.

On May 29, in order to impress his followers, De Gaulle—everybody was surprised that he had not resigned—paid a visit to his old friend, the torturer Massu, in his barracks in Baden-Baden. Even as all his ministers were panicking to a laughable extent (especially, if witnesses are to be believed, Peyrefitte), or were going to ground in hope of being overlooked in the event of conflict, De Gaulle was about to seize the situation by the throat.

Negotiations with the trade unions had already gone his way. The CP would prove a loyal ally: they shared a common enemy and they would act in concert.

In order to point up the dangers of civil war, De Gaulle had the army cordon off Paris. Then he made the announcement that he would be staying and dissolved the National Assembly (which had not lifted a finger in any case!). This left people absorbed by an upcoming election. That would provide a distraction from the struggle.

A demonstration in support of De Gaulle was organized and it drew 100,000 people on to the Champs Elysées. The regime was making a comeback like some horrible smell from the basement. The SAC (Civilian Action Service), whose bar-bouzes (para-police) carried tri-color warrant cards, was very active, especially through the less militarized CDRs (Committees to Defend the Republic). Recruitment of these parallel police agents, overseen by people like Comiti or the sinister Foccart, often focused upon the underworld and former OAS personnel. The SAC drew up a plan to round up leftists to be penned in stadiums in each town. The lists were furnished by the DST, no less. As we can see, the CRS was closer to turning into the SS than they themselves may have thought. The roundup was scheduled for May 24, before being postponed to a later date and eventually called off.

But paranoia did cost one life in Calvados when a gendarme killed a young man he had mistaken for a saboteur.

On May 31, the new Pompidou government was announced: the ministerial line-up was the same as before…but they had swapped portfolios! Marcellin was now Interior minister and Ortoli took over from Peyrefitte. The cabinet had lost its fear. They were keeping their counsel, that was all. "Of course, the bourgeoisie had not departed France; it had merely been struck dumb by terror," the S.I. was to pronounce. Sector by sector, the government was to renegotiate a return to work in return for the concession of petty advantages.

The movement split in two, with the moderates swallowing the bait. The trades unions did their bit to break the revolt at all costs. To that end, the CGT deployed powers of imagination of which it would never have been suspected.

Among the farmers, the FNSEA was to thwart any liaison with the workers. Fear of bankruptcy, of produce or petrol shortages, scared off the easily deterred. De Gaulle played it for all he was worth.

However fighting resumed on June 5 in Flins. In the midst of all the excitement, a vote was held on a resumption of work at Renault: the ballot boxes were "stuffed" with votes in favor of a return. A thousand CRS were sent in. The battle of Flins was to drag on for four days. The students, led by Geismar, joined the strikers. The CGT was in a furious rage. The fighting spilled over into the surrounding fields.

On several occasions the CGT helped the police to thwart the students. It ensured that its delegates who were regularly dismissed by the assemblies of the factory soviets were paid.

On June 10, a 17-year old Maoist high school student, Gilles Tautin, was drowned in the Seine as he fled in the midst of the rout.

On that very day, the fighting also started up again in Sochaux-Montbéliard at the Puegeot plant. It lasted for two days.

Two workers were killed: one was shot (24-year old Pierre Beylot) and one was killed by a falling grenade (49-year old Henri Blanchet). Angry workers smashed everything in certain premises. There were street fights, essentially involving workers, right across France right up until June 13.

On June 12, De Gaulle dissolved eight leftist organizations, among them the 22 March Movement. Expulsions and searches led up to eviction from the Odéon at police hands.

The trade unions (CGT and CFDT) were furious, but the students were in the same boat. Their stewarding at the Sorbonne had, for some time by then, been provided by unemployed workers and déclassé sorts, a few of whom were (rumor had it) legionnaires and even mercenaries who were referred to as the "Katangese." Annoyed by this unpleasant image, the students politely turned them away (and their leader was to be murdered a short time later in bizarre circumstances by his own colleagues).

There was no one left to defend the movement's last remaining symbolic site. On June 16, the police cleared it. On June 18 work resumed at the Renault plants.

Séguy and De Gaulle had won.

It only remained now for the elections to see the seal upon this trend. The UDR expanded its vote considerably, while the vote for the left—especially the CP vote—plummeted. Fear had carried the day. During the election campaign, three more people had lost their lives in the French West Indies. But something in the French mind-set had snapped and many still could not grasp this fact yet. One of the signs of it was that Gaullism's fate had been sealed. De Gaulle was removed one year later over a trivial matter.

To quote Delale and Ragache: "In reality, the popular uprising in May had paved the way for the development of an authentic 'cultural revolution,' that is, a revolution in the realm of day-to-day culture and social relationships. Hundreds of thousands of intellectuals, cadres, students, high school students, teachers, artists, doctors, and researchers had thrown themselves into activity and had tried to 'remake the world' by 're-inventing society.' In an even broader sense, May '68 represented, for the vast majority of French people, a real shock, a rupture: for some, the upheaval had all the appearances of an earth tremor and evoked terror as a response; others saw it as an awakening, an abrupt revelation of teeming life, the brutal eruption of energies bottled up for too long, followed by an unleashing of spontaneous initiative and individual expression."

In the universities, collectives had taken charge of publications, telephone services, health, nursing, fire fighting, catering, secretarial tasks, cooking, dormitory services, nurseries, and in Besançon there was even a "revolutionary police." All these new tasks turned these students into well-rounded citizens.

The splendid slogans admired the world over, the superb posters from the (former) Fine Arts Workshop and the particularly acute sense of humor to be encountered everywhere, the close relations established between artists and workers, between academics and proletarians, all of this—and it is famous—is indicative of the richness of May. A new world was being sketched there. Or rather, the world had taken on the mantle of a new way of living.

And this left its mark on every mind, even if it was kept very private. Proof of this came in the form of all the little compartmentalized struggles that cropped up during the restoration of the old order in the wake of May: women's issues, issues affecting education, gays, prisons, migrants, racial minorities, doctors, psychiatrists, soldiers, etc. Day-to-day living was to feel the impact of this for a long time. Every aspect of life had felt its touch (there was even the spectacle of cadres taking over the CNPF premises). There was a crucial need to get the point across that "nothing could be the same ever again." Evidence of this could be discovered in the renaming of streets, lecture theaters, high schools, and even ships. The only thing missing was a revolutionary calendar.

Some die-hards fought on into July. The CMDO fell to pieces. Its well-known Situationist members (Debord, Vaneigem, Viénet, Khayati) or Enragé members

(Riesel and Sébastiani) later came together within the S.I., but the S.I. itself was not to survive May. Once the action ceased, the luminaries fell to pieces and succumbed to alcohol, drugs, boredom, or despair: and the S.I. was no exception. It is not easy to survive defeat.

In May, most working class people had failed to appreciate the originality of their own struggle. Let us not speak of the students, who, in the end, were a letdown. There was no one who ventured to assert in practical terms the power of councils. Yet one last straw and the whole thing might have come tumbling down.

Their adversaries, though, had sized up the danger correctly: De Gaulle, the CNPF and Séguy had realized that their world had developed fatal cracks. Though it may be hard to envisage today, the terror inspired in the bourgeoisie was very real indeed. That those under threat should have linked forces is quite understandable, but equally understandable is the conspiracy of silence they maintained over the 12 years that have passed since then. Such was their fear that it took ten years before Cohn-Bendit was able to return freely to France. Having moved on to activism in the German communes and then becoming a pioneering ecologist, Danny had been a bookseller, before moving to France to work in the publishing sector. Sauvageot (who dropped out of public life after May) and Geismar (who was for a time linked to Maoist dilettantism) went on to become lecturers.

"For the very first time in France, the State was ignored: It was the first practical critique of the Jacobinism that had for so long been the nightmare of French revolutionary movements, including the Commune," as Viénet was to put it.

Those who lived this strange period first hand will remember the overwrought, amorous, passionate atmosphere and the physical and intellectual excitement that washed over their minds. They loved everybody, knew one another by sight, and enjoyed themselves without inhibition. It was a tremendous outpouring of affection. "People looked with amusement upon the curious existence that they had been leading just eight days before, an existence they had outgrown." (S.I., No. 12)

One other crucial facet has been covered up by ALL of the historians of May '68. Yet, as I see things, it is the most important of them all. Over those few weeks, and over the weeks that immediately preceded or succeeded May, this same groundswell arose or was replicated in every corner of the world, West and East alike, in "socialist" regimes as well as in capitalist ones, in highly developed as well as in Third World nations, in dictatorships as well as in liberal countries. Judge for yourselves: there were upheavals along similar lines in Italy, Spain, W. Germany, Switzerland, Belgium, England, Sweden, Greece, Turkey, Poland, Czechoslovakia, Yugoslavia, China, Japan, India, Indonesia, Thailand, the USA, Brazil, Santo Domingo, Venezuela, Uruguay, Chile, Argentina, Congo-Kinshasa, Senegal, Algeria, Tunisia, Morocco, Mauretania, etc.

This phenomenon, without parallel in History, is still unexplained and diligently distorted by everybody, including the protagonists of May, doubtless

207

because it makes a nonsense of absolutely every traditional school of thought on History and of every ideology and flew in the face of every political and social interest and blew everybody's mind.

In that regard, May '68 may well have been, not the final fling of the classical workers' movement, but perhaps the first stirrings of a new revolutionary age, the second stage of which may not be visible to the naked eye (by naked, I mean an eye not informed by modern dialectical consciousness). This gives us a better understanding of the despair of our contemporaries, who have deserted every ideology; we have the Stalinists' own disclosures about all the Gulags, the widespread distaste for party membership and for political militancy (and an option instead for activism in a cause—ecology, feminism, minority rights, neighborhood committees, etc.), for voting and politics (the repeated failures of the left, even though it may enjoy a majority in France, are but one signal of this) and many other symptoms.

Denmark, 1971
CHRISTIANIA

We can destroy everything, because we built it all and we can rebuild it all.

Bakunin

We are the heirs of the men who, though living in an age of ignorance, misery, oppression, ugliness, hypocrisy, iniquity, and hatred, kept their gaze fixed upon a city of knowledge, well-being, liberty, beauty, candor, justice, and brotherhood and who strove with all of their might to construct that wondrous city.

Sébastien Faure

In the heart of Copenhagen, in the Christianhavn district, the armed services decommissioned a 22-hectare site which had belonged to them and on which a few deserted buildings were allowed to stand. This was in the spring of 1971. They left everything in working order but fenced it off. They had no plans for the use of the site.

That autumn, a few squatters started to settle into the 170 buildings. They numbered around 25 people. They placed ads in the alternative press, "Use your imagination with the No. 8 bus," that being the route that passed nearby. In October they held their first meeting and made provision against anything that might pose a threat to these living quarters. Their commune was to take the name of "Christiania." It was launched on September 26.

In November, the decision was reached that "the object of Christiania is the construction of a self-managing society wherein every individual is free to do his own thing while remaining answerable to the community as a whole. This society must be economically autonomous and our shared aspiration is to demonstrate that all pollution—physical and moral alike—can be avoided." This was already a full-blown political program and it only remained to get down to the details and put it into effect. Which is what the Chrisitianians were to do over the ensuing years and what they may well be doing yet.

Straight away, spontaneously, with no preconceived planning, numerous would-be Christianians flooded in and settled wherever they pleased, wherever took their fancy. Each of them built or rebuilt to suit themselves, in the most motley town-planning arrangements, but the overall blend of all this architectural folly was in fact to endow Christiania with a real town "feel."

209

By the start of 1972, their numbers had grown to 400. Even then there were some who wanted to "organize" the commune and take it in hand, self-managed or not, and to introduce a measure of planning. Others were against this. A few cleaned up the worst of the filth, disposed of the rubbish and tidied the place up a bit. Others resolutely let things go. Numerous conflicts cropped up. They held general assemblies, setting up working groups and think-tanks, an information office, a community hall, a weekly paper, *Ordkløveren*, shops, a restaurant, flea markets, workshops (including some producing the wood stoves so useful in the countryside), concert rooms, etc...

A veritable alternative township, Christiania looked to the needs of her (many) unemployed. And the unemployed also took the commune in hand. Unemployment benefit payments were turned over to the commune and the jobless put their free time to good use by working free of charge for the commune. Rents were paid on time. Bar profits swelled the coffers and the economic team redistributed the money once all bills had been settled.

Some people even renounced their own names and plumped as a group for the name Lovetand "Lionheart"—a name to which around 40 of them answer at present.

In May 1972 came the first indication of unease on the part of the authorities: a negotiated settlement was in the making when the (Social Democratic) government cut off the power supply. It was at about this time that a theater troupe called Solvognen arrived in Christiania; from then on it would be at the center of all parties, shows, and street activities and commune demonstrations, not to mention propaganda tours in the world outside. A year was to pass peaceably as a life of leisure was organized.

Once up and running, Christiania had a thousand inhabitants, about a hundred of them children. Three hundred dogs, goats, pigs, horses, and poultry

roamed its streets. There were 750 permanent residents, plus those passing through, and it became a place to visit. They adopted a violet-colored flag that fluttered majestically above the district.

In June 1973 they secured recognition as an experimental society. The government acknowledged them, yet launched an architectural competition on the future use of the site. In return, they had to look to the proper maintenance of the premises, carrying out the necessary repairs—or see the buildings levelled. Right-wing politicians capitalized upon them in their denunciation of the left-wing government's muddle-headedness. In the ensuing elections (January 1974) the right came to power.

This complicated matters for the commune-dwellers. The right was firmly determined to bulldoze the place in order to let building speculators—their natural constituency—have their way with the 22 hectares.

From then on, in every election, Christiania was to field its own candidates—the "Valborg Found"—comprising feminists, gays, crazies, dropouts, ecologists, etc. They had one of them returned, a woman called Tine Smedes. This was the signal for great celebrations. In the outside world, they attracted extraordinary popular backing. A "Help Christiania" campaign was launched. Tine Smedes often scolded the rather lame parliamentary deputies. She caused a public sensation by breast-feeding her child in the chamber.

In May 1974, they managed to have the demolition order rescinded (they were granted a period of grace up until 1976).

In February 1975, the left was returned to power, but the Parliament's finance commission still refused to assume responsibility for the requisite repair work. The right pushed through a scheme to do away with Christiania and in the end it was passed by a slim margin. The site was to be cleared by April 1, 1976.

All of a sudden, the Christianians started to carry out the repairs themselves, when demolition was what they were supposed to be preparing for. They set up social centers and even a school.

Then, out of the blue, in December, they attacked the government for having failed to honor its commitments (vis-a-vis their status as an experimental society). They got themselves organized properly, mobilizing the media. Books about their venture appeared and public opinion tilted in their favor. Christiania turned into the number one tourist attraction and public debates were held pretty well everywhere. In order to assist the media against making too gross errors, everybody wore a color-coded armband according to his role (building schemes, propaganda and theater work, children and teachers, traders, poets and dealers, garbage collectors and therapists, nonviolent stewards). An army of female pacifists was even organized in order to pre-empt incident.

In March, a great Spring Festival was laid on. Three thousand people marched on the town hall and Parliament in Copenhagen. The upshot was that, on the eve of the expiration of the period of grace, the Parliament backed down. The fateful day was postponed indefinitely.

A Christiania record brought them in some money, on which basis they were able to mount a counterattack and fund other projects of the same sort across Denmark. At Christmas, they laid on a few spectacular actions such as a banquet for 1,000 homeless people. Meanwhile their court case was coming to a head. In February, they won the case. Their lawyer, Carl Madsen, who was terminally ill, mustered enough strength to win the case before succumbing to his cancer. He had been involved in everything they did.

By June 1977, Christiania was in its heyday. Windmills turned on the hills and everything had been rebuilt and given a fresh coat of paint. Every home was different from its neighbor and they came in all shapes and sizes…domes, caravans, chalets, hut-like constructions, etc., abutted the converted houses. There were enough schools and hospitals to cater for their requirements. People from surrounding areas were sending their own children or their sick folk there. There was an entire lecture theater built of recycled timber.

The only real problem was the problem of the drug users. There was a large number of these and they simply flooded in from outside to buy their dope in the free district. Often they settled there. Grass smokers did not create much bother but hard-drug users did, being perpetually spaced out, suicidal, and idle. But beer

Carl Madsen

drinkers were a problem too, making up the most aggressive section and generating silly fights. They did a lot to discredit the commune residents in the eyes of the outside world.

From the outset, one of the only two laws the Christianians had passed had been: No hard drugs. The other one was: No cars. There never were any of those.

Christiania lived off its festivals and the Solvognen's many theatrical performances which would make all aficionados of less than po-faced agitprop green with envy. At Carl Madsen's funeral in June 1978, his wishes were observed:

yellow and red flowers, rainbow-colored flags, demonstrations of joy, merry-making, music, group singing of the Internationale—all of it out in the countryside where he was laid to rest.

Meanwhile, negotiations with the authorities were continuing. Ten women led the Christiania representation. The police gave them a hard time of it but not openly: the police would afford entry to hard-drug users and dealers in an attempt to sour relations between the residents. Their battles had strengthened and tightened these relations, even between those who did not see eye to eye on everything: they were united in their determination to defend this enclave in the old world. In spite of this ghetto mentality, their links with the outside world were extensive. A large number of Christianians lived outside the commune, travelling in on a daily basis. Some left, but carried on supporting them, and their places were taken by fresh blood. Rather than a ghetto, rather than a reservation for dropouts, crazies, drug addicts, sick people, deviants, leftists, and the like (as their most rabid—albeit resigned—opponents had long regarded them), Christiania was an outpost. Some people were alive to this fact. Even their adversaries, even the authorities preferred to see all the subversives concentrated there, where they did not pose too many problems, rather than scattered across Denmark. Or worse: obliging them to find room for them in prisons, mental hospitals, and the like, with the responsibility for watching over them.

Inside Christiania, it was the residents who controlled them and controlled one another. This was good value for the extraordinary freedom afforded them in return. Then again it has to be conceded that, on average, the crime rate there was very low, which suggests that Christiania was a success—in social terms, at any rate.

Their approach to medicine, for instance, was extremely revolutionary: the doctors available only offered treatment in their areas of competence. When unsure about a given ailment, they said so and looked up books on the subject, asking for some time or referring the patient to others who were more au fait with the complaint. They were assisted by non-doctors who picked up elementary knowledge on the job. All of this was free of charge. There were plenty of herbalists and they were very up to date.

In Christiania, problems were broached openly and frictions were not covered up. Social relations were open and above board. Frictions sometimes appeared overblown because they were played out in public, but in the end they were less serious than in "normal" society. The most serious problem, though, was that the women were well outnumbered by the men, which led to the sort of tensions one might expect. One rapist (a Frenchman, as it happens) was expelled from Christiania and his picture was posted up everywhere as a warning to women.

One Christiania resident, Marianne, states in Catpoh's remarkable book: "That's why Christiania was so provocative. Because its residents dared to live what the rest could only dare dream." Not that there was any shortage of hostility toward them. The Danish Communist Party regularly cited them as the perfect example of what was rotten in the state of Denmark.

Nor was there any lack of support for them, either, (they even received fraternal messages from the LIP workers). Christiania was part and parcel of the whole ecology, anti-nuclear, anti-psychiatry, feminist, new school, nonviolent, alternative scene bequeathed by the years of the counterculture. But all of this was also grafted onto a flesh and blood utopia, a living utopia. One had only to see the radiance of the children, the bloom in the faces of the active women, the serenity in certain faces and the look on the faces of some of the men who had been through the experience of social organization, the thought behind their entertainment and the unbridled, knowing imagination behind their

building projects to realize that Christiania was one of this century's great alternative success stories. One that many a communitarian would not even have dared dream about.

But the credit for this belonged exclusively to their own determination and thoughtfulness. As one of the residents, Soren-Ib, commented: "The only thing one ever has is what one takes and we have Christiania because we took it."

By 1980, Christiania could well have disappeared, but by then could look back on nine solid years of freedom, nine years of demanding, exciting freedom, which is why it can be said that Christiania will remain one of the greatest success stories of the proletariat in the history of mankind.

Portugal, 1974-1975
THE REVOLUTION OF THE CARNATIONS

Under socialism, everybody will take it in turns to govern and will quickly get used to no one's governing.

Lenin
The State and Revolution (1917)

A people always has too much government.

Anselme Ballegarrigue
Come to the Point! Come to the Point!
(1848)

The essential, fundamental point of dissension is quite different: socialists are authoritarians, anarchists are libertarians.

Malatesta
Umanità Nova (1921)

Could there have been anything less like a revolution than what happened on April 25, 1974? It was a putsch, and an army putsch at that. The populace played not the slightest role in it and only found out what had happened from the radio or from the newspapers the following day. At which point they took to the streets and made "their" revolution, with the complaisance of the military.

By a stroke of luck, the latter had as a whole been won over by a radical change in society. The officers had been promoted from the ranks and had not forgotten their proletarian roots. Which was to invest this revolt with a special cachet.

As we know, the coup d'état mounted by the left-leaning "captains" was made under the leadership of one of them, Otelo Saraiva de Carvalho, who, within a year had been promoted general, before being stood down earlier than anticipated. Putsches were a Portuguese tradition as the army had always been on hand to resolve political difficulties.

But then there was the kindly nature of this revolution, effected without much bloodshed (as for the members of the PIDE, the sinister secret police force of Salazar and then of Caetano, they doubtless found it regrettable that by 1980 the Portuguese no longer had them on their backs). It was in fact the people who placed carnations into the gun barrels of these good soldiers who had been kind enough to drive out the squalid tyrants.

There was nothing so comforting as this young, dynamic army—the very image of what Portugal meant to become. They were the envy of the outside world. The M.F.A. (Armed Forces Movement) which was to run operations had drafted its program as long ago as 1973 and it was one Captain Melo Antunes who had drawn it up. He was a moderate who was later to play a regrettable part. Moreover, at the outset, everything was hunky-dory between these "proletarian" captains and the enlightened bourgeoisie represented by Spinola, the general whom they had immediately pushed to the front. While he had laid his plans well, Spinola aroused the captains' misgivings. And rightly so. They were not from the same world as this monocle-wearing aristocrat who was eager to manipulate them. He had not even been briefed on their plans for April 24. But had reacted quickly.

On April 25, the movement was set in motion in the early hours by the broadcasting over the airwaves of a banned song (banned but familiar to all), *Grandola, vila morena*, written by José Afonso a decade earlier. The refrain went: "Grandola, dark city / Land of brotherhood / It is the people who command / Within your precincts, O city." As Afonso was to tell us six years later, this was a reference to a fraternal gathering held shortly before the revolution, a gathering that the P.I.D.E. had been unable to prevent. At any rate, the song "carried a message."

Troops dispatched to crush the mutiny defected to the insurgents. Within 24 hours, the dictatorship had been swept away. The prisons were emptied, especially those run by the P.I.D.E. Caetano and his cronies fled the country. To pre-empt the lynching of P.I.D.E. personnel, they were locked up in their own prisons.

The first of the opportunists and profiteers scurried home. In the van of this influx came Mario Soares, a social democrat, who announced on arriving that he was ready to lead the government with the Communists, although no one had asked him. This Communist Party-Socialist Party-Catholic leftist alliance might appear bizarre and it did paper over a lot of contradictions. The people (as a whole) wanted to abolish capitalism, whereas the parties (especially the P.C. and the P.S.) had ambitions of running it to their own advantage (adopting a more modernistic approach), while the army was all that was left of the old State (and would not be spared a challenge, in spite of the initial superficial unanimity). May 1 was the occasion for a huge demonstration. Censorship had been completely lifted. Spinola did what he could to apply the brakes to the process. The revolutionaries were in control of the banks and newspapers. Bosses were being given a kick up the ass all over the country and were fleeing abroad. The first soviets were being set up. And the first strikes were halting production (the strikes at Lisnave, Messa, etc.) Radio Renaissance was under workers' control and this was to create problems with the army.

Spinola took over the leadership in a government in which the secretary of the Portuguese P.C., Alvaro Cunhal, accepted a ministerial appointment. Which came as a surprise only to the naive. Jorge Semprún has proved that (like Franco and Stalin before them) Spinola and Cunhal shared a common enemy: a people taking

216

its affairs into its own hands.

The euphoria lasted until that summer and the people pretty much enjoyed the peace and did as they pleased. All of the parties, which had been weaklings under the dictatorship, were swamped by the countless initiatives of the populace. Sailors and marines—who had not initially been in on the coup—were found mounting belated mutinies with an enthusiasm that startled onlookers and escaped the control even of the M.F.A. itself. The populace did likewise. Discipline broke down all but completely. The officers had not anticipated any of this. What they had planned was simply a putsch. The upshot was that by June the first arrests were being made among the leftists.

But by then the political parties were raring to go. Each wanted power for itself. Even if there was not one of them that could speak for as much as 10 percent of the Portuguese population. There was a calamitous paucity of political leadership of quality. The likes of Cunhal or Soares stood for the most mediocre segments of their parties.

While the people were often illiterate, they displayed more resolution and delicacy in their spontaneous activities. In the Alentejo, they seized the estates of landowners who had left them fallow (that old story again). The Alentejo is a rural province in the south of the country. In conservatism's base in the north, by contrast, the right was biding its time, just waiting for its time to arrive.

The only thing that the Communists, Socialists, the right, the bourgeoisie, the parties, the Church, the great landowners, the bosses, the civil service, the notables, and the military had in common was an interest in bringing such spontaneous popular initiatives to a speedy end: the people were tearing up the rule book and preventing the players from getting on with the game.

There was one movement that played an important part in these initiatives: the L.U.A.R. (Revolutionary Unity and Action League), launched in 1968 by Palma Ignacio, an organization that had carried out quite a number of operations under Salazar (which in itself set it apart from all the rest). The L.U.A.R. helped with squats, cultural activities, and groups and operated at grassroots levels.

July saw the formation of the C.O.P.C.O.N. (Continental Operational Commandos)—rangers and paras brought home from the colonies to enforce law and order. Independent of the M.F.A., they were quite repressive to start with, before swinging behind the M.F.A. in September upon detecting dirty work afoot on the right. They were led by Carvalho, who was also appointed military governor of Lisbon. This endowed him with tremendous authority.

In addition to C.O.P.C.O.N. (not one, but several commandos), the spearhead of the M.F.A. was the Fifth Army. After the C.O.P.C.O.N., the progressive regiments were the R.A.L.I.S., the R.I.O.Q., the E.P.A.M., the Military Police, and the Lisbon Transport Regiments.

In fact, much power was in the hands of the C.T.s (Workers' Commissions, or

Strike Commissions, or Defense Committees, or Trade Union Commissions, or Workers' Commissions—it depended on the location). These were, in effect, soviets.

As in any self-managerial upheaval, there were all sorts caught up in it, including quite a few enemies of self-management (that, after all, is the definition of self-management: the offering of the widest choice, even the option to be a fascist or a ninny, just as long as there is no imposition upon one's neighbor). Wherever the parties were strong, they set up self-styled C.T.s, which they manipulated to suit themselves: on the other hand, wherever they were weak, soviets were democratically elected, especially in the larger firms (Messa, or Timex—which made contacts everywhere, with LIP among others). There was a large number of women involved in this. And there were grassroots assemblies everywhere as well.

The position of the Portuguese P.S. could not have been plainer. From its first meeting on May 24 onward, when Cunhal had announced: "General strike may lead to chaos." Another favorite refrain which the Stalinists were quicker to intone than the bourgeoisie. The P.C.P. very quickly came out against self-management, strikes, and soviets and invoked "fascist manipulation" at every opportunity. Swept along by the workers, the P.C.P. watchdogs therefore had to look for support to whoever was left: the reactionary businessmen and middle bourgeoisie who feared for their threatened former privileges.

They dispatched scabs to break strikes by Communists replacing the strikers. Brezhnev offered encouragement in this, and Russia was to be seen to provide fish to the fisheries employers so as to break the Matosinhos fishermen's strike.

August 21 saw the issuing of a very reactionary ordinance on the right to strike. Police, screws, judges, civil servants and, servicemen were denied the right altogether. Every strike had to be notified...37 days in advance! In the event of infringement of this order, a lockout would be lawful. In any event, things had to be handled through the trade unions (which were in the pocket of the political parties). The P.C.P.—make no mistake about it—had lobbied heavily for this law.

The first governments had governed not at all. Power was dispersed and atomized throughout. The situation was outside of the control of the power crazy. The inevitable occurred. On September 28, 1974, after five months of "shambles" or of "freedom" (it all depended on where one was standing), Spinola tried to seize power alone. He even placed Carvalho, his main obstacle, under arrest, as well as Vasco Gonçalves who was close to the Communist Party. But the attempted coup failed.

By the following day, Spinola had been dumped. Everyone joined forces on the left and the progressives carried the day in the behind-the-scenes fighting. From then on, the M.F.A. was the only credible authority and became a permanent element in government, which most of the officers had not wanted.

From the outset, the demand from the grassroots had been for a healthy purge of the administration, unchanged since Caetano's time. Spinola had appointed a right-winger, Galvão de Melo, to head the Commission to Dismantle the P.I.D.E.. His appointee was to do all in his power to support him on September 28, before being brought down with him. Now the left was in control of the files compiled by the fascists, but they took great care not to destroy them. As for the network of informers, they made do with turning it to their own service! As Jorge Semprún succinctly puts it "gradually, the Commission to Dismantle the P.I.D.E. turned into a commission on the organization of the political police of the future."

In passing, let us note that that same month, the former Portuguese colony of Guinea-Bissau obtained its independence, ahead of Mozambique's independence which followed in 1975.

Power now lay with the M.F.A. and with the Council of the Revolution, a smaller spin-off from the M.F.A.. Since things had started, the strong man had been Otelo de Carvalho. He was to remain such until November 1975. Carvalho was no politician. As he himself often admitted, he had no real interest in politics. But he was a good listener and felt that, in his guts, he was on the side of the rank and file, though he was not always clear as to what he should be doing and sometimes he made mistakes. He refused to take power. He was under pressure from all sides: it would have been so simple and Portugal yearned for her own Castro. But he declined on every occasion. The M.F.A. was in the process of breaking up and only he would have stood any chance of holding it together. But what would that have meant? A military dictatorship? His lack of political education made him back off. In any event, by this time the M.F.A. was supporting the occupation of the estates. It enjoyed the right to veto the choice of ministers and president and was a break upon the reactionaries and chicanery.

In January, the P.C.P. moved that there should be only one trade union confederation (which it would then be able to control with ease). The M.F.A. agreed to this.

Spinola had not surrendered his weapons. This time he was to attempt a putsch rather than a palace revolution. This came on March 11, 1975. Again he failed and fled to Spain. Carvalho was never in a stronger position. But others were close on his heels—people like 41-year old Major Melo Antunes, the brains behind the M.F.A., who was keeping his cards close to his chest.

While the first nationalizations (banking and insurance) were carried out and while the P.C.P. commandeered the P.I.D.E. dossiers, elections were scheduled for the first anniversary of the revolution. The united left won. A pact was reached between the government and the M.F.A., that the process would be carried forward but closely monitored. We should point out that the parties of the far right and far left, who were treated the same, had been refused the right to offer themselves to the voters for election. The so-called "united" left was made up of course of the Socialist Party, the Communist Party and the P.P.D. (a centrist party somewhat further to the left than the other two and that was in government in 1980).

219

On the other hand, the soldiers' soviets were starting to question how representative the M.F.A. was (this was especially the case in Oporto). In May came the República affair—a newspaper taken over by its workforce who were unhappy with the (socialist) editors of the paper. The Socialist Party went all out for open crisis, which suited its purposes. Its aim was to topple the government so as to increase its own power, which the elections had left indeterminate (it had taken only 37 percent out of the 75 percent of votes cast for the left). And it succeeded.

Soares capitalized upon all this to launch a somewhat pointless struggle against the P.C.P.; it was hoping to win over a few voters and to improve its own image abroad. This did not take much work, for Soares had never been a worry to anyone—not on the right, at any rate. Delighted, the right raised its head again. The Church threw its weight behind Soares immediately. The bourgeois parties did too, but more discreetly.

By the beginning of the summer, the P.C. was in control of most of the media excepting Radio Renaissance and *República*. In August, its protector, Gonçalves, was brought down. Also at around this time came the launch of what was to be termed the "Group of the Nine," an ambiguous pressure group, further to the left politically than the P.S. or the P.C., but at the same time, unmistakably to the right of the revolutionaries. Its leader and the author of its foundation document, Melo Antunes, was a moderate, but he was of the mind that the revolutionary process should carry on. Essentially, he wanted to see a follow-through of April 25, whereas many military in the M.F.A. had given up, and the left-wing parties wanted to see April 25 thrown into reverse and the right simply wanted to see the old state completely restored. The group's other supporters were Pires Veloso, Franco Charais, Vasco Lourenço, Pezarat Correia, Vitor Alves, and Vitor Crespo—names that we will be meeting again.

Power was still hovering between these people, Carvalho and would-be moderate arbiters such as the president Costa Gomes. Gonçalves's replacement as prime minister was Admiral Pinheiro de Azevedo and he held that position up until the presidential elections. It was he who used the paras from Tancos to wrest control of Radio Renaissance from the leftists. The paras blasted their way in with dynamite.

The grassroots of the M.F.A. were the A.D.U.s (Unity Assemblies), the soviets whose officers were elected, where discipline was freely consented to, and where there were delegates from the soldiers, officers, and N.C.O.s. All in all, this arrangement never worked very well. So in September there was the launch of the S.U.V. (the soldiers, united, will never be defeated), a still moderate but clandestine (this was a novelty) rank and file organization.

On the day after the recovery of Radio Renaissance, the paras who had carried out the operation mutinied: they had had their fill of being used this way and that way this by one person or another. The P.C. tried to talk them round.

Carvalho had had enough too: he resigned from the Council of Revolution and its endless palaver. The crisis was entirely political and the rank and file's patience was running out. Their fate had yet to be decided and they were indifferent to the dissension at the top.

The government and others called upon Carvalho one last time to take power by way of a resolution to the situation or to step down once and for all. Carvalho was reluctant to do either. Allowing these buffoons to assume control of the army was out of the question. Moreover, his men were against his being replaced as head of the C.O.P.C.O.N. or as military governor of Lisbon.

The Tancos paras had no clear fix on the situation. They were to let themselves be manipulated beautifully. Their mutiny played into the hands of the right, which peddled a rumor about a left-wing coup d'état (although, as we have seen, Carvalho had rejected that). The equally blinded far left never lifted a finger when the R.A.L.I.S., commanded by Dinis de Almeida, was taken in hand (and Almeida arrested).

There was no putsch, but people reacted as if there had, because that suited the soft left and the right equally. The M.F.A.'s left-wing found itself being edged out of power by the P.C.P., the P.S.P., the P.P.D., and the Group of Nine. Normalization was now the order of the day. A few officers were placed under arrest. The commandos from Amadora oversaw the takeover and from then on, they were to be the forces of "order." For the time being, the Group of Nine had won. None of the nine (in fact there were 12 of them on the Council of Revolution) could see that they had just signed the revolution's death warrant and guaranteed their own downfall. Now there was nothing to stop the swing to the right, for there were no forces remaining on the left.

One of the leaders of this coup was Lieutenant-Colonel Ramalho Eanes of the military police regiment, who went on to be president. It was he who tipped the scales when an attempt was made to impose Vasco Lourenço in place of Carvalho. The troops would have none of this and he had to make provision against them.

The Nine were able to preen themselves: aside from Lourenço, Antunes became Foreign Affairs minister, Vitor Alves Education minister, and Rear-Admiral Crespo became minister for Cooperation. Also they held all four military regions in Portugal, the other three (outside of Lisbon) being the North (held by Pires Veloso), the South (held by Pezarat Correia), and the Center (by Charais).

The unity of the radicals had been shattered. The populace had not lifted a finger in their defense: for most of them, the burden of dictatorship still weighed too heavily upon them and they were not ready for revolution, could not comprehend what was going on and in any case would be happy enough with a moderate liberal democracy. The elections were to bear this out. The revolutionaries had been cut off from their grassroots for too long.

The M.F.A. was, all intents and purposes, no more. The A.D.U.s and S.U.V.s alike had no links to the people. Moreover, the army was soon going to be whipped back into shape.

The government had not really played any part in this putsch disguised as a counter-putsch. The protagonists had been the military right-wingers (Eanes, who would go on to be a general) who had acted even as the government was negotiating with Carvalho without government=consent. Carvalho was dismissed from all his posts, as was his alter ego, General Fabião, the 46-year-old chief of staff of land forces, an erstwhile Spinolist who had swung to the far left along with the revolution.

Eanes was the former director of television. He disbanded the C.O.P.C.O.N. which was attached to headquarters staff. As for the mutineers, they were outwitted by Colonel Jaime Neves, a man of the far right. The last remaining left-wing members of the Council of Revolution resigned, as did Admiral Antonio Alva Rosa Coutinho, who had earlier been posted home from Angola where he had headed the provisional junta on the grounds that he was unduly sympathetic to the M.P.L.A. The L.U.A.R. was threatened.

The Socialist Party was cock-a-hoop, but it distrusted Antunes, finding him a touch too much the leftist. The right raised its head. It would soon be able to attack its real enemy—the self-managing agrarian reform. It was at this point that the four arrests were made at Torre Bela—of which more detail anon.

In January 1976, for the first time, the army and the G.N.R. (Republican National Guard) opened fire on the crowd (killing three people in Oporto). The responsibility lay with Pires Veloso, a right-wing general and governor of the North. The first former P.I.D.E. agents were freed from prison. On the other hand, Carvalho was arrested for conspiracy on November 25! The blame for events was laid at the door of the only people who had done nothing, that is, everybody except the right and the P.S.—the P.C.s, the L.U.A.R., the C.O.P.C.O.N., and the far left. Carvalho was to be freed in March but placed under house arrest.

In the Alentejo the attack on the agrarian communes was pressed home. Neves was in charge of this. Attacks were also mounted against occupied factories which were then restored to the bosses, just as the estates were restored to the landlords.

For as long as Antonio Lopes Cardoso (a Socialist Party member who was without question the only one even slightly to the left) was minister of Agriculture, not many peasants were driven off the land. But this had to be pressed home and Mario Soares would not let up, until Lopes Cardoso quit his ministerial post and his party and went on to form a sort of Portuguese version of the French P.S.U.

The heartland of Portuguese fascism was Rio Major, near which was located the most renowned of the agrarian communes, Torre Bela (see below). That was where the C.A.P. (Portuguese Farmers' Association=the landowners)—a right-wing organization that set itself the target of evicting the commands—had its headquarters. It is worth noting that the local P.S.P. branch was anti-Cardoso and joined forces with the fascists to oust the peasants. The latter were accused of "communism" because the P.C.P. had not in any way opposed the occupations and had even supported them when it was in control of them.

In April 1976, legislative elections gave the edge to Soares and his allies, but it was notable that the right-wing vote was rising. Presidential elections followed in June. Eanes was returned as president with 61 percent of the vote, with P.S. and right-wing backing. Carvalho took 17 percent of the vote, which came as a surprise. At the age of 41, Eanes was a youthful head of state and he made a big impression on the others. Portugal had found, in him, the man she needed to restore the preceding regime shorn of the unseemly appearences of dictatorship. Soares was prime minister and drew his salary just long enough, for the next person to be thrown overboard was himself. The poor wretch had nothing but fine talk with which to defend himself and talk comes cheap. Note that his minister of Defense was Firmino Miguel, Spinola's one-time deputy.

Just for the record, remember that at the end of the summer, the government set about attacking squats which had begun under Gonçalves. Abandoned hotels and houses were returned to their owners and to the rich as they all flooded back into Portugal.

Carvalho's supporters and the far left had set up the G.D.U.P. (Group to Galvanize Popular Unity) and from here on they were the only ones trying to prevent the liquidation of the revolution and of the communes.

Campaigning by the communards made possible the granting of legal recognition of 200,000 hectares seized in March 1977. It was still being held, but not really under self-management. It was more a case of State-supervised agrarian reform. Cardoso's successor, a dyed-in-the-wool SP member, Barreto, never had any hesitation in deploying the GNR against the populace.

Carvalho was put in prison again for having spoken in public from a G.D.U.P. platform (this was in October). At his trial in March 1977, he stood alongside Rosa Coutinho, personnel from the R.A.L.I.S. (Almeida), from the Military Police, and from C.O.P.C.O.N..

While all of this jiggery-pokery was in progress, Soares's disastrous leadership had brought Portugal to the brink, and her economic straits were worse than ever. On the other hand, in the agrarian communes, output was rising spectacularly. A good slap in the face for those who dismissed self-management as utopian.

In 1980, while incidents continued every time land was returned to its "rightful" owners, Carvalho declared at the Gramsci Insititute in Paris: "We were naive dreamers. We ailed to divine the snares and traps of the politicians. Victims also of our own contradictions, the majority of the young officers aspired primarily to a restoration of a bourgeois parliamentary regime..." One can only agree with him there.

One French journalist, François Pisani, has devoted a wholly remarkable volume to the Torre Bela commune. I reckon it might be of interest if I were to offer a summary of it, in view of the exemplary nature of the struggle, the problems confronted, and the solutions devised prior to the final crackdown.

Torre Bela is a 1,700-hectare estate in the Ribatejo (a central province adjacent to the Alentejo), belonging to the Duke of Lafoes (royal family), who had allowed it to go to rack and ruin. Half of it was forest and the estate itself is enclosed within a four-meter high wall. The peasants from the surrounding village were impoverished, illiterate, victims of alcoholism and unemployment. And the events of April 25 made not one iota of difference to them.

It was only one year later that they began to wake up. In fact, on April 23, 1975, a few peasants and farm laborers arrived in Torre Bela to seek work from the Duke, who refused to see them. Whereupon they occupied the estate and set up a cooperative that was to work the land on their account.

Torre Bela is well situated. The land seizure movement which started in the Alentejo was sweeping northward. That autumn, their attempt to band together with other communes under the eyes of the military came to nothing. Initially the P.C.P. kept an eye on developments in hopes of making recruits but never quite managed it and stayed inactive.

Their organizational setup was a simple one: cooking was done out of doors, under a rippling tarpaulin, around a wood fire (the flues indoors were too narrow). That was where the commune was to be found. They had, initially, 600 hectares of arable land. Their bookkeeper always carried their cash on his person for fear of mislaying it. Anyone could come into Torre Bela. Many an alcoholic forswore their drinking. They bartered goods with other communes and sold some to outsiders as well. With the aid of volunteers, they did not have to tackle the toughest tasks alone, as they had been reached by radio and newspaper propaganda.

From then on, everyone could eat his fill in the communal refectory. And this helped cut the consumption of alcohol. General assemblies were held in the cultural center, which had been established in an old residence of the Duke's. These assemblies were the source of all power. The cooperative had about 50 members. At the assemblies everyone was free to air his thoughts and to speak his mind.

Their first leader was Wilson Felipe (son of a small holder called João Felipe, a goat farmer) and it was he who had incited the others to proceed with the seizure. At the time, he was 27 years old. An astounding fellow—ex-soldier, ex-criminal, ex-pimp, brawler, and bad character—he had served six years in prison for a hold up and owed his release to the revolution. He had given things a lot of thought and what was to happen was to represent for him his way of "redeeming himself" in the eyes of the village to which he had returned.

Another leader was Camilo Tavares Mortagua, one-time activist. Highly placed in the L.U.A.R., he had dropped out of that organization at Wilson's invitation in order to come to Torre Bela to offer his expertise. A supporter of Enrique Galvão under Salazar, he had been a member of the commando that had hijacked the liner Santa Maria in 1961, creating quite a sensation, as well as a participant in the L.U.A.R.'s raid on the bank in Figueira da Foz.

Only slowly did women get involved in politics. This was one of the most macho areas in the world and in Torre Bela women were too heavily outnumbered by the men. Sexual misery prevailed.

The school was under the supervision of a former priest, José Rebaça, who led a drive against universal illiteracy.

Wilson had planned the land seizure down to the finest detail. He had selected just 30 people out of the original 100 considered. Those who belonged to a party were not to wear any badges: "This occupation is the work of the people, not of any party." Soon their numbers grew to 400 and then to 1,000. The Duke screamed at them down the telephone and refused to talk to the "populace." Peaceably, touching nothing and to the sound of "Granola, Vila Morena," the squatters broached the suggested cooperative with the estate's workers, who were agreeable. The Duke caved in a little and agreed to a meeting with representatives from the M.F.A., the government, and the trade unions.

All of the parties marched out to Torre Bela (where, all in all, the outlook was communist), but none of them was allowed to remain and they were discouraged from trying to (Wilson was not aligned with any party).

To begin with, the cooperative was to be made up of 32 men and 8 women (out of the then 1,500 residents), the largest number it could sustain. Members were chosen from among the most deprived, which is to say, the least radical and most resigned (alcohol abusers), the least gifted and least politicized (such is the implication of poverty).

Camilo looked after production, management, and bookkeeping, as well as distribution and marketing.

There was tremendous assistance from outsiders in the form of collections taken up, visits from soviets, committees, servicemen, and radicals from every country you could name. The Duke and his supporters peddled all sorts of rumors (about conspiracy, orgies, training camps, and drug use).

To begin with, self-management was not all plain sailing: they got drunk, failed to argue things out, and ended up in slugging matches. But the work that Camilo did carried them through all of that. "The prime quality of a revolutionary cadre is flexibility," he said. Everyone received the same wage. They lent a helping hand with other undertakings in the locality. The Church and the Socialist Party closed ranks against them. However, local socialists were divided in their attitude to them. Soares, who was totally paranoid, was the one who saw Communists everywhere and it was he who made the decisions. His members merely followed his lead.

On December 1, 1975, after the right-wing putsch, the army invaded Torre Bela—one scout car (the famous multipurpose machine-gun carriers, the very symbol of the revolution) and ten terror-stricken soldiers who announced: "We're here to carry out a search for weapons." The search proved fruitless. The estate was ringed by six more scout cars and 50 men. An aircraft circled overhead! There was a rumor to the effect that they had concealed missiles...even mines and anti-aircraft guns. In fact some planes had mistakenly identified some long-shafted carts as anti-aircraft batteries!

Wilson and some of the others were arrested. Foreigners present were to be deported. Some were released very quickly but the right, tipped off (by whom?), had already sent its supporters in to attack the commune. Five hundred people belonging to the Socialist Party and the P.P.D., safe in the knowledge that there were no weapons there, flooded the area, hurling abuse at residents and backing down only when confronted by the army.

Army inquiries were insistent: once the allegations of conspiracy had been disposed of, criticisms of farming methodology followed (in a way, this amounted to an admission that self-management was indeed the point at issue). João Felipe was to state: "Yesterday we were heroes, but today we are nothing but bandits." November 25 made its impact felt in the area. Wilson was still in prison.

Then four others—including Camilo and João Felipe—were placed under arrest, the last remaining leaders. Torre Bela was helped to survive by money from abroad. They marketed a record. Camilo had picked up the money, which was the cash found on his person. He was accused of being a "new duke" to the peasants,

Wilson. Torre Bela. 1975.

with a fleet of cars and Wilson was written off as a common criminal. Naturally, the money in question would not be handed back to the members of the cooperative who really needed it.

Even in prison the communards carried on: they pooled all of their resources. Lopes Cardoso had inquiries made in Torre Bela. At the same time (by a curious coincidence?), the Duke stopped paying wages.

In spite of a press conference in Torre Bela and a meeting with Cardoso's deputy, nothing was done. The Socialist Party newspaper, *A Luta*, vented its spleen against them nationwide.

Even so, they had to free the four most recently arrested communards, with Wilson remaining in custody. They really did not have any charges to bring against them. There was rejoicing when they came home.

Life carried on. They established a livestock farm (with 120 goats, 2 cows to provide milk for the children, 100 hens, and 50 pigs) and planted cereals, forage plants, vines, and olives. They had two tractors, a harvester and they irrigated and cleared the land and their bellies were full. They had even turned down their wages, being content to be self-sufficient.

They were still short of comfort, electricity, and a windmill. But their little enclave worked, like a host of others across Portugal. It was at this point that the right raised its head again and the campaign to stamp them out was to escalate.

It was plainly stated in their statutes that their aim was to build upon a collective class consciousness to transform the workers' technical and cultural levels, to assist them in achieving political awareness, and to create a new man. Nothing more.

The workers' commission included five cooperative members (including Wilson and his father) who oversaw the work. Camilo, on the other hand, had been unwilling to join the commission.

At the same time as the investigators, the trade unions arrived. The latter were very hostile to their venture and refused to acknowledge their concrete results.

By March 1976, their position was changing. The Union of Cooperatives had secured government recognition. Camilo became chairman of the Producers' Association locally. Their cooperative was renamed the "April 23."

Wilson, now released, had reluctantly joined the P.C. in search of a little backing. In September 1977, there was an arson attack. Four hundred people from Rio Major tried to evict them. There was fierce fighting with the fascists, whom the army dispersed.

However, in March 1979, they were to be driven out by the GNR itself. The Duke was to recover his lands with the assistance of the Agrarian Reform Institute [sic]. The belongings of cooperative members were tossed out into the streets or their equipment was simply stolen by the Duke. In reply, the Duke found his land being confiscated by the State for redistribution (to whoever wanted it).

The Socialist Party had thrown its support behind the Duke, capitalizing upon this chance to mop up the last commune left in the region.

The peasants were to look after things in the meantime, milking the cows and pruning the vines. Some of them emigrated, their dreams at an end. Those who had previously hired out their labor now found themselves blacklisted. Quarrels set them against one another. Camilo left for Mozambique to work in a cooperative there. Wilson married and moved away. Everything returned to how it had been under Salazar.

A few, the ones who had fallen furthest, trotted off to seek the Duke's forgiveness! The Middle Ages are still with us.

As Carvalho said: "If only a few of them had been shot…" April 25 might never have come to pass. And yet the likes of Soares flourish like couch grass.

France, 1971 — Until ultimate victory
LE LARZAC

You ask that we select a territory where we might like to live, should we have to quit this one which has always been our home. Can you see those graves yonder? They belong to our fathers and our grandfathers (...) We have always lived here. We prefer to die here. Just like our fathers did. Abandon them, we cannot. Our children were born here— how could we leave? Even if you were to give us the best land on earth, it could not be better than this. Here, we are at home... We cannot live anywhere else (...) We want this place and no other... For us, there is no other land. There is no point in your buying another for us. If you drive us from this place, we will go like the quail into the hills and perish there, the old, the women, and the children. Let the government be content and proud! It may kill us (...) If we may not live here, we want to go into the hills to die. We do not want to live in any other place.

Cecilio Blacktooth
addressing the U.S. Government's
commissioners in Warner's Hot Springs.

It is only right that we should conclude this book with a current struggle. A struggle still raging, still being waged before our very eyes. And, I hope, waged with the support of every one of us.

Le Larzac is a plateau in the Aveyron department of France, undoubtedly one of the loveliest places in the whole country. Hitherto it was the site of a few, rather

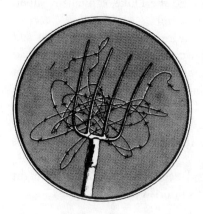

beautiful farms, grazing sheep, a few ploughed fields, and nothing to affront the eyes. Since 1890, there has been an army camp on the edge of the plateau, adjacent to the village of La Cavalerie. Curiously, that village and its environs are of a repugnant filthiness that clashes with the neighboring townships: sticky wrappers, plastic bottles, broken glass, all manner of rubbish is scattered across whole hectares in the wake of the army. The contrast strikes every visitor. It is as if mud had been smeared across silken bed sheets.

The camp covers an area of 3,000 hectares. Previously, there had never been any difficulty about the army's coexisting alongside the peasants. In any case, the area was gradually being depopulated. To take one example out of a thousand: during the war in Algeria, Le Larzac was turned into a concentration camp for captive Algerian freedom-fighters, most of whom were peasants themselves (and remember that there were four such camps within France proper). Well, at the time, there was not the slightest objection raised by the region, neither by the peasants nor by the town-dwellers. Only a few politicians passed any comment. Not the local population who blithely approved. Not until 15 years had passed and they found themselves being treated so badly did it occur to them to examine their consciences.

The late 1960s introduced two new factors. For one thing, there was an upsurge in the population of the plateau and its environs—an upsurge consisting chiefly of peasants, with young people moving in and the region starting to undergo a revival. For another, the army was on the lookout for a vast tract of land for the maneuvers of N.A.T.O. troops practicing for large-scale operations. The plateau looked very tempting. An investigation was even launched to discover if the local sinkholes might be used to store nuclear weapon.

In the 1960s, prior to these events, the local elected representatives (who included M Roger Julien, the mayor of Nant, a small, nearby town, of which more later), backed by a few peasant families (including the Guiraud and Jonquet families who were to be in the van of the fight) even asked for the camp to be extended! Which accounts for the astonishment felt by the deputy mayor of Millau, Delmas, later on when he realized the extent to which people's minds had changed in just a few years (and, naturally, he took his stand on the old "demand" by the inhabitants of the plateau). It was the economic recovery enjoyed by the plateau that had altered the outlooks of most of those concerned, a recovery that Delmas and the authorities were to strive to deny, and with good reason!

It was the mayor who was to press for the project: he did not live regularly in the area. Louis-Alexandre Delmas controlled the region politically. He enjoyed a majority and at a U.D.R. congress (actually, in those days it was the R.P.R.) in the region, he publicly announced the scheme. The secretary of State for National Defense, André Fanton, confirmed this. This was in October 1970. It ought to be noted that Delmas was a former member of Michel Debré's staff and had Debré's ear.

In fact, the announcement was public only for members of the U.D.R., but two future "Larzac-ers" found out anyway: Pierre Laur (an industrialist from Roquefort, producer of the famous Roquefort cheese which is the source of the region's wealth. We should note that a few years earlier he had been thinking of settling in the Var department...but had been evicted by the army which wanted to build the Canjuers camp! So he had seen it all before), and Guy Tarlier (ex-officer, former settler in Africa, a bundle of energy and fine public speaker. He worked the Devez-Novel farmstead).

229

This announcement confirmed rumors that had been circulating over the previous month. In La Cavalerie, the mayor, Marcel Lapeyre, was whole-heartedly in favor of the camp. Indeed, he had long been returned in elections on that very program. Peasants were never to be the majority within his town, which was little more than some bars catering for soldiers and a few businesses wholly dependent on the military for their survival. Moreover, Lapeyre was the camp's civilian procurement officer, so he had an axe to grind. To each his own.

The village priest was also for the camp. After all, he was.the camp padre! As we can see, the army is adept at placing its people in strategic positions. And remember, the army is France's largest landowner.

In fact, all of the people who were to oppose the extension plans were, to a man, those with no direct financial or ideological interest in its proceeding. The opponents included the peasants, of course, (they being the chief victims), and the Roquefort cheese producers, the ecologists, and nature-lovers. (The region possessed great geographical, mineralogical, paleontological, and tourist potential).

Tarlier was the one to get the opposition campaign underway, along with the Burguière and Galtier families. The Burguières worked the L'Hopital farm in the north. They were a very devout family—Léon Burguière, the father, his sons, Jean-Marie and Pierre, and their wives. Jean-Claude Galtier was a shepherd who had joined with Philippe Fauchot and Michel Courtin (now no longer with him) a few years before to launch the G.A.E.C. in Les Baumes. A G.A.E.C. is a Cooperative Farming Group.

An initial published text, Some Peasants from Le Larzac, was issued and it aroused public opinion. The F.D.S.E.A. (Departmental Federation of Farmers' Unions, of which Marcel Debatisse was the national leader) was led locally by Louis Massebiau, among others. Massebiau and his wife worked the Le Clot farm outside La Cavalerie.

That January, they launched the Association to Safeguard Le Larzac, which was to be chaired by Henri Ramade, a retired school teacher and former mayor of Saint-Jean du Bruel, a little village close to the plateau. Its secretary would be Roger Julien, a centrist lawyer and mayor of Nant, whom we mentioned earlier. Léon Burguière was vice-chairman and Pierre Laur the treasurer. This was the first of the organizations which were to "mount" resistance over Le Larzac.

In the spring, a first public campaign against the camp was launched in Millau. It was not the doing of the farmers who had not yet mobilized. It was the doing of the Secours Rouge (Red Aid), a leftist organization which has since disappeared but that was very active in the 1970's and that was close to Gauche Prolétarienne (Proletarian Left). At their instigation there even surfaced a strange *Open Letter to Camp Supporters*—the work of Jean-Marie Cassan, a farmer who had dabbled in Maoism and whose part in the initial operations was to be significant, but who passed away a few months later following an illness. The letter carried the signatures of Léon Burguière, Massebiau, and Tarlier.

For its part, the Association issued a *White Book* which offered statistical proof that Le Larzac was a viable farming proposition.

The first march for Le Larzac was organized by leftists and covered the distance from Millau to La Cavalerie (about 20 kilometers, climbing all the way!) on May 9. Fifteen hundred people took part but very few of them were country people. Most of these had yet to wake up to the threat. Members of the L'Arche community based in the Hérault department not too far away—(a community that had grown up around the guru Lanza del Vasto)—showed up, only to quit on account of the violent sloganeering. In any case, Roger Julien had forcefully counseled the country people against coming: they were afraid of leftists.

Summer came and with it, for the first time, people from outside, young people, coming to work alongside the country folk. One theater group, the Teatre de la Carriera, which staged production in the Occitan language, staged "*The Death and Resurrection of Mr. Occitania*," a play that was to cause something of a sensation in the region.

On occasion, the meeting of these two worlds was jarring, but very telling. Cassan drew in the Maoists, many of whom were utterly ignorant of country life and above all of the mind-sets by which it was characterized. The country folk on the other hand, most of whom were very religious, had problems understanding the mores, thinking, and practices of the young folk from the city. But even so there was a political awakening to their position within society and this problem which was staring them in the face, and how! They were taken aback by the support from outsiders.

In September, 107 farmers dumped manure and rubble outside the home of the mayor in La Cavalerie. Massebiau, Cassan, and Tarlier were among them. Massebiau delivered a violent address which showed the influence of Maoist jargon. This was the first "peasant" operation. The real struggle was beginning.

In October, Defense minister Michel Debré formally announced the decision to extend the army camp by a further 14,000 hectares! A propaganda film on television showed Le Larzac as a wasteland where only a few old people remained. This was the straw that broke the camel's back. More than anything else, it was these two synchronized developments which were to open the eyes of most of the country people to what was going on.

A demonstration followed in Millau (the nearest town of any size, upon which the camp was administratively and politically dependent). Six thousand people mustered in the Place de Mandarous in the town, and the town itself resembled a "ghost town." The F.N.S.E.A., which was to operate throughout this crisis as the government's preferred go-between (at national level at any rate), attempted to nudge the peasants in the direction of conciliation.

Churches on the plateau tolled their bells—the faithful accompaniment of

2,000 years of peasant revolts. There was a rift between the peasants and the leftists, the latter being four-square behind violent activity which went against the grain of the country folk.

Then again, local church leaders had no hesitation. Such was their hold over the peasants that they exercised a measure of authority in spiritual and intellectual matters, and this they must not lose. Most of the priests of Millau sided with the peasants. Then the Bishop of Rodez, Monsignor Ménard, spoke up in their favor (but he died in June 1973).

Negotiations with Debré came to nothing (although the delegates from Le Larzac did not include a single farmer, only industrialists from Roquefort or F.D.S.E.A. members). Debré announced a short time later: "Since a decision in principle has been taken, plainly the debate has been opened." But this was not some piece of theater by Courteline.

On the occasion of a by-election in Rodez, the U.D.R. and the Independent Republicans showed their true colors. They frantically announced to all who might listen that they were against the camp. In La Cavalerie, a model helicopter indicating the entrance to the camp was blown up by the Maoists. In January 1972, the Monte Carlo rally faced sabotage on the local stage. Support committees were mushrooming pretty well everywhere. In Millau, the driving force behind them was Lutte Occitane. One Maoist farmer was even arrested.

The powers that be increased the number of conferences about the camp extension. Molotov cocktails were thrown at the U.D.R. and C.G.T. offices and later at the Rodez prefecture—by Maoists. They were disowned by the country people.

A "son et lumière" show was staged in Millau. Huge bonfires were lighted on the heights of the plateau overlooking the town, while the siren screamed from the Belfry in Millau. For the first time, residents of Millau and country folk were caught up in the same activities (this was unheard of!). When they saw firefighters and police getting stuck in the mud on their way to fight the blazes, once the sirens wailed across the valley, the tide of peasant laughter was the finishing touch. The authorities started to panic as a result.

This was also the first time that the womenfolk of Le Larzac made their voices heard through a collective text, a satirical document called *The Flea Market in Le Larzac*.

On March 1, Lanza del Vasto gave a talk in Millau on nonviolence. Though 80 years of age, he embarked upon a hunger strike (as was his wont) in solidarity: the peasants took it in turns to sit with him during his protest. A little later, the anti-militarist priest Jean Toulat took his turn to speak before 1,500 people on "Le Larzac and peace." These two interventions, closely monitored by the devout residents who were, of course, disinclined to use violence, injected some pacifist and anti-militarist content into the protest. Thus far, there had been no license from the spiritual authorities for attacks on the army (which was as much respected as the church itself). Leftists could scarcely hold out the promise of such license, and in any case were not trying to.

All of a sudden, they tried. Peasants in shackles were delivered to an officers' ball in La Cavalerie. An astonishing sight was to meet their eyes: they had a parcel of angry bees placed among the dancers.

These were the circumstances in which the caussenard country folk (and Le Larzac is one of the main causses=limestone areas) made one another's acquaintance. Their exacting lifestyle had scarcely encouraged such contacts. Most of them had never set foot inside a neighbor's home. Only rarely were they on friendly enough terms to use the familiar forms of address. All of these impediments which their enemies had traditionally used against them, evaporated within just a few months.

And there was plenty of support from the outside world. A gathering of mayors from the Aveyron department came out in their favor. On March 28, the Bishop of Rodez, Monsignor Ménard, and the Archbishop of Toulouse joined Lanza del Vasto in his fast. The bishop of Montpellier gave them his blessing. Misgivings were starting to evaporate. This double reassurance, from a highly respected pacifist and from the Church was to swing even the most dubious of resisters behind action against the camp. Resignation was no longer the fashion. This led to the birth of the 103.

One hundred and three out of the 107 peasants whose holdings were directly threatened by compulsory purchase pledged not to back down, not to sell, and to consult with one another about everything.

"Peace marchers" from all over France arrived on April 1 to greet the ending of Lanza del Vasto's fast. The aged mystic and guru soon realized that he would not have the same control over the situation as he had hoped, so he left the area.

Lanza proved unable to impose his line upon the 103, as did the leftists (300 of whom had attacked the police station in Millau in an act that simply defied the understanding of the local populace). Over the many long years which the struggle was to take, no group, no party, no personality, and no body was ever able to assume the power exercised by this handful of peasants alone. This was undoubtedly the most attractive aspect of their exemplary campaign. From then on, Tarlier was to be Lanza del Vasto's "heir apparent."

For their part, the leftists simply could not comprehend this bizarre fight which did not quite fit with their rigid Leninist models. By now almost entirely cut off from the peasants, with no more initiative other than whatever the 103 allowed them to have, most of them quit. It rankled with them that they had failed to lead the campaign. Such is the fate that awaits those who would meddle in a self-managed struggle. The campaign uses them, accepts them...and then forgets about them.

"Operation Open Farms" which was the culmination of the march lasted for three days. It was to draw 3,000 visitors. There were discussions, they listened to

Marti singing and ate mutton. The country people, hitherto guarded about the long-haired young people, these "hippies" (hardly!) made their peace with them or at least with the sight of them and got used to seeing them around the plateau. Massebiau had organized it all. But the operation was to prove too demanding for him. He threw up his arms, and left it to a new team to galvanize the campaign: the Burguières, Robert Gastal (a farmer from La Cavalerie who was to prove a very effective public speaker, although he had no previous experience of speaking in public) and Léon Maillé (a farmer from the little hamlet of Potensac).

The alliance between peasant and worker and town and countryside was to be made effective by a significant strike, the strike by the workforce of the Samex Company that made trousers in Millau.

In order to show them their life and how they were exploited, the girls from Samex occupied their factory and set one production line in motion for the visiting peasants. The C.F.D.T. backed this idea. It was a real eye-opener for the peasants. They were horrified: how was this degree of exploitation possible, how could an employer impose such a life upon them in return for such starvation rates of pay? The very next day, they were back with enough victuals to withstand a siege. And they came back every day. They were to mount a joint procession through the town and another on May 1—another first for Millau, where that feast had usually been quite pathetic.

The Samex girls went on to win, so in the end their strike proved a success. That salutary example was to be grist to the mill of the 103: it showed that it paid to fight.

By the way, Janine Massebiau was arrested along with another two people, for…spying! What was her crime? She had trespassed on an army-owned field in order to take a shortcut! They were released after two days.

The peasants regularly traipsed around France to explain just what was happening. Larzac committees were founded. An initial support rally in Paris was held in the Mutualité hall (with 5,000 attending). Debré and Sanguinetti delivered themselves of angry declarations.

On July 14, 1972, 70 tractors driven by the 103, led by Tarlier, drove down the road to Rodez where they were acclaimed by 20,000 people. Robert Gastal declared: "If need be, we will travel up to Paris by tractor. Le Larzac must become a national issue." It did.

It was at this point that a ministerial delegate took a high profile on the plateau. Henri Tournier was a former barbouze with the S.D.E.C.E. A regular sight in Africa. He had quite simply been charged to look into the practicalities of the Le Larzac issue. One day the peasants cornered him in the town hall in L'Hospitalet du Larzac and subjected him to two hours of questioning. In spite of which his report to the minister was to point out the weakness of the government position. Plainly he had not been convinced by the case for extension.

Moreover, Debré, like his successors, was on several occasions to give the impression that they were on the point of backing down. After all, it was not one of them who had come up with the idea. They had merely inherited it, that was all. But it was embarrassing to be seen by N.A.T.O. to be backing down. Which accounts for the subsequent worsening of the situation.

A large sheep-station, La Grande Jasse, beside highway N 9 (which cut through the planned camp and cut the plateau in two) was to be used as a tourist information office from then on. "Smile operations" were mounted there. Throughout the summer, the peasants were pinned down by the harvest season and the Samex employees gave up their holidays to man the center.

During one live television broadcast of a public game, some peasants wearing "Let's save Le Larzac" hats mingled with the crowd on screen. Simone Evesque, a young peasant girl from Mas Bas was arrested for "desecration of the monument to the fallen." She had not been responsible but it took a blockade of the courthouse to secure her release.

October saw the opening of the public inquiry. In an effort to disrupt the opening, the 103 released 2,000 sheep outside the town hall in La Cavalerie. They all jotted the same message on the register: "In my estimation, this extension is a catastrophe for the region and for all men. I will never quit, no matter what means may be employed to drive me off."

On October 25, over a two-hour period, Pierre Burguière, his wife, Tarlier, and Michel Courtin released 60 sheep daubed with the slogan "Let's save Le Larzac" under the Eiffel Tower. In Millau, another seven people did the rounds. Three days after that, they solemnly planted 103 trees along the N.9.

At a rally in Millau, General de Bollardière spoke out against the camp extension. At Christmas, the prefect declared "public interest" in the State's acquisition of 14,000 hectares spreading across 14 different towns.

On January 7, 1973, 26 tractors set off for Paris, arriving there on January 13. Funded by sponsors at five francs per tractor kilometer, the operation was mounted in several stages, and met with a rapturous reception at every stage. A ban was slapped on the final stage after Orléans. Immediately, the F.D.S.E.A. and the C.N.J.A. (Young Farmers' Union, another very moderate farming union) washed their hands of them. The pathetic buffoon Debatisse, the then leader of the farming unions, was nothing better than a government agent planted inside the organization. His role was to be exposed plainly shortly afterward when he was offered a place on the majority's list of nominees for the European Parliament. That such a character should have prospered in a farmers' union says a lot about the antiquated structures of the traditional organizations and about the political indifference of the French farmer. One of the achievements of Le Larzac was that it had shattered this mind-numbing image of the peasant eternally obedient to the central authorities.

Also, no political or trade union organization displayed any great eagerness to help them. They seized upon any excuse whatever to get offside. They made exceptions of this group or that whereas the 103 issued appeals to everyone on an equal basis.

The only ones to stand by them were the Orléans support committee and the Paysans-Travailleurs (Peasant-Toilers) whose leader, Bernard Lambert, stood up for them. This was the only trade union independent of the authorities and it had been quick to spot the essential novelty of the campaign by the 103.

Among the memorable "snapshots" of the campaign, there was the sight of a national serviceman spending his year's pay on tractor-bonds. In the letter they brought to the Matignon palace to premier Messmer, might be read the words: "That one should have slaves is nothing. What is intolerable is that one should have slaves and yet call them citizens."

The march ended on foot, face to face with the C.R.S.

That same month, Louis Balsan, the curator of arts and antiquities in the Aveyron department, was dismissed after 28 years in office, under pressure from Debré. Balsan had backed the protestors from the outset. He was a figure of some authority in the area and objections to his dismissal were unanimous. The following month, deputy Delmas died of a heart attack. He was replaced by his locum, Doctor Gabriac.

The 103 offered support to no candidate in the legislative elections in March 1973, but they called for rejection of the authorities in office. In Rodez, even Olivier Giscard d'Estaing, the brother of the French president, campaigned for rejection of the camp extension! The U.D.R. lost 6,000 votes in Millau, but a candidate from the majority party, Gabriac, was returned as deputy (he had been mayor for the past month). The left had taken an unexpectedly high number of votes, especially through Gérard Duruy, the local Socialist Party leader and an ardent champion of Le Larzac.

A little after this, the Résistance-Action-Larzac organization stole a shelf of documents from Henri Tournier and photocopies were sent out to all peasants. Now his "plan" was public knowledge: he thought a climb-down by the powers that be, would be an interesting hypothesis. Shortly after that, Tournier left the area.

April saw the beginning of the tactic of returning military records by 50 peasants, although they were not anti-militarist (which shows how far things had moved on). The aged Elie Jonquet from the little hamlet of La Blaquière, wrote to the minister: "It is with a heavy heart that I find myself obliged to take this course of action, but my conscience requires it. I cannot serve a regime that is following in the footsteps of the one I fought in 1940."

Robert Galley took over from Michel Debré.

In May there was international brotherhood day, with visiting Native Americans—notably the popular Little Feather—and singers from Ireland's I.R.A., who mingled with the Occitans.

June saw the beginning of—unauthorized—construction work on the New Blaquière Sheep-station, smack-dab in the middle of the extension area. This was Tarlier's idea. There was a great party. People flooded in from all over to lend a hand. The protestors themselves sent the L.I.P. workers a telegram expressing support for their struggle, then at its height. This was the start of close solidarity between the two epicenters of self-management at the time. And "cement-bonds" were on sale there at 8.60 francs.

In August, even as the C.R.S. was occupying L.I.P., the peasants symbolically halted their harvest and travelled in a tractor motorcade from Millau to La Cavalerie. On August 25, the Paysans-Travailleurs marched on the plateau. The F.D.S.E.A. announced that peasants had no interest in the big Le Larzac festival.

It did not have long to wait for an answer: the Rajal del Guorp, a favorite location for all mass gatherings with its characteristic cropped boulders, played host to some 80,000 people.

There was a march on La Blaquière, there was a festival, there were discussions. Bernard Lambert, no pacifist, was to state: "I am with you. We must try every nonviolent resource and the truth is that I am ready to turn the other cheek when one is struck...But the Lord did not say anything about using one's feet!" The impact of this declaration was predictable. One of the Burguières was to say later, after a bridge had been blown up, that it was a fine example of "hard-line nonviolent action"!

The L.I.P. workers were there, so was de Bollardière, some Palestinians and some I.R.A. men (the British army was on a training exercise in Le Larzac at the time) and there were singers too, like Marti, Colette Magny, Kirjuhel...Anarchists who usually welcomed a bit of a shambles were eventually to be found acting as stewards, at the malicious request of the country people who were just overwhelmed by the crowds!

One of the most popular peasants from the 103 group lived and worked in La Blaquière—Auguste Guiraud. When he spotted from some distance the tens of thousands of marchers on their way out to pay a visit to his illegal sheep-station, he went out to meet them and led them in. The L.I.P. workers brought him a large shaved sheep with one testicle removed. Marie-Rose Guiraud stated: "This sheep-station belongs to everybody in France and from around the world who carry their heads held high and wish to live on their feet." In his enthusiasm, her husband was even to raise a clenched fist while the *Internationale* was being sung. Not that this was to please everybody.

For the record, *L'Humanité* was to devote a total of 18 lines to the whole event. The nearest Communist newspaper *la Marseillaise*, gave it seven: and on its front page carried a report, in glowing terms, on the army's Operation Road User Assistance, complete with accompanying photograph. The Communist Party and the C.G.T. were alone in having declined an invitation to participate in the festival.

In the elections that September, Duruy and Colon (another Socialist Party candidate) were returned. In the canton of Nant, mayor Julien defeated Lapeyre. The 103 were organized in six districts (La Cavalerie, Les Liquisses, L'Hospitalet, La Blaquière, Larzac-Nord, and Larzac-Nord Ouest). Each district had two delegates and these were rotated whenever possible. In matters of importance, all decisions were made by the General Assembly. This was soviet power, though it would probably surprise them to learn it.

There were around 50 of them on permanent call. The de facto leaders numbered around 15 and Tarlier was one of these. The telephone was used to coordinate and this accounts for the illicit installations later on. The Assembly changed location every so often so that those on the periphery would not always be the same people. They had a number of commissions: a G.F.A. (Farmland Group), propaganda, actions, workshops (under the supervision of the worker-priest Robert Pirault), festivals, press, finances, and legal affairs.

They had indeed set up a G.F.A. which saw to the buying up of land from those who were willing to sell. Under the law, they had first option on such land (peasant priority), even ahead of the army!

Large numbers of unpaid volunteers worked at the sheep-station. They did not get on too well with the country people who gently eased them out before relations soured. On matters of morals, the country folk were punctilious, and some of them almost choked when they discovered that they had had unmarried couples under their roof! It was a stark contrast to encounter such antiquated views in folk who were on the cutting edge of self-managerial campaigning. It was a contrast that was

238

to startle all who had not made a sufficiently close study of the effects of alienation. One can appreciate the shallow formulas and ignorance on the part of ordinary leftists foundering upon such unexpected findings.

In any case, the peasants took a rather traditional approach to working arrangements. The volunteers tended to be quite libertarian and hostile to overpowering, hierarchical organization. It was time for them to go their separate ways.

They secured the building of a school in Le Causse, over objections from the local town council and thanks to a campaign by parents of the pupils. This was just outside the boundaries of the planned camp. But it was the only instance in France in many a long year of a new school's being opened in a rural setting (they were shutting them down everywhere else).

In December, they made a start on the ploughing of fallow land belonging to the U.D.R. deputy, Christian de La Malène. Bought in 1966, the land had never been put to any use. It had merely been acquired when plans to extend the camp were being hatched in high places, and for speculation purposes only. Placards proclaimed: "Plough through warfare." Furthermore, 19 peasants left the running

of parts of their holdings to poorer peasants. To anyone who has spent any time in the French countryside, that gesture by itself will have much to say about the changes to the outlooks of the 103.

In February 1974, the illicit sheep-station in the hamlet of La Blaquière where the Guirauds and the Jonquets lived, was formally inaugurated. In the purest Biblical traditions, little children carried lambs in their arms.

In May, Bigeard, no less, arrived to give a pep talk to the paras whom he was then to post on plateau farms, while aircraft buzzed the flocks. The peasants treated them as trespassers and chased them off. Tarlier was especially active in this regard.

Galley in turn was replaced by Jacques Soufflet, then, after a short while, by Yvon Bourges, whose ignorance was to become the stuff of legend, as were his blunders.

We might as well record in passing that Giscard d'Estaing became French president, whereas the peasants had called upon people to cast their votes for Mitterrand. On the other hand, Lanza del Vasto had come out in favor of Giscard, which just goes to show the gulf existing between him and the peasants.

In June, a missile strayed off course and exploded over a campsite in Lozère. This was not an unusual occurrence and on occasion shells "went astray" on purpose, to hit, say, an irksome sheep-station.

On a tract of land purchased by *Le Canard Enchaîné*, a newly excavated duck pond was inaugurated. At the same time, Henri Ramade, the Association chairman appeared, in a letter sent to elected representatives, to be coming around to Tournier's arguments. This caused outrage among the peasants.

In August they laid on the Harvest Festival under the device "Wheat brings life. Weapons take it away." It was a festival in support of the Third World, which would be the first to suffer from the new weapons being tested in Le Larzac. The money raised would go to sub-Saharan Africa. One hundred and three thousand people would attend!

There was one minor incident upon which I should like to dwell briefly, since I was, quite by chance, an eye-witness to it. Without telling anyone in advance, François Mitterrand had decided to come along on a public walkabout. Much has been written about what happened next. The right-wing newspapers had a field day with it, quite wrongly. The left-wing press pointed the finger at "provocateurs" in the pay of the police, which was patent nonsense.

The facts of the matter are that the incidents started in front of a Third World stand where there were some young Algerian militants. Some of these, on seeing Mitterrand pass by, remembered that the Socialist Party leader had also been one of the "left-wing" ministers responsible for a certain policy of brutality in colonial Algeria. Such facts are readily overlooked today, and Mitterrand's personal responsibility was no doubt minimal (as he was not a person of much note in those days).

But the fact remains that slogans were shouted, especially one that went: "Mitterrand, butcher of the Algerian people!" A small crowd started to follow the

240

unfortunate secretary who, while keen to have people recognize him, had probably not wanted recognition of this skeleton from his past.

The heckling turned ugly because of some extreme left-wing militants (Maoists or maybe Trotskyists), some of them only too delighted to take the leader of a rival party down a peg or two, or (mostly the anarchists) who were simply eager to give a party leader (any party leader) a piece of their mind.

Some Socialist Party stewards volunteered their services, but there on the plateau there was no particular exit to be had and the group swirled around pitifully. The folk from Le Larzac were furious that they had received no notification and they had some difficulty in calming the attackers. The members of the Socialist Party protection squad displayed courage in placing themselves between the attackers and their leader—something they should never do as professional politicians get paid to take their blows. Mitterrand was stoned, but less severely than his makeshift bodyguards.

The Socialist Party secretary had to run the gauntlet of shame for a hundred meters before he was able to make his getaway by car, swearing, albeit in a raging temper, that that was the last they would see of him.

From the country folk, there was widespread condemnation of the incident. It has to be said that, while it was not a bad lesson to learn (reminding a leader of his past record is always a good idea), the location was undoubtedly poorly chosen and it did a disservice to the 103.

In October, the Les Truels farm, army property, was squatted by some young farmers, with support from around a hundred people. In spite of the physical threats from paras and legionnaires, they stood their ground. The authorities caved in and Claude Voron, a member of L'Arche, was able to move in, as was Roger Moreau, secretary of the 103. In January, they were helped to lay gravel on the path and then on other paths elsewhere.

It was only afterward that illicit plumbing of a water supply took place within the perimeter of the planned camp extension. The Gardes mobiles were sent in to deal with them. Tarlier, Pirault, and Voron were to be summoned before a magistrate for obstructing traffic and damaging a public thoroughfare.

In February 1975, they took over the civil airfield in Millau, which the army had decided to commandeer. There was also the opening of a land registration. The peasants barricaded the town hall in Millau using a chain. Papers needed for the survey were burned. The scene was the same in other town halls. Hence the arrests and several days of brawling.

Three peasants had talks with Bourges. Exasperated, the latter had ended up by letting slip the question: "How much do you want?" The trio burst out laughing in the minister's face.

In March, there was an attack upon the Guiraud family. A charge of plastic explosives went off but miraculously no one was hurt. Their farmhouse was partly destroyed. The peasants arrived to rebuild the farmhouse. Before making a start on seven new homesteads.

March 15, 1975 was Le Larzac Day right across France. Route N.9 was blocked by 900 sheep. Millau was turned into a ghost town once again. There was a pitched battle with the C.R.S., and the bars on the subprefecture were staved in by a tractor: the struggle was plainly taking a radical turn. A convoy approaching the camp along N.9 was intercepted. The colonel in charge wound up having to complete his journey on foot with his men, in order to stop them from spending any more time perusing leaflets.

June saw the publication of the first issue of *Gardarem lo Larzac*, the official mouthpiece of the movement, a precious source of exemplary sincerity and sardonic tone. It was under the supervision of Léon Maillé from the village of Potensac.

Purchases began of tracts of land falling within the intended camp perimeter. Les Homs, which was bought up by the G.F.A., was to be farmed by P.Y. de Boissieu. At the same time, a new structure, Larzac-Université, bought up land which was promptly ploughed in Montredon.

Larzac-Université, association 1901, an amalgam of peasants, militants, and university personnel, went on to organize training courses and looked after the welcoming and accommodation of thousands of visitors, producing booklets and carrying out investigations of all manner of subjects directly or indirectly connected with Le Larzac, looking into economic prospects as well as the nesting sites of birds of prey, carrying out map-making inquiries, laying the groundwork for the sign-posting of the entire plateau to help visitors find their bearings, etc. It was doubtless one of the few "universities" in France with anything to pass on and where people had a smile on their faces.

One of the people in charge of greeting visitors to Le Larzac was the worker-priest Robert Pirault (who recently left the priesthood...to marry). For two years he ran the La Blaquière site and settled in Saint-Martin-du-Larzac, in an old presbytery. It was he who was the head of the second G.F.A. (now a fourth one is being set up and should be up and running by the times these lines see publication).

People from Le Larzac regularly attended all anti-militarist gatherings in Canjuers and Fontevrault. In October, Les Cuns, an army property, was taken over and converted into a nonviolence center. In December, they were to halt the maneuvers that the artillery had scheduled on their land.

1976 witnessed desperate scheming by the prefect and demonstrators being arrested briefly in June. The second G.F.A. was sustained by money coming in from the outside in the form of gifts, etc. As for evidence of the banks' neutrality vis-à-vis the State, the Crédit Agricole abided by the instructions it had received that not a penny was to lent to be Le Larzac peasants. In July, 22 demonstrators were tried and factories struck in support of them. Sentences were light (at under six months).

The courts refused to order the eviction of the squatters. The military were infuriated and systematically destroyed farmhouses they owned in order to forestall further squats. Public opinion took a very dim view of this act of war and the army back pedaled and decided to occupy these premises physically. Watchtowers and barbed wire became part and parcel of the countryside in Le Larzac after that. It was a good foretaste of what lay in store for the plateau. Work began on another sheep-station in Saint-Sauveur.

Then the peasants occupied Cavaliès, another army property. The army used violence to evict them. Whereupon the squatters settled down nearby in a sheep-station belonging to the S.A.F.E.R., the organization charged with buying up land on which peasants had a first option. The squatters and the military confronted one another and the situation was tense.

In Millau, they spoiled an army parade which the authorities abandoned. But vengeance was not far behind: the squatters in Les Cuns were evicted and the next day a captain by the name of Pichon punched in Pierre Burguière's face. That same month, the deputy mayor, Gabriac, passed away. In the municipal by-elections, five new left-wing representatives were returned to the town hall. They included Léon Maillé.

The protracted skirmishing with the army was hard. And it would take us too long to retail all its ins and outs. It ought to be understood that more and more national servicemen were identifying with the peasants of Le Larzac. Whole regiments had refused assignment there (in some of the exercises live rounds were fired, the food was disgusting and the locals were hostile). In 1977, there was not a single political party prepared in election times to speak up in favor of the camp, not even those on the majority side of the house!

The summer of 1977 was to see another 50,000 turn out for the big rally. But in September, and for the first time, one of the 103 was to cave in and sell the Le Pinel farm to the army. Immediately, the others moved in and ploughed the land. In December, eight peasants from La Cavalerie agreed to swap some land with the army, while publicly expressing their opposition to the camp.

In May 1978, they occupied the Le Bénéfire farmstead. That year, the 103 carried out a review. Out of the original 103 peasants, three had died (although their holdings were still being farmed), one had packed in farming, twelve had seen their lands requisitioned by the army for its planned extension, two (in 1976) had failed to renew their pledge (but had not sold their holdings), and another twelve had "turned their coats" and sold out. That left 71, to which should be added some new occupiers, making a total of 84 members.

The army had secured less than 10 percent of the land it had earmarked and then only in tiny parcels with which it could do nothing.

The succeeding elections returned a member of the R.P.R., Godfrain, as deputy (although Duruy had racked up a good number of votes which the breakdown of the Union of the Left had prevented from being translated into a victory), while one M.R.G. dissenter, Manuel Diaz, became mayor of Millau, having indicated his support for the peasants while severing his connections with the left. Diaz was a shifty, ambiguous person who managed to play both sides against the middle.

In September 1978, in La Cavalerie and La Roque Sainte Marguerite, another of the townships involved, compulsory purchase orders on the land were issued. It was at this point that some peasants were to launch a hunger strike in Rodez cathedral, while the visiting Giscard was booed at every turn.

In November, there was the "long march" (another legacy from the Maoists of the early days, perhaps?) by the peasants of Le Larzac, from Millau to Paris on foot, a march that won them the admiration of all and a rapturous reception everywhere they went. This remarkable public relations operation was also a pilgrimage of faith, an amalgam of various traditions, from fighting to folklore, from religion and from revolution alike.

The 700 kilometers ended in disappointment when the Parisian "autonomists" could not resist the opportunity to do battle with the C.R.S. The wreckers' failure to understand what the peasants were all about was equaled only by the peasants' bewilderment at these wreckers whose rebelliousness and methods both eluded them. There was poor liaison with Parisian sympathizers with Le Larzac on account of the political inconsequentiality of the autonomists and that was a shame, for violence is not the same as radicalism and righteous anger is no excuse for political irresponsibility.

In Millau in February 1979, a referendum organized by the municipality found 89 percent of the population opposed the camp! In Creissels, another neighboring village that was also concerned, the figure was 93 percent! The morale of the camp's supporters slumped.

From 1979 onward, the magistrate in charge of the compulsory purchase orders was regularly to attempt to approach the targeted holdings. He never quite succeeded, due to physical resistance on the part of the peasants. There were to be numerous clashes with police.

That summer there was a new initiative, the Chantiers du Larzac. Centered upon Saint-Martin, they would see hundreds of folk of every sort and drawn from every part of Europe pass through. As unpaid volunteers, these transients (often tourists weaned off the idea of bovinely sunbathing) were to repair roads and paths, dig trenches for water courses, touch up deteriorated buildings, erect signposts on the plateau, etc., during the time when the farmers were busiest with the work in the fields. The operation was due to resume the next summer and to focus upon La Blaquière, seizing upon Heritage Year as an excuse.

There are many organizations under the umbrella of the 103: there was the returning of military records, the withholding of 3 percent of the tax bill, the G.F.A., and the A.P.A.L. (Association to Promote Agriculture in Le Larzac).

Life went on in Le Larzac in spite of the provocations (the Guirauds were

244

knocked down, while trying to redirect it, by a truck that had "strayed" on to their land in La Blaquière). At the start of 1980, the Millau town council issued an ultimatum to the government to negotiate or else. Thus far, there has been no response.

There was also the matter of the railway that crosses the plateau in the south. For years it had been neglected by the S.N.C.F. (French National Railway Company) which had assessed it as "unprofitable": we know that the S.N.C.F. has shut down all the country lines throughout the country, but now this line is to be reopened…but for army use only! In the light of this scandal, the peasants showed no hesitation: they erected a festival hall out in the open on the track.

In May 1980, the courts revoked the compulsory purchase orders on appeal. For the authorities, this meant beginning all over again. This success was going to be an incentive to them. Again the land could be purchased and they were not about to miss their chance. After the LIP-Le Larzac twinning, we were now into the (longer-lasting) era of the Le Larzac-Plogoff twinning.

I do not mean to say that the fate of the peasants of Le Larzac and that of the inhabitants of Plogoff are the same. Of course not. The latter also were never consulted about the sauce in which they were to be served up, they too self-managed their own campaign, they too enjoy no support from any of the left-wing parties (who are all fans of nuclear power these days). The slogan "Gardarem lo Plogoff" is a fair encapsulation of this mingling of battles which comes in the wake of a mingling of situations. To create one, two, three, twenty Larzacs across the country— what better way of liberating the country, which is our common inheritance?

A look at the balance sheet for Le Larzac is revealing. They have erected 17 sheep-stations and other buildings, six of them within the camp boundaries. They have laid 25 kilometers of roads, installed telephones in around 20 farms (as an essential means of rapid communication with one another) in spite of obstruction from the P.T.T. (Posts and Tele communications) which was banned from installing any—yet supplied the equipment to those wanting to install their own. Running water has been supplied to a further five families. In Les Homs, a magnificent windmill has been meeting the hamlet's energy requirements since 1978.

The people from Le Larzac have given flesh and blood to the emergence of the "new country-dwellers," this new type of peasant (new I mean, since the appearance of capitalism, for they fit in with the old tradition of peasant uprisings) who act in concert, when until very recent times each of them would have acted in isolation.

In spite of important economic or ideological forces manipulating them (the Roquefort cheese industry, whose interests and their own do not overlap exactly; the Church; the political parties; the farmers' trade unions; etc.) they managed to fend off every attempt to hijack their struggle. They did it their way, with that mixture of naiveté (lack of political experience) and imaginative spontaneity which characterizes them. Undeniably, they amazed the world and took it by surprise.

Nobody believed they could succeed, or at any rate, not like that. They forced everyone to admire them, even their opponents and their "critical" supporters (myself among them). We can only speculate what could happen if the mighty political or trade union organizations were to deploy even one-tenth of their imagination, their courage, their obstinacy, their energy. The whole of society would be turned upside down within a week. Like the L.I.P. workers, like Plogoff, they have taught us all a great lesson. The inconsequentiality of the C.P., the Socialist Party, the ecological organizations, the C.G.T., the C.F.D.T. and the F.D.S.E.A. and the rest is highlighted by the power of this spontaneous struggle.

And all of this in a department which boasts 600 priests, where Mass attendance is the highest in France, where the votes have traditionally gone to the most conservative candidate, if not the wealthiest or the most fascistic.

It took the clash of two radically opposing outlooks on the world and on life to light the fuse.

Le Larzac has also changed utterly. The life of the peasants…a life of weariness, upsets, and lassitude…has nothing to do with it. Their real life may well have started only with their struggle, which opened their eyes to their circumstances better than anything else could, and also revealed to them certain things about themselves, affording them that "intuitive wisdom which springs directly from living conditions" as Pannekoek has it.

When the action slowed down, they were gripped by an emptiness. They sensed that they were the main protagonists for once and may well have acted because driven forward against their will. This feeling on history on the move which grips revolutionaries at the time is a familiar phenomenon. There is an abrupt realization that one has some power over one's own existence. This intoxicating sensation leaves an indelible mark upon those who have felt it. As Jean-Marie Burguière was to put it, "We have a lifetime to absorb everything that has flooded in on us from every side."

And there was a change in mind-sets also. On contact with other people, other ideas, other mores, other practices, the peasants have matured through an experience exceptional in peasant life. One winds up posing questions about one's own choices. "It would take Le Larzacs all over the place to move people forward," said one Le Larzac woman, Jeanne Jonquet.

Elie Jonquet explains the inception of a sturdy political awareness, acquired solely through battle, in these terms: "I watched British troops at their war games in the yard, on the roof of my home, and that evening I saw the savage repression that those same troops were enforcing in Northern Ireland."

In uncovering the modern forms of oppression and resistance, it is their own roots that they have stumbled upon again. Take for instance, the Tax Refusal campaign (the 3 percent deducted from the tax bill and passed to the 103 instead), which was an earlier practice of the Camisards, the very same Camisards of whom a few went to ground in this very region when their rebellion ended.

Their campaign will shortly complete its first ten years. And their success is that old, for at the moment their land is still being worked, their flocks still have their pastures, and the army does not have the use of "its" extended camp. And in all that time not a life has been lost, and serious incidents have been few (which often accounts for the silence maintained by the sensationalist press—by which I mean all newspapers, including those of the left—about their struggle which is no longer "news").

To finish on a magnificent note, let us quote an extract from an exchange at one meeting of the 103, reported by the participants themselves. Somebody suggested, apropos of I know not what problem: "That's worth taking a vote on." To which somebody else replied: "Oh no, no vote. We have to come to a decision together."

What better definition could there be of direct democracy and the common struggle, self-management, soviets, and all that goes to make up the subject matter of this book?

247

The following titles were used as source materials for this book or offer further insights into the events discussed. All are available from AK Press. Call or write for a full catalog.

A Short History of Anarchism, Max Nettlau
Anarchism, Daniel Guerin
Anarcho-Syndicalism, Rudolf Rocker
Revolution of Everyday Life, Raoul Vaneigem
A Cavalier History of Surrealism, Raoul Vaneigem
Beneath the Paving Stones: Situationists and the Beach, Dark Star
Society of the Spectacle, Guy Debord
Ringolevio, Emmett Grogan
Louise Michel, Edith Thomas
History of the Makhnovist Movement, Piotr Archinov
Facing the Enemey, Alexandre Skirda
Struggle Against the State and other Essays, Nestor Makhno
Memoirs of a Makhnovist Partisan, Ossip Tsebry
La Revolucion Desconocida: Ukrania 1917-21, Hector Schujman
From Lenin to Stalin, Victor Serge
Russian Tragedy, Alexander Berkman
Rosa Luxemburg: Writings and Reflections
Durruti the People Armed, Abel Paz
Spain 1936-39 Social Revolution Counter Revolution, Various
The Lifestyle of Buenaventura Durruti
Anarchist Collectives: Workers Self Management in Spain 1936-39
Spanish Civil War, Abel Paz
Anarchists in the Spanish Revolution, Jose Peirats
Jumping the Line, William Herrick
Spanish Anarchists the Heroic Years, Murray Bookchin
To Remember Spain, Murray Bookchin
Friends of Durruti Group 1937-39, Agustin Guillamon
Sabate: Guerilla Extraordinary, Antonio Tellez
1936: The Spanish Revolution, The EX
A Day Mounful and Overcast, Iron Column
Hungary 1956, Andy Anderson
A Testament of Revolution, Bela Liptak
Great French Revolution, Peter Kropotkin
No Gods No Master Vol. 1 and 2, Daniel Guerin
Obsolete Communism, Daniel and Gabriel Cohn-Bendit
Basic Bakunin: Writings 1869-71, Mikhail Bakunin
Anarchy in Action, Colin Ward
Since Predator Came, Ward Churchill
Encyclopedia of American Indian Wars 1492-1890, Jerry Keenan
Children in Society, Stephen Cullen
Deschooling Society, Ivan Illich
Talking Schools, Colin Ward
By Any Means Necessary: Outlaw Manifestos & Ephemera 1965-70, Peter Stansill

Albert Meltzer
Anarchism Arguments For and Against
$5.95   1 873176 57 0

Everything you wanted to know about anarchism. A new, revised and updated edition of the definitive pocket primer on anarchism. From the historical background and justification of anarchism to the class struggle, organization and role of the anarchist in authoritarian society, this simple tome walks the reader through both theory and practice. The book concludes with a set of questions and objections from a variety of political positions: Leninist, Fascist, Social Democrat, and apolitical Chris on the corner.

The perfect introduction for those who wish they were better informed, the mildly curious, and especially those looking for a place to start their new anarchist life.

Daniel and Gabriel Cohn-Bendit
Obsolete Communism: The Left-Wing Alternative
$17.95   1 902593 25 1

In May 68 a student protest at Nanterre University spread to other universities, to Paris factories and in a few weeks to most of France. At the center of the fray from the beginning was Daniel Cohn-Bendit, expelled from Nanterre for his agitation. Obsolete Communism was written in 5 weeks immediately after the French state regained control, and no account of May 68 or indeed of any rebellion can match its immediacy or urgency. Daniel's gripping account of the revolt is complemented by brother Gabriel's biting criticism of the collaboration of the state, the union leadership and the French Communist Party in restoring order, defusing revolutionary energy & handing the factories back to the capitalists.

Antonio Tellez
Sabate Guerilla Extraordinary
$10.00 1 902593 10 3

A new edition of the incredible story of the life, the actions, and the death of an anarchist guerilla. Sabate was the most famous of the anarchists who never stopped - after the defeat of the Spanish Revolution - fighting Franco. Until his death, in action, in 1960, he and a few brave comrades physically carried the fight against fascism into Spain.

Agustin Guillamon
The Friends of Durruti Group: 1937-1939
$9.95 1873176546

Spain 1936-1939: This is the story of a group of anarchists engaged in the most thoroughgoing social and economic revolution of all time. Essentially street fighters with a long pedigree of militant action, they used their own experiences to arrive at the finest contemporary analysis of the Spanish Revolution. In doing so they laid down essential markers for all future revolutionaries. This study - drawing on interviews with participants and synthesising archival information - is THE definitive text on these unsung activists. This volume is translated, edited and introduced by Paul Sharkey, acknowledged internationally as the foremost expert on the Friends Of Durruti Group.

Murray Bookchin
The Spanish Anarchists: The Heroic Years 1868-1936
$19.95 1 873176 04 x

A long-awaited new edition of the seminal history of Spanish Anarchism. Hailed as a masterpiece, it includes a new prefatory essay by the author.

"I've read The Spanish Anarchists with the excitement of learning something new. It's solidly researched, lucidly written and admirably fair-minded.... Murray Bookchin is that rare bird today, a historian."
–DWIGHT MACDONALD

"I have learned a great deal from this book. It is a rich and fascinating account.... Most important, it has a wonderful spirit of revolutionary optimism that connects the Spanish Anarchists with our own time." –HOWARD ZINN

Murray Bookchin
To remember Spain: The Anarchist and Syndicalist Revolution of 1936
$6.00 1 873176 87 2

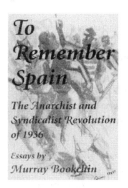

In the essays that make up this book, Murray Bookchin places the Spanish Anarchist and anarcho-syndicalist movements of the 1930's in the context of revolutionary worker's movements of the pre-World War II era. These articles describe, analyse, and evaluate the last great proletarian revolution of the past two centuries. They form indispensable supplements to Bookchin's larger 1977 work, The Spanish Anarchists: The Heroic Years, 1868-1936. Read together, these works constitute a highly informative and theoretically significant assessment of the anarchist and anarcho-syndicalist movements in Spain. They are invaluable for any reader concerned with the place of the Spanish Revolution in history and with the accomplishments, insights and failings of the anarcho-syndicalist movements.

Abel Paz
The Spanish Civil War
$12.95 2 85025 532 7

An intimate account of the Spanish Revolution, from the perspective of a then 15-year-old newspaper boy in Barcelona. Illustrated with 150 photographs from the archives of the CNT. This pocket book offers the best first hand visuals available.

The EX
1936: The Spanish Revolution
$24.95 Hardcover Book/Double 3" CD

Originally released in 1986, this 144 page photo-book about the Spanish anarchists' fight against the fascists is finally available again. Within the deluxe hard-cover, you'll find previously unpublished photographs from the CNT (the Spanish anar-chist trade union) archives, documenting the heroic revolutionary struggle from 1936–1939, with text in English and Spanish. Includes two 3" CD singles with two Spanish Anarchist songs and two original compositions, all performed by the Ex, everyone's favourite anarchist - art - agitators.